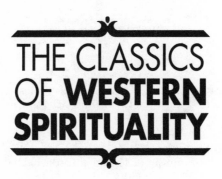

THE CLASSICS OF **WESTERN SPIRITUALITY**

Enigma

Robert Harris

THE CLASSICS OF WESTERN SPIRITUALITY
A Library of the Great Spiritual Masters

Anglo-Saxon Spirituality
SELECTED WRITINGS

TRANSLATED AND INTRODUCED BY
ROBERT BOENIG

PREFACE BY
RICHARD K. EMMERSON

PAULIST PRESS
NEW YORK • MAHWAH, NJ

Cover art: King David Playing the Round Lyre (from Cott. Vesp. A.I f30v; photo no. 1000336.051). Courtesy of The British Library. Used with Permission.

The Scripture quotations contained herein are from the Revised Standard Version Bible.

The publisher gratefully acknowledges the following editions of the original language texts from which the translations in this volume were made:

The Blickling Homilies (EETS OS 58, 63, 73, Homilies X, XIV, XVII, and XIX), edited by R. Morris; *The Vercelli Homilies and Related Texts* (EETS OS 300, Homilies II, VI, and XI), edited by D. G. Scragg; *Aelfric's Lives of the Saints*, vol. 2 (EETS OS 82, St. Oswald and Saint Dionysius) edited by W. W. Skeat; *Aelfric's Catholic Homilies*, Series I (EETS SS 17, St. John the Apostle), edited by P. Clemoes; *Aelfric's Catholic Homilies*, Series II (EETS SS 5, On the Sacrifice of Easter), edited by M. Godden; *Old English Homilies from MS Bodley 343* (EETS OS 302, The Temptation of Christ, The Transfiguration of Christ, and The Transience of Earthly Delights), edited by S. Irvine. Used with permission by The Council of the Early English Text Society.

Anglo-Saxon Poetic Records, ed. Krapp and Dobbie (*Genesis A* [Selection]: *Abraham and Isaac* and *Genesis B* [First Fragment]: *Satan in Hell* [vol. I]; Cynewulf: *The Fates of the Apostles* and *The Dream of the Rood* [vol. II]; *Guthlac A, Advent Lyrics, The Lord's Prayer I, Soul and Body II, Judgment Day I*, and *The Phoenix* [vol. III]; *Judith* [vol. IV]; *Psalm 121* [vol. V]; *Cædmon's Hymn* and *Maxims II* [vol. VI]). Used with permission by Columbia University Press.

The Homilies of Wulfstan (*Sermo Lupi ad Anglos*, On the Sevenfold Gifts of the Spirit, and On the False Gods) edited by Dorothy Bethurum (Oxford: Clarendon Press).

Library of Congress Cataloging-in-Publication Data

Anglo-Saxon spirituality : selected writings / translated and introduced by Robert Boenig.
    p. cm. — (The classics of Western spirituality ; #100)
    Includes bibliographical references (p.) and index.
    ISBN 0-8091-3950-2 — ISBN 0-8091-0515-2 (alk. paper)
    1. Spirituality—Early works to 1800.   2. Christian literature, English (Old). 3. Spirituality—England—History—Sources.   4. England—Church history— 449–1066—Sources. I. Boenig, Robert, 1948–   II. Series.

BR749 .A54 2000
274.2'03—dc21

00-031386

Published by Paulist Press
997 Macarthur Boulevard
Mahwah, New Jersey 07430

www.paulistpress.com

Printed and bound in the United States of America

TABLE OF CONTENTS

TABLE OF CONTENTS

Translator of This Volume

ROBERT BOENIG received his M.Div. in biblical studies from Princeton Theological Seminary and the Ph.D. in medieval English literature from Rutgers University and is now Professor of English at Texas A&M University. He is the author of *Saint and Hero: Andreas and Medieval Doctrine*, *Chaucer and the Mystics*, and *The Acts of Andrew in the Country of the Cannibals: Translations from the Greek, Latin, and Old English*. He is co-editor with William F. Pollard of *Mysticism and Spirituality in Medieval England* and editor-in-chief of the journal *Studia Mystica*. His articles have appeared in a number of journals, including *JEGP*, *The Chaucer Review*, and *Speculum*.

Author of the Preface

RICHARD K. EMMERSON received his Ph.D. in English and medieval studies from Stanford University. He has taught at Walla Walla College, Georgetown University, and Western Washington University and is now executive director of the Medieval Academy of America and editor of *Speculum*. He has authored numerous essays on medieval apocalypticism, drama, illustrated manuscripts, and visionary literature and has published five books: *Antichrist in the Middle Ages: A Study of Medieval Apocalypticism, Art, and Literature*; *Approaches to Teaching Medieval English Drama*; *The Apocalyptic Imagination in Medieval Literature*, with Ronald B. Herzman; *The Apocalypse in the Middle Ages*, edited with Bernard McGinn; and *Antichrist and Doomsday: The Middle French Jour du Jugement*, translated with David Hult.

Acknowledgment

I acknowledge with gratitude the College of Liberal Arts of Texas A&M University for awarding me a Scholarly and Creative Activities Grant in 1997 to support my work on this volume.

FOREWORD

"What does Ingeld have to do with Christ?," wrote the Anglo-Saxon scholar and statesman Alcuin from the Carolingian court back home to monks in England who were fond of heroic poetry near the beginning of the disastrous years of Viking violence there. Ingeld was a traditional hero of secular Germanic legend, and Alcuin saw this chasing after the pagan heroes of the past as morally suspect, contributing to the troubles of society. The answer to his question, at least from the point of view of the student of Anglo-Saxon culture, literature, and spirituality is "Everything." The Anglo-Saxons, among the earliest peoples of Western Europe to forge a native vernacular literature, developed a fusion of the Christian and the pagan/heroic that made their culture distinguished, their literature compelling, and their spirituality unique.

The Anglo-Saxon age extends from the mid 400s, when warriors from Germanic tribes in northwest Europe arrived in what we now call England as mercenary soldiers, through their gradual conversion to Christianity in the seventh century, to their downfall before the Norman cavalry brought to England in 1066 by William the Conqueror. For a little over six hundred years the Anglo-Saxons expressed themselves in songs and then in the writing their conversion to Christianity taught them. They saw their religion through the lens of their heroic past, depicting apostles and saints as thanes of their leader, Christ, and writing sermons that sought understanding of their world through apocalyptic musings on the Day of Judgment and the troubles and victories of the church they embraced so enthusiastically.

FOREWORD

This volume presents a wide-ranging selection of their writings both in poetry and in prose. There are sermons extolling the heroism of saints, homilies explaining church festivals and customs, poetical paraphrases of excerpts from the Bible, and visions of Judgment Day both in poetry and prose. Together they bespeak a vigorous spirituality that was eschatological, heroic, and liturgical in nature.

PREFACE

Before the brave Beowulf arrives at Hroðgar's highly cultured court, the poet of *Beowulf* establishes the basic framework for this heroic narrative of distant ancestors. This structure is radically dualistic, based on binaries coded good and evil. Into Heorot, Hroðgar's hall, comes the "sorry soul," the "hellish demon," "that ghastly grim one, Grendel."[1] Unable to abide the "human happiness" (l. 89) of the hall—the "sweet . . . singing, sound of harping" (l. 90)—Grendel, the "kin of Cain" (l. 107), "grim and greedy, was gripped at once/by wrath and raging" (ll. 121–22). He is harassed particularly by the *scop*'s Creation song:

> One learnèd in lore　　made a lay singing
> how the mighty King　　molded creation,
> fair shining fields,　　far streams circling.
> The proud Victor placed　　pure light to brighten,
> moonbeams and sun's rays　　for mainland dwellers,
> decorated　　downs and meadows
> with limbs and leaves.　　Life, too, He gave
> to each quick creature　　that courses earth's paths.
>
> (ll. 91–98)

Thus the binaries are set: God versus demon, the Creator versus the destroyer, the giver of life versus the first killer's kin, the brightness of Heorot versus "the murk" (l. 87) of Grendel's lair, song versus rage. The struggle in which Beowulf will become the primary participant is linked to the great controversy between good and evil rooted in the origins of the world. As Beowulf says when relating his victory over Grendel, the "dark-stained" (l. 977) defeated monster must now await

> the day of doom   when his dismal fate
> must follow his course   as the Father decrees. (ll. 978–79)

The struggle, in other words, continues until Doomsday, yet, as the poet comments,

> God governed all,   as he yet guides mankind. (l. 1058)

As a primarily secular heroic poem in which Wyrd and pagan rites remain much in evidence, *Beowulf* is understandably excluded from a collection of poetry and prose exemplifying the range of Anglo-Saxon spirituality. Nevertheless, this earliest masterpiece of European vernacular literature may be linked to the more explicitly Christian works anthologized in this volume. They share, for example, a dualistic understanding of the world, an Alpha-and-Omega-like notion of the origins and conclusion of the human struggle between good and evil, and, most importantly, an affirmation of the ultimate power of the Creator despite the continuing cruelty of the kin of Cain. They also share a common inherited oral tradition—Christianized yet sensitive to the Germanic past—and a profound sense of the communal nature of life. Both of these features, for example, are evident in the first recorded English poem, *Cædmon's Hymn* (p. 168), which as Robert Boenig notes in his very helpful introduction (p. 24), resembles *Beowulf*'s Creation lay that so enraged Grendel. Orally composed, yet divinely inspired, it intertwines the formulaic forms from the pagan past with the biblical account of the Creator God, now sung in the monastic community rather than the heroic hall. Although, as Matthew Arnold once noted, Cædmon should not be compared to Milton, the *Hymn* is a remarkable achievement, not simply because it is a "first," but because it so symbolizes the seamless mixing of sound and sense possible in Anglo-Saxon poetics. The poetic device of variation that characterizes the alliterative line is not rote repetition; instead, it is the primary means by which the poet heaps fulsome praise upon God (Guardian, Measurer, wonder-Father, eternal Lord, holy Creator, Leader), who is manifest to humankind through his fulsome creation.

Divine deeds, miraculous might, powerful praise, wonderful works—it is remarkable how the alliterative phrases that typify Anglo-Saxon poetry come tripping off the tongue and how the ancient poetic forms are appropriated by the new Christian tradition. In the following passage from *Judith*, for example, the Hebrew heroine could well be Beowulf when he receives his sword before seeking out Grendel's mother:

> She found there ready
> help from the famous Lord when she found herself in most need,
> grace from the greatest Judge, that he should guard
> her from the worst terror, the Wielder of creation. The Father in
> heaven
> gave her a shining gift, since she ever had firm faith
> in the Almighty. (p. 179)

Here and throughout, the power of God and his followers is stressed. This is true whether the poet is retelling biblical stories, as in the selection from *Genesis A* ("Then the powerful King began to prove," p. 169), or hagiographic legend, as in the selection from *Guthlac A* ("There the warrior/overcame many dangers. Many of God's martyrs/became great there," p. 199). Anglo-Saxon spirituality is as far removed from a feeble religiosity as one can get. Year after year I have watched students, many who detest sentimentalized religious verse, marvel at the power of Old English poetry. This is not the opiate of the people; it is for the mighty, not the meek.

Unlike much of the tradition of spirituality associated with medieval Christianity, Anglo-Saxon spirituality is muscular, not mystical. This attribute is best exemplified by *The Dream of the Rood* (pp. 259–63), one of the finest religious poems in English from any period. Here the cross is seen in a dream, but unlike the visionary cross of Julian of Norwich, it is not dripping in blood nor is it the object of years of mystical contemplation.[2] Unlike the Gothic emphasis on the suffering Christ that is so distinct in late medieval spirituality—as evident in the popular mystery plays linked to the feast of Corpus Christi and focusing on the literal as well as the figurative body of Christ³—the Crucifixion account of *The Dream of the Rood* is active, not passive. Rather than a silent Christ who must be stretched and pushed to be conformed to the cross by the gabbing soldiers of the York Crucifixion play,⁴ Christ is now the warrior king who climbs the cross like a hero mounting his steed and seizing his sword. As the editor rightly states, "Christ is no sacrificial victim in this poem; he is a hero with whom a Germanic warrior could readily identify" (p. 42). The poet's praise of Beowulf, moreover, applies to the victorious crucified Christ: the "great and good leader,   met a glorious death" (*Beowulf*, line 3037).

The poetic emphasis on God's victorious might in battling evil and on divine providence and its active intervention in human affairs is evident as well in Old English prose. The timeless and timely nature of the present is due to its inextricable connection with biblical past and apocalyptic future as evident throughout salvation history from the origins of the world to its end. Even a homily on Christmas day, which one would expect to focus on a meek and mild child, begins by emphasizing the glory and fame of the event, its transformative potency, and its victorious nature. Thus Homily VI of the *Vercelli Book* notes that Jesus "filled all of this middle earth with the new light of his coming," that this coming was expected "from the beginning of the world," and that he will bring all humankind "to the glory of the heavenly kingdom" (p. 93). The sermon continues by describing a series of marvels signifying the child's birth, including a miraculous victory over the martial, who "softened themselves for peace and could fight no more" (pp. 93–94).

Not surprisingly, descriptions of Christ's second advent at the end of the world are equally powerful. *Judgment Day I*, for example, mixes the exaggerated horrible with ironic understatement:

> Our Lord has set himself an advent here
> on that proud day, highest of powerful kings.
> Then the King of humankind will kindle
> the land with fire. That will not be a little
> gathering to convene! (p. 236)

The second advent is also preceded by signs, but in the hortatory mode of apocalyptic sermons, the signs are now contemporary rather than historical. Thus *Blickling Homily* X mourns the tremendous flourishing of evil (p. 61), and it links the very end of the world with its very beginning (p. 64). Like the spirituality of the poetry, the more traditional spirituality of Anglo-Saxon prose links Creation and Doomsday and heaven and earth and stresses God's unwavering will for humankind in the continuing moral battle. As is typical of much eschatological thought, the individual is understood in terms of the universal, each person playing a role in the moral conflict raging since the beginning of time and continuing to its culmination at Doomsday. Until then, the power of evil must be matched by good. As the most famous piece of Old English prose, Wulfstan's *Sermo Lupi ad Anglos*, notes, "we know full well that too great an offense needs a great remedy and too great a fire not a small amount of water, if that fire must at all be quenched. And it is very necessary for everyone henceforth to obey God's law with zeal and honestly pay God's dues" (p. 141).

The present collection will surprise those unfamiliar with Anglo-Saxon literature, who will learn much from Boenig's insightful introduction both surveying and contextualizing these wonderful texts. These fine translations will delight those who only vaguely remember reading *Beowulf* in high school English. Those more familiar with the heroic and elegiac poetry that is usually emphasized in surveys of Old English literature will find that this rich collection both confirms their sense of its artistry and supplements the secular works that most often receive attention, such as the *Battle of Maldon, Seafarer, Wife's Lament,* as well as *Beowulf.* Other readers, interested in the eclecticism of medieval Christianity and its complex history of popular belief, will be fascinated by the interlinking of cultural and religious traditions, evident, for example, in "Satan in Hell" (pp. 172–78), in which the fallen angel is portrayed as if he were a defiant retainer who rebels against his Germanic overlord. Those whose personal searches seek meaning in the apparently chaotic events of mundane existence and who desire a more active spirituality in which the divine is fully engaged in human affairs will also be rewarded by the wide-ranging selections included in this volume, from the wisdom of the Maxims (pp. 264–66) to the promises of the Advent Lyrics:

And the Savior of the nations deals out every day
his pardon as help to the people,
going forth like this, the God of hosts.
Therefore we should loyally laud him
with words and works. (p. 229)

All will enjoy the artful blending of Germanic and Christian traditions that makes Anglo-Saxon spirituality so unique.

Notes

1. *Beowulf*, trans. Ruth P. M. Lehmann (Austin: University of Texas Press, 1988), lines 86, 101, 102. All citations of the poem are from this translation.

2. See, for example, *Julian of Norwich: Showings*, ed. Edmund Colledge, O.S.A., and James Walsh, S.J., Classics of Western Spirituality (New York: Paulist Press, 1988).

3. See V. A. Kolve, *The Play Called Corpus Christi* (Stanford: Stanford University Press, 1966); and Peter Travis, "The Semiotics of Christ's Body in the English Cycles," in *Approaches to Teaching Medieval English Drama*, ed. Richard K. Emmerson (New York: Modern Language Association, 1990), pp. 67–78.

4. "The Crucifixion," in *York Mystery Plays: A Selection in Modern Spelling*, ed. Richard Beadle and Pamela King (New York: Oxford University Press, 1995), pp. 211–21.

INTRODUCTION

Anglo-Saxon England and Its Church

In the spring of the year 1066, not that very long after the death—on the day before Epiphany—of Edward the Confessor,[1] last of the royal family of Anglo-Saxon England to wield a scepter in his kingdom, a comet appeared in the night sky. It was the comet later identified by Edmund Halley and now bearing his name.[2] Its appearance heralded important events, among other things the invasion of England by the Norman French. At least this was the interpretation of it suggested by those who some twenty years later embroidered the celebrated Bayeaux Tapestry.[3]

Halley's Comet is embroidered into the events depicted there not quite halfway through its length of almost sixty-nine meters. Immediately preceding it, King Harold, the earl whom Edward may have designated as his successor as he lay dying, has been crowned by Archbishop Stigand while his retainers, or thanes, as the Anglo-Saxons called them, look on. But they quickly turn, pointing up to the sky, where we see the words *isti mirant stella* ("they marvel at the star") as the comet sweeps by. An attendant with a troubled look on his brow brings the news of it to the king, who bends his ear, grasps a spear, and allows worry to cloud his face. He has, of course, just received intimation that a change was about to take place, that his shaky reign, though only begun, is nearing its end: William the Bastard, Duke of Normandy, is gathering forces to lay claim to the kingdom of Edward, his distant cousin by marriage, and to oust the usurper not of royal blood from the throne. But the comet heralded more than the fall of a recently crowned

1

king; it heralded the end of an era—the end of a form of government unique to early medieval Europe, the end of a vernacular literature (the first, save those of the Celts, in the West) and for our purposes the end of a distinct form of spirituality.

When did that era begin? There are two ways of answering that question. The first, of course, is when the tribes that would later be termed variously the Anglo-Saxons, the Saxons, or the English, first arrived on the island of Britain and began their slow ascendancy toward power, expelling the long-established Celtic tribes from most of their land.[4] The second, of course, is when the Anglo-Saxons converted to Christianity, gradually abandoning their pagan Germanic beliefs and accepting simultaneously literacy and the faith at the hands of missionaries from the Mediterranean. The first was the work of the latter part of the fifth century, while the second spanned the seventh.

Before the Anglo-Saxons arrived, the land they would conquer was inhabited by Celtic peoples, the Britons—a fairly peaceful, educated, and Christian folk. Conquered first by the Roman legions during the reign of the Emperor Claudius in the mid-first century, they had adapted well to the Roman culture, the rich among them speaking Latin, living in villas, and luxuriating in Roman-style baths. They had become Christians, responding to the new faith brought to their shores by Roman soldiers. Their celebrated martial ferocity had long atrophied, for the Roman legions became their defenders against their cousins, the non-Romanized Celtic tribes to the north. When the Romans retreated to attend to their own problems closer to their home, as the Germanic tribes pushing westward sent the empire into decline, the Britons were left without their aid in their struggles with their enemies, notably the Picts, inhabitants of roughly the eastern portion of the region we now call Scotland. As the well-known story goes, the British compensated by hiring mercenaries among the Continental Germanic tribes, who helped fight their enemies but soon saw the possibilities Britain offered for expansion and thus turned on their patrons in a series of "rebellions." The migration of the Anglo-Saxons was under way.

Gildas (mid sixth century), the British bishop and saint, is a primary source for the events attending the migration[5] of the

INTRODUCTION

Anglo-Saxons to Britain, with the Anglo-Saxon monk Bede (early eighth century) following him. In his work *The Ruin of Britain* Gildas delivers a jeremiad against the British: their sins have occasioned the judgment of God, who has allowed the Anglo-Saxon tribes to harry them and lay their land waste. (It is worth noting in passing that the Anglo-Saxons suffered the same fate at the hands of the Vikings late in the Anglo-Saxon period; Wulfstan, using Gildas as a source, delivered a similar jeremiad to the conquerors now turned into the ones about to be conquered. It is his famous *Sermo Lupi ad Anglos*, translated in this volume.)

Gildas begins by inscribing the disaster come upon his people with meaning taken from the Bible: "I gazed on these things and many others in the Old Testament as though on a mirror reflecting our own life...."[6] At the outset of Anglo-Saxon England, their enemies and their victims evince the same interpretive tendencies—to seek among spiritual things an explanation for the temporal. Gildas's problem is, in essence, the "problem of pain" debated among theologians and philosophers: in a world created by a just God, how can a good and religious people be conquered by violent, godless pagans? His answer is, of course, that the sins of the Britons have called down God's judgment upon them: "...when they strayed from the right track the Lord did not spare a people that was peculiarly his own among all nations."[7] Interesting is Gildas's description of the fierce Anglo-Saxons:

> Then a pack of cubs burst forth from the lair of the barbarian lioness, coming in three *keels*, as they call warships in their language. The winds were favorable; favorable too the omens and the auguries, which prophesied, according to a sure portent among them, that they would live for three hundred years in the land towards which their prows were directed, and that for half the time, a hundred and fifty years, they would repeatedly lay it waste.[8]

With Gildas's interest in prophesy, tribulation, and a set time for the tribulation to last, it is not difficult to hear echoes of St. John's Apocalypse (see, for instance, Rv 11:1–3). After a lengthy struggle, the Britons lost, largely being assimilated into the Anglo-Saxon populations, retreating to the hills of what is now called Wales to join other Britons not yet conquered, or fleeing across the waters to that area of modern France now named for them, Brittany.

Relatively little is known of the Anglo-Saxons in their original pagan phase, before they became Christians. What is clear is that they brought their pagan, heroic beliefs with them and for a time worshiped Woden and the panoply of Germanic gods and goddesses in their new home. It is also clear that they originally maintained the tribal distinctions among them on the Continent, resisting any impulse to consolidate into a unified kingdom. These tribal divisions eventually evolved into further divisions, with finally a fair number of petty kingdoms and principalities emerging.[9] The most important were Bernicia and Deira (later amalgamated as Northumbria) to the north; Lindsey bordering on Deira to the south; Mercia in the West Midlands; East Anglia to the east; Essex, Sussex, and Wessex stretching from East Anglia to the south and west; and Kent (originally a Celtic name) in the extreme southeast, entry point to the Roman missionaries who were soon to evangelize the Anglo-Saxons. These regions were constantly in conflict with each other, even after the conversion, and the vicissitudes of warfare kept borders and allegiances in flux.

The Conversion was Pope Gregory the Great's grand missionary project, initiated right before the end of the sixth century. Bede, writing a century and a quarter later, recounts the likely legendary incident that led to the Conversion, a story whose charm demands quotation at length:

> I must here relate a story, handed down to us by the tradition of our forebears, which explains Gregory's deep desire for the salvation of our nation. We are told that one day some merchants who had recently arrived in Rome displayed their many wares in the market-place. Among the crowd who thronged to buy was Gregory [not yet elected pope], who saw among other merchandise some boys exposed for sale. These had fair complexions, fine-cut features, and beautiful hair. Looking at them with interest, he enquired from what country and what part of the world they came. "They come from the island of Britain," he was told, "where all the people have this appearance." He

4

then asked whether the islanders were Christians, or whether they were still ignorant heathens. "They are pagans," he was informed. "Alas!" said Gregory with a heartfelt sigh, "how sad that such bright-faced folk are still in the grasp of the Author of darkness, and that such graceful features conceal minds void of God's grace! What is the name of this race?" "They are called Angles," he was told. "That is appropriate," he said, "for they have angelic faces, and it is right that they should become joint-heirs with the angels in heaven. And what is the name of the province from which they have been brought?" "Deira," was the answer. "Good. They shall indeed be rescued *de ira*—from wrath—and called to the mercy of Christ. And what is the name of their king?" "Aelle," he was told. "Then," said Gregory, making play on the name, "it is right that their land should echo the praise of God our Creator in the word *Alleluia*."[10]

As soon as Gregory became pope, Bede assures us, he put into effect the mission to evangelize the people of these slave boys. Gregory's delight in punning should not deafen us to the allegorical implications of the text: their servility is both literal and figurative.

The mission was headed by Augustine, a monk from Gregory's own monastery of St. Andrew's, who set out with a company of missionaries, abandoned his mission as hopeless while traversing Gaul, was redispatched by a stern Gregory, and landed on the Isle of Thanet outside Canterbury in A.D. 597. King Æþelbert ruled Kent, and his wife Bertha, a Frankish princess, was already a Christian, living unequally yoked with her pagan husband, attended by a private chaplain.[11]

Æþelbert was sympathetic and, after a time of hesitation, accepted the faith. A sub-mission was soon dispatched to the north under Augustine's companion Paulinus. Another famous story from Bede captures the spirit of this time of conversion. Paulinus presents the gospel before the court of King Edwin of Northumbria, and its merits are debated among the leading men, one of whom, a pagan priest named Coifi, delivers this speech:

> Your majesty, when we compare the present life of man on earth with that time of which we have no knowledge, it seems to me like the swift flight of a single sparrow through the banqueting-

hall where you are sitting at dinner on a winter's day with your thanes and counselors. In the midst there is a comforting fire to warm the hall; outside, the storms of winter rain or snow are raging. This sparrow flies swiftly in through one door of the hall, and out through another. While he is inside, he is safe from the winter storms; but after a few moments of comfort, he vanishes from sight into the wintry world from which he came. Even so, man appears on earth for a little while; but of what went before this life or of what follows, we know nothing. Therefore, if this new teaching has brought any more certain knowledge, it seems only right that we should follow it.[12]

Arguably the most important development of the early phase of the Conversion was the missionaries' attitude toward the paganism that they encountered.[13] Germanic paganism included worship of a pantheon of gods and goddesses, chief among them Woden and Thunor (i.e., Old Norse Odin and Thor).[14] Animal and possibly human sacrifices were important. The Germanic religion, moreover, had not eradicated a Celtic paganism that had survived somehow the Britons' conversion to Christianity. Celtic paganism,[15] dominated by the priestly/philosophical Druid caste, involved such sacrifices and a kind of nature-oriented cultus dominated by sacred oak groves. Celtic solstice and equinox celebrations were vestigial among the Germanic pagans. As Coifi's speech demonstrates, the pagans, even their priests, were not always hostile toward the new religion. Yet there were often periods of widespread or sporadic resistance; old beliefs do not die out readily. Augustine thus wrote Pope Gregory for advice, asking the pope what he should do about the pagan customs, temples, and sacred groves.

Gregory's response, known as the *Libellus Responsionum* and recorded at length by Bede (Book I, Chapter 27),[16] is remarkable, for he counseled no widespread destruction of the pagan past but instead an accommodation with it that would lead to its coopting:

...we have been giving careful thought to the affairs of the English [Gregory writes], and have come to the conclusion that the temples of the idols among the people should on no account be destroyed. The idols are to be destroyed, but the

> temples themselves are to be aspersed with holy water, altars
> set up in them, and relics deposited there.[17]

Thus the people will worship God in an accustomed place. Pagan sacrifices must be replaced by devotion to the slain martyrs. Animals may be killed but not as sacrifices being offered but instead as food for Christian priests. There is evidence that Augustine and even the Celtic missionaries from Ireland, who soon became busy in the north and to whom much if not most of the credit for the conversion of the Anglo-Saxons is due, saw wisdom in such accommodation: Augustine's first meeting with British bishops was in a sacred grove,[18] and St. Columba established the monastery of Dearmach in another sacred grove.[19]

The signs of the coopted paganism are still with us today: mistletoe at Christmas, the winter solstice date of Christmas, the summer solstice date of St. John the Baptist Day with its bonfires (sacrificial "bone" fires), the wildness of Halloween (originally the Celtic festival of Samhain, its New Year, when the dead, for the moment not subject to time, could return in the night between the old and new years). The word *Easter* is taken from the Anglo-Saxon deity Eostre, associated with a springtime cultus.

Not only did the Roman missionaries have to negotiate an accommodation with Germanic and vestigial Celtic paganism, they also had the native Celtic Christianity to deal with. The Celtic Church was largely isolated from the rest of Western Christendom: much of Europe's continent was pagan, and there had been little contact between the Celtic Church and Rome in the years before and during the Anglo-Saxon Migration. As a result the Celtic Church had developed a number of idiosyncrasies that set it apart from the rest of Western Christendom, or at least that is how those adhering to the Roman version of Christianity, like Bede, saw it.

Celtic Christianity was dominated by strong abbots and monasteries and characterized by relatively weak bishops (with St. Patrick, a missionary to Ireland from Britain, of course, an exception). This was largely opposite to the condition that obtained in the Roman Church. The Celtic Church followed, moreover, the eighty-four-year cycle of the dating of Easter rather than the nineteen-year cycle of the Roman Church. There were some other, to our eyes minor, differences that loomed in importance, most notable the shape of the monastic tonsure, with the Roman monks shaving the crown of the head so their hair resembled a halo and the Celtic monks preferring a different tonsure (possibly shaving the front part of the crown with the back part left long—a coopted survival of the tonsure of the Druidical caste).

Another important difference between the two churches was the nature of penance, with the Celtic Church favoring private oracular confession for both grave and minor sins and private penance geared to sever the cleric (and, also, layperson) from the sin, and the Roman Church favoring public confession of grave sins and liturgical reconciliation.[20]

The two churches had separate hierarchies, with the clerics in Augustine's mission and its successors in close contact with the pope and the Celtic abbots and bishops acknowledging only a token obedience to Rome. This problem was soon confounded by the Celtic Church's rival mission among the Anglo-Saxons, particularly in the north, where earlier Columba had founded the monastery on the island of Iona, and where Bishop Aidan wandered about among the northern Anglo-Saxons preaching his Celtic-flavored gospel, particularly at the court of the Northumbrian King Oswald. (Ælfric's sermon on the life of that sainted king, translated for this volume, gives much information about the relation between the two men.) The two churches, in short, were at odds and often clashed.

Augustine himself made some efforts to bring the Celtic hierarchy under his domination, meeting with them, as mentioned earlier, in a sacred oak grove, as Bede recounts in Book II, Chapter 2. But, no diplomat and in this unlike his mentor Gregory, Augustine was inflexible, and his efforts failed. While the Roman missions were struggling with periods of relapsed paganism successively in Kent, East Anglia, and Northumbria (where the chief missionary there, Paulinus, once had to flee for his life), this conflict did not appear grave. But as the Roman Church gradually won over most of the potentates and thus the people of Anglo-Saxon England to its cultus, the Celtic idiosyncrasies appeared to be a threat to the Roman party's hegemony.

Often it would produce some annoying confusion, the most famous instance of which was the Northumbrian King Oswiu's celebrating the feast of Easter (following the Celtic dating cycle) while his queen (following the Roman dating) was still laboring under the fast of Lent. Thus in A.D. 661 a synod was held to debate these matters. It was convened by the Northumbrian King Oswiu and Hild, abbess of the double monastery of Streaneshalch, later given the Norse name Whitby. Bede recounts at length the issues at this so-called Synod of Whitby (Book III, Chapter 25). According to him, it was mostly a debate over the date of Easter, but it also touched on the other matters with, of course, the overriding issue the hegemony over the Anglo-Saxon Christianity. Oswiu, nominally the synod's arbitrator, and Hild, together with a number of Celtic and Celtic-influenced clergy, supported the Celtic position, while Oswiu's son Alchfrith, Agilbert, bishop of the West Saxons, and a young abbot, later bishop of York, Wilfred, represented the Roman interests. Colman, bishop of Lindisfarne, and Wilfred were the chief spokesmen for either side. Surprisingly, the Roman position won out, and a converted Oswiu ruled in favor of it.

It would, of course, be naive to assume that the Synod of Whitby settled all differences in favor of Rome. Few immediate changes took place, and there was no immediate large-scale submission of the Celtic Church to the Roman. But the balance had been tipped in favor of the Roman party. Over the next few decades the Roman Easter date took precedence over the Celtic, as did the Roman tonsure over the Celtic. Roman-aligned clerics gradually gained the hegemony, for the Anglo-Saxon kings gradually loaded the scales of preference and investiture in their direction. It was not a total victory, however, for the Celtic form of penance was eventually coopted by the Anglo-Saxons, most notably by the Archbishop of Canterbury, Theodore of Tarsus. Accompanying Anglo-Saxon and Celtic missionaries, it gradually permeated the churches of the newly converted Continental Germanic tribes, eventually gaining acceptance in Rome and finally becoming mandatory for all Western

Christians at the Fourth Lateran Council of 1215, long after the Anglo-Saxon era ended.

In Book IV of his *Ecclesiastical History* Bede recounts the appointment of Theodore of Tarsus as archbishop of Canterbury shortly after the Synod of Whitby. Since Pope Gregory's days, Western Europe had been suffering from an outbreak of bubonic plague. Archbishop Deusdedit died of it, and his successor, Wighard, contracted it while in Rome for his consecration. Pope Vitalian thus nominated Hadrian, a north African then serving as abbot of a monastery in Naples. He declined in humility, suggested the scholar Theodore, a Greek-speaking cleric of his acquaintance, and agreed to accompany the sixty-six-year-old Theodore to England. This unlikely choice for archbishop was, in retrospect, the wisest choice the pope could have made.

When Theodore and Hadrian arrived in England, they set in motion some basic changes in the Anglo-Saxon Church, ones that would propel England to the forefront in church organization, missionary work, and scholarship.[21] Theodore, in fact, deserves as much credit as his predecessor, Augustine, for founding the English Church, for during his archepiscopacy he laid the foundations on which the English Church in some sense still stands.

When he arrived, there were only three bishops, including Wilfred, now enthroned at York. (York, originally intended by Pope Gregory to be a metropolitan see equal in dignity to another in London—the place he intended for the see of Canterbury—was not yet an archbishopric, only reaching that dignity some seventy years later.) Theodore immediately found able administrators and established a number of new dioceses, particularly in the south. Wilfred resisted him for a time in the north, initiating a series of conflicts and depositions that would plague his turbulent ecclesiastical career for the next several decades.[22]

Even more important, perhaps, than this ecclesiastical reorganization, Theodore with Hadrian's help established centers of learning and encouraged scholarship. The monk and abbot Baducyning, better known as Benedict Biscop,[23] had already begun labors of intellectual renewal in the Anglo-Saxon Church by his monastic foundations (including Bede's Wearmouth and Jarrow) and his travels to and from Rome bringing back books and other ecclesiastical items. But Theodore embodied and thus encouraged the scholarly life, even, it seems, introducing some knowledge of Greek to the island.[24] The pupils, trained under his program of education, most notably Aldhelm, were promoted to positions of authority, thus fostering learning throughout the English Church.

Aldhelm[25] (d. 709–10), is a particularly interesting figure in the Anglo-Saxon Church. After studying under Hadrian and earlier under the Irishman Maeldub, he became abbot of Malmesbury and then bishop of Sherborne, the diocese created by Theodore to serve the extreme southwest portion of England. William of Malmesbury recounts,[26] in an endearing anecdote, Aldhelm's habit of standing on a bridge singing songs in Anglo-Saxon to catch the people's attention, so that they would receive the gospel. More important than this evangelistic activity was his scholarship, for he produced a significant corpus of religious writings—a series of poems, a treatise on meter addressed to King Aldfrith of Northumbria, including a body of interpolated riddles, a treatise *On Virginity*, a series of letters, and a couple of charters. His style is characterized by convoluted syntax, neologisms, and verbal gamesmanship, including puns and much alliteration.

The greatest of all the scholars trained in the new learning Theodore and Hadrian brought to Anglo-Saxon England was, of course, Bede (d. 734),[27] the Northumbrian monk who dominated Anglo-Saxon scholarship in the next generation. The subject of much scholarly and critical interest, Bede needs little treatment here. Like Aldhelm he wrote in Latin. He was a prolific author, producing a series of biblical commentaries in the allegorical mode, treatises about the schemes and tropes of rhetoric and about the dating of Easter, some hagiography, and his famous *Ecclesiastical History of the English Nation*, the primary source for reconstructing Anglo-Saxon history until A.D. 731, the year of its completion.

The third representative of the scholarship that graced the Anglo-Saxon Church and affected its spirituality is Alcuin (735–804) (the Latinized form of the name Ælhwine), the cleric from York who migrated to the Continent and became one of Charlemagne's chief advisors.[28] Like his predecessor Bede, Alcuin was a prolific writer, particularly known for his biblical commentaries. While at the Carolingian court he helped foster Anglo-Saxon-style learning throughout the empire and helped fashion a taste for classical Latinity and allusion. He also wrote a number of epistles, including an interesting appeal to Anglo-Saxon monks to forsake the heroic and pagan-inspired native poetry in favor of more piously edifying fare. In a letter to Higebald, bishop of Lindisfarne, the locus of the first major Viking attack on Anglo-Saxon England, he relates the recent violence to the Lindisfarne monks' prediliction for the literary violence found in heroic poetry: "What," he writes, "has Ingeld to do with Christ?"[29] This is significant, as we shall see later in this Introduction, for understanding the peculiar mix of the Christian and the heroic in Anglo-Saxon spirituality.

Not only did the Anglo-Saxon Church export scholarship to the Continent, its missionaries also helped convert the remaining pagans there.[30] The Anglo-Saxon missions started in 678 with Wilfred, who did evangelistic work among the Frisians on his way to Rome to protest his deposition. After him Willibrord (d. 739) in Frisia, Black Hewald and White Hewald (d. 789) among the Saxons and Frisians were notable. The greatest of all Anglo-Saxon missionaries, though, was Boniface, who helped organize the church among both the Germans and the Franks before he was martyred at Dokkum in 754, helping to establish the Frisian Church. The problematic nature of mass conversion imposed from above aside, the work of the Anglo-Saxon missionaries was energetic and remarkable—a major development in European history.

Another major development, though, was soon to curtail this missionary activity and have widespread and disastrous consequences for the Anglo-Saxon Church—the incursions and, later, invasions, of the Vikings.[31] The term *Viking* is loosely applied to Scandinavian seafaring pirates; they mostly came from what is now Norway and, particularly later in the period of Viking activity, Denmark. In 793 Viking ships appeared off the northeast coast of Anglo-Saxon England, landing on the holy island of Lindisfarne, where St. Cuthbert had been a hermit and where a monastery had been built that housed his relics. The Vikings sacked the monastery, carrying off much of its treasure. Anglo-Saxon England had experienced a long period of relative peace, in which conflicts were inter-insular and no foreign powers attempted invasion. Its coasts were largely undefended, and the helpless monks could, of course, mount no resistance to their savage pagan adversaries. For approximately the next seven decades Anglo-Saxon England was vulnerable to similar raids. The Vikings would appear in their long ships; they would pillage and rape and then be off to sea with their booty. Monasteries, for they usually contained liturgical treasures and housed groups of men untrained in the arts of war, often were the targets of such raids. The Vikings not only were intent on the material gain from their raids, they were also, it seems, delighted by the violence itself.

Anglo-Saxon England was not, of course, the only victim of the Vikings, for the ninth century witnessed an explosion of Scandinavian activity throughout northern Europe. Eastward through the Baltic into what is now Russia, westward to what is now Normandy, and northward and then westward to Ireland and Iceland, the Vikings sought places to raid and, in a more peaceful mode, trade. Dublin was founded by the Vikings, and Ireland became an outpost from which later attacks on Anglo-Saxon England would originate.

From the 860s to the end of the ninth century the tactics of the Vikings changed. In 865, a Viking band first spent the winter in Anglo-Saxon England. The *Anglo-Saxon Chronicle* records the event:

> ...in the same year came a great heathen host to the land of the English people and took winter quarters among the East Angles and were there horsed, and the East Angles made peace with them.[32]

They had decided on full-scale conquest rather than sporadic raiding. For the next three decades and more, the *Anglo-Saxon Chronicle* relates with a desperate monotony their brutality. The entry of 870, for instance, reads:

> In this year the [Viking] army rode over Mercia into East Anglia and spent the winter at Thetford. And in this winter King Edmund fought against them, and the Danes won the victory and killed the king and went about throughout all that country.[33]

This is the Edmund later honored as a saint and martyr, in whose honor the powerful abbey of Bury St. Edmunds was founded. He was actually killed as a ritual sacrifice to the Norse gods by the method known as slaughter by the blood-eagle, one that involved flaying and beheading.[34]

Gradually the Vikings conquered most of the north and east of Anglo-Saxon England, reducing the petty kingdoms there to servitude or destroying them entirely. Mercia and, further to the south, Wessex held out the longest, with Mercia eventually submitting as a client principality and Wessex suffering intense pressure from the Vikings.

The kings of Wessex during this period were the sons of Æþelwulf—Æþelberht (860–65), Æþelræd I (865–71), and, most important, Alfred (871–99).[35] Æþelberht died at the beginning of this period of conquest, and the resistance against the Vikings was led by his younger brothers Æþelræd I and Alfred. The two fought back vigorously and with some success, but the Vikings gained ground sporadically. Æþelræd I died in 871, and Alfred, known to history as King Alfred the Great, succeeded to the kingdom at age twenty-three. At first he fared badly, at one point in the mid 870s apparently being forced in desperation into the life of a guerrilla leader and outlaw. In 878 his army won a decisive victory at Edington, which in effect stopped major Viking expansion for over a century. Eventually a truce involved setting up an independent Viking principality known as the Danelaw in what is now Essex, the East Midlands, and East Anglia, and, perhaps more important, the conversion to Christianity of the Viking leader Guthrum. Alfred's children—his son Edward the Elder and his daughter Æþelflæd led the resistance against the vestigial Viking menace throughout the next generation. Edward's son Æþelstan fought off a further Viking offensive launched in part from Ireland, winning the Battle of Brunanburh in 937.

Alfred was of course a writer as well as a king, his prose works of the educational program he established for his reign entitling him to his epithet "the Great" as much as his military successes. In a preface to an Old English translation of Pope Gregory's *Pastoral*

Care, Alfred talks about the effects the Viking incursions and conquests had on his portion of Anglo-Saxon England:

> ...it has very often come to my mind what wise men there were formerly throughout the English people, both in sacred and in secular orders; and how there were happy times then throughout England...and how men from abroad came here to this land in search of knowledge and instruction, and how we should now have to get them from abroad....So complete was [the] decay [of learning] among the English people that there were very few this side of the Humber who could comprehend their services in English, or even translate a letter from Latin into English....When I remembered all this, then I also remembered how, before it was all ravaged and burnt, I had seen how the churches throughout all England stood filled with treasures and books....[36]

The Anglo-Saxons, once pagan invaders themselves, had, it seems, the tables entirely turned upon them. Alfred's response was to promote learning, and, significantly, it was learning in English, not Latin. He instituted a campaign of translations of what he deemed essential books to replace those the Vikings had destroyed or stolen among a people no longer adept at Latin. Among them were Old English versions of Gregory's *Pastoral Care*,[37] Bede's *Ecclesiastical History*,[38] and Orosius's *History of the World*.[39] So the effect of the Viking depredations was not only widespread destruction but also a vernacular program of learning. Much more important was the emergence of Wessex, with Alfred's house as rulers of an increasingly united England.

In the last half of the tenth century Anglo-Saxon England underwent a monastic revival that brought the English Church back from the Viking disruptions to the level of both learning and devotion that Alfred looked back to so longingly.[40] This revival was led by three men—Dunstan, abbot of Glastonbury and later archbishop of Canterbury; Æþelwold, abbot of Abingdon and later bishop of Winchester; and Oswald (interestingly an Anglo-Saxon of Danish ancestry), monk of Fleury on the Continent and later bishop of Worcester. Each was interested in reforming and thus revitalizing monastic practice in Anglo-Saxon England. The path of each one's career brought him from his monastery into the administration of the church as a whole, which in turn caught the spirit of monastic reform and revitalization. The church they reinvigorated became dominated by monk-bishops, and their pupils of the next generation were men of distinction, most notably perhaps the prolific writer and homilist Ælfric (955–1012), abbot of Eynsham, a student of Æþelwold.

A golden age of the Anglo-Saxon Church did not, however, quite materialize, for the third and in many ways most vigorous wave of Viking activity was about to break upon England's shores. During the reign of Alfred's great-great-grandson Æþelræd II (978–1016), the Danes invaded England with great vigor, eventually deposing him and setting up a Viking as king of England. This Æþelræd is usually referred to as "Athelred the Unready," a pejorative epithet that seemingly bespeaks his unpreparedness for this new wave of Viking violence. In Old English he is *Æþelræd Unræd*, and this actually means something different. *Unræd*, ancestor of the Modern English word *unready*, actually meant "no counsel," for the second element in that word, *ræd*, meant "advice or counsel," and the first element, as today, "un." It is actually a pun on his name given by his doubtlessly frustrated countrymen, for *Æþelræd* means "noble counsel." So to his contemporaries he was dismissed as "Noble-counsel, no counsel"—a slur on his penchant for listening to the wrong advice from the counselors closest to him. The pun actually has a further level, usually overlooked by those who explain it. The morpheme *un* not only meant "un" in Old English, it also meant "very," as in the line in *Beowulf, þær Hroðgar, sæt,/eald ond unhar*,[41] "There sat Hrothgar, old and very gray." So the pun actually ran something like this: Æþelræd, whose name means "noble counsel" received "no counsel" because he listened to too many ("very counsel") bad advisors.

The Viking attacks began in 980. The best known of them, of course, was the Battle of Maldon, fought in August 991, for it was celebrated in a famous Old English poem.[42] There alderman Byrhtnoth of Essex lost a fiercely fought encounter with the Vikings, being killed along with most of his troops after allowing the

Vikings, who were disembarked on a tidal island, access to the mainland across a narrow causeway in the interests of a "fair" fight. From this point on, the English were forced to pay tribute money to the Vikings.

By 1013 the Danish leader Swein Forkbeard had landed with an invading army with conquest in mind. By the end of that year Æþelræd fled to Normandy and Swein was declared king, but Swein soon died, allowing Æþelræd to return, the battle against the Vikings led by his son Edmund Ironside. The Vikings were now under the command of Swein's son Cnut. Æþelræd died in 1016, Edmund Ironside was proclaimed king and for a time led successful resistance against Cnut. But he lost a battle at Ashingdon in Essex near the end of that year and died shortly thereafter, leaving the Danish Viking Cnut as king of England.

Cnut was eager to consolidate his gains in England. Already king of Denmark, he surprisingly did not use his English ascendancy as a means of benefiting and promoting his co-nationals. In this he differs from William the Conqueror, who, fifty years later, would begin a radical Normanizing of the English Church and government. Cnut quickly married Emma, born into the Norman ducal house and Æþelræd's second wife and queen, and he accepted into his service Anglo-Saxon clerks and ministers as holdovers from the last reign. Foremost among them was Wulfstan, archbishop of York and bishop of Worcester, who helped him codify English law. This is the same Wulfstan who wrote sermons, most notably his *Sermo Lupi ad Anglos*, translated in this volume, that decry the Viking atrocities as judgments of God against a sinful nation. The wheel had come full circle since the days of Gildas.

Cnut's reign was a peaceful one in which Anglo-Saxon identity and culture were not overwhelmed by those of the Danes. Many of the great monuments of Anglo-Saxon literature, in fact, were copied into manuscript during his reign. A benefit of his reign, of course, was the cessation of Viking violence, and this peace helped foster a late flowering of Anglo-Saxon culture and spirituality. Cnut died in 1035 and was succeeded by his sons Harold Hairfoot (d. 1039) and Harthacnut (d. 1042), the last his son by Æþelræd's widow, Emma, both of whom died after brief reigns.

Cnut's surviving male relatives were embroiled in Scandinavian affairs, so Emma's surviving son by Æþelræd, Edward, known as the Confessor,[43] who had lived in Normandy for most of his life, came back to England to reestablish the Anglo-Saxon dynasty. His twenty-four-year reign was fairly peaceful, with the major conflicts being with Earl Godwin, his most powerful magnate. Edward, Anglo-Saxon in birth, did what Cnut refrained from doing—began a widespread preference for non-nationals in government and church, importing many Normans into positions of authority in England. His relationship to the English was ambivalent. He married Edith, Earl Godwin's daughter, sister of his successor King Harold, but banished her for a while to a convent in 1051 during a crisis in his relationship with Godwin over the arrogance of power among his Norman friends and supporters. Edward and Edith remained childless.

Much is murky about the succession and the events leading up to the Norman Conquest. Did Edward promise the kingdom to Duke William of Normandy, his distant cousin through his mother, Emma? Or did he indicate on his deathbed that the son of Godwin (who had died shortly after the crisis of 1051), Harold, would succeed? Did Harold—as is related in the Bayeaux Tapestry—swear homage to William? The events are, of course, well-known. When Edward died in early January 1066, Harold had himself crowned king. William began to prepare an invasion, as did Harald, king of Norway, who intended to annex England as heir to Cnut. Harald of Norway, aided by Harold of England's disaffected brother Tostig, landed first, in Yorkshire. Harold of England marched an army north and defeated this first invader at Stamford Bridge. William's forces arrived in the south almost immediately, occasioning Harold's rather heroic march to his last battle. They met at the field of Senlac, some distance from the coastal town of Hastings, and the Norman cavalry prevailed over the English foot soldiers, Harold was killed, and Anglo-Saxon England came to an end,[44] leaving its church in turmoil.

Anglo-Saxon Literature

Anglo-Saxon literature[45] is remarkable for a number of reasons, not the least because it was, with the exception of some monuments in the Celtic languages, Western Europe's earliest surviving full-scale vernacular literature. A partial reason for this early emergence of the vernacular may be found in King Alfred's statement, already quoted, that the Viking incursions had largely wiped out the knowledge of Latin both north and also south of the River Humber. Anglo-Saxon England's insularity, and the survival of a native verse form from its pagan past into its Christian present, may also be factors. What is perhaps more significant is that Old English literature, both poetry and prose, reached very high levels of sophistication—the prose toward the end of the Anglo-Saxon period in the second generation of the Benedictine Revival and the poetry somewhat earlier, with the composition of the greatest monument of Old English literature, *Beowulf*,[46] a heroic work out of the scope of this present volume.

The Anglo-Saxons shared a common poetical technique with the other Germanic nations in the early Middle Ages, a prosody that stretches back before the Middle Ages into the prehistory of those peoples. For the Anglo-Saxons, moreover, only this prosody amounted to poetry; we find among them little of the variety or experiments with verse or stanza forms of, say, those writing in Old Provençal or Old French, or, for that matter, their successors among the Middle English poets. The longest Old English poems, like the epic *Beowulf*, and the shortest, like *Cædmon's Hymn*, all share this prosody.

It is characterized by alliteration and is based on stress, not quantity. All Germanic languages and dialects (even their survivors today, including Modern English) are stress-timed languages,[47] in which what we call the primary accent falls on, usually, a word's first syllable. Rhyme, the characteristic most associated in the popular mind with poetry, is, of course, a property of the ends of words, not their beginnings, but it began to dominate English poetry only during the Middle English period, when it was imported from France along with the huge influx of French words that accompanied the conquerors from Normandy into their new realm. The ear of the Germanic peoples, however, was attuned because of their language's persistent initial accentual stress to the beginnings of words, so their poets preferred alliteration and avoided rhyme, except for a couple of instances in the surviving poetry where it is used as an ornament.[48]

There have been many attempts to describe Old English poetics, the dominant being Eduard Sievers's five types (with many subtypes) of metrical foot;[49] among recent descriptions, those employing musical[50] and, lately, computer-generated modeling are among the most interesting. Much of the complexities attending the debate over the nature of Old English meter has to do with the variable number of unstressed syllables in a line of poetry. A metrics based only on stressed syllables, however, is surprisingly simple.

Lines of Old English poetry generally have four stressed syllables and are divided by a caesura so that each half-line contains two stresses. The number of unstressed syllables varies greatly. There are also the so-called hypermetric lines, usually with three stresses in each half-line, and these may be found scattered about the whole corpus of Old English poetry. (In the translations included in this volume the reader may detect a number of lines that seem inordinately long. These are the hypermetric lines one encounters in the original texts.) The words that alliterate within Old English poetical lines are the stressed words.

There are only three patterns of alliteration in the normal four-stressed Old English poetical line. They are:

a	a	/	a	x
x	a	/	a	x
a	x	/	a	x

The slash represents the caesura in the middle of each verse, the a represents an alliterating stressed syllable, and the x represents a non-alliterating stressed syllable. The first pattern was likely the ideal, but in Old English (as, for that matter, in Modern English) the sense does not always admit alliteration, for there are a finite number of words available for any given approximate meaning. Thus the less rigorous second and third patterns are prevalent. Notice that each pattern is identical in the second half line, one usually termed the b-verse. The first accented syllable of the b-verse always alliterates, while the second never does. It is therefore fair to say that the accented syllable immediately after the caesura controls the alliteration of the entire line.

We can see each of these three patterns in lines taken from Cædmon's *Hymn*. Line two, for instance, follows the first pattern: *meotodes meahte   ond his modgeþanc.* Line one follows the second pattern: *Nu sculon herigean   heafonrices weard.* And line 4 follows the third: *ece drihten   or onstealde.* This last line deserves three comments: (1) All vowels in Old English alliterate with each other. (2) Words beginning with a prefix resist the persistent Germanic accent on the first syllable; thus *onstealde*, where possible alliteration would be on "st" rather than "o." (3) Words beginning with "sc" (pronounced "sh"), "st," and "sl" alliterate neither with each other nor with "s" but only with words beginning with those two letters. In my translations for this volume I have not, of course, attempted to reproduce into Modern English this scheme in its rigor. I have striven first of all for accuracy in meaning, but, realizing that the alliteration gives Old English poetry its distinctive flavor, I have attempted where at all possible to include at least something that alliterates in each line.

Another feature of Old English poetry worthy of note is its persistent variation with its corollary apposition. Unlike Old English prose, the poetry abounds in repetition of roughly synonymous words and phrases, piling up (as it sometimes seems) needless redundancies. Sympathetic readers of Old English poetry, though, must imagine themselves back into the poetic ideology of Anglo-Saxon England, shedding modern value-driven conceptions like redundancy, efficiency, and straightforwardness. The Anglo-Saxons, it seems, delighted in richness of vocabulary and the ingenuity of developing alternative ways of saying things. A few examples, this time from the modern English translations included in this volume, will serve as explanation:

In the poem named for her, Judith saves the nation of Israel from the army commanded by the general Holofernes by killing him as he lies in a drunken stupor. She prays for courage to do the deed, and says, "Avenge now, mighty Lord,/wondrous Giver of glory,/what makes me angry in spirit,/hot in my heart!" (lines 92b-94a). Here "mighty Lord" is roughly equivalent to "wondrous Giver of glory" as is "angry in spirit" to "hot in my heart." The poet needs only one of each pair to communicate the necessary information. Or, in Cædmon's *Hymn*, we find in its short length of only nine lines eight variants that refer to God—Heaven's guardian, Measurer, wonder-Father, eternal Lord (twice), holy Creator, mankind's Guardian, and almighty Leader. One of these, of course, would do—at least with modern notions of redundancy in mind.

This type of variation, where roughly synonymous terms are set off against each other in grammatical apposition and woven over the course of a couple or several or even occasionally many lines with other syntactical elements, is a characteristic of Germanic poetry from its origins. Pagan poetry and post-Conversion secular poetry also employ it. But it is consonant with the poetry the Anglo-Saxons could find in the Bible, particularly that of the Psalms, where almost every important term has an appositional variant. The effect of such variation is not that, of course, of modern poetry. We learn to admire its ingenuity, its weaving of strands of apposition almost like the interwoven lines in Anglo-Saxon art, where limbs and tails of birds and animals curl about in intricate and elaborate patterns. This poetic technique has been termed interlace,[51] and it is wholly consonant with the patterns and designs that Anglo-Saxon material culture has left us.[52]

One major effect of the appositional[53] variation is an enrichment in vocabulary not evident in modern poetry (and one fiendishly difficult, devilishly challenging, infernally taxing to reproduce in translation!). It is also not evident in Anglo-Saxon prose. In the secular poetry like *Beowulf*, *The Wanderer*, *The Seafarer*, and *The Battle of Maldon*, the vocabulary abounds in terms for swords, shields, warriors, ships, and all the accouterments of heroism. We see many of these secular terms transferred over into the religious poetry in part because they comprised a "poetic diction," in part because the poets invested their religion with much of the spirit of pagan Germanic heroism. But there is also a proliferation of terms that are religious—names and expressions for God, for instance, or words roughly meaning "glory" or "heaven."

A related issue is the special type of metaphorical variation known as the kenning. Not only did Anglo-Saxon poets vary with individual words, they sometimes did so with artificial metaphors that employ in microcosm some of the properties of riddles. Again, this is a characteristic of secular as well as sacred poetry, where swords are "battle-lights," the sea a "whale's road," and a king the "people's shield." Thus in *The Dream of the Rood*, for instance, people are "speech-bearers" and the cross a "victory-beam." Or in *Judith* Holofernes is "the warriors' gold-friend," the sky a "roof of clouds," Judith herself "the one with wound [=curly] locks." The Anglo-Saxons were fond, it seems, of riddles, judging at least from the collection of them Aldhelm penned in Latin and the grouping of them contained in the Exeter Book. A masterful interpretation of *The Dream of the Rood* even claims it as a riddle writ large,[54] with the Rood's first-person speech so similar to the first-person discourse of the riddles, where various objects dare the reader to "guess what I am." In this literary environment, it is no surprise that the variants often become the micro-riddles that are the kennings. What is a whale's road? Tell me what I am! The sea, of course!

A final—and very important—aspect of Old English poetry to be considered is its origin in song. The orality of early poems among the Anglo-Saxons cannot be disputed. That an almost identical verse form exists in the other Germanic cultures and languages—Old High German, Old Saxon, and later Old Norse, for instance, is proof that the Anglo-Saxons inherited their poetry from their Germanic forebears. That a kind of literacy, doubtless extremely limited demographically, existed among the Germanic tribes is also evident, but the writing system—the runic futhark[55]—was primarily used for inscriptions, not the recording of what in later times came to be known as literature, even though stray lines of verse did survive in runic form throughout the early medieval Germanic world. This means, of course, that a type of poetry existed before an adequate means of recording it—hence the oral roots if not nature—of Old English poetry.

References within the surviving poetry, moreover, attest to some kind of oral performance, one evidently accompanied by a musical instrument the poets name as a harp. This should come as no surprise, even to such latecomers as ourselves, for whom poetry has become a quiet, individual activity almost always mediated by the printed page. For from its earliest times among the ancient Greeks, the poetry of Western European culture has been associated with public and musical performances. We need only think of the bard in Homer's *Odyssey* singing his account of the Trojan War,[56] or Sappho singing her lyric poetry to the accompaniment, of course, of the lyre.

In *Beowulf* we have more than one reference to an oral poetry. Near the opening of the poem, for instance, the malice of the monster Grendel as he eavesdrops on the rejoicing in the hall of the Danish king is directly related to an oral performance of poetry:

> Then the fierce spirit painfully endured hardship for a time, he who dwelt in the darkness, for every day he heard loud mirth in the hall; there was the sound of the harp, the clear song of the scop [= poet]. There he spoke who could relate the beginnings of men far back in time, said that the Almighty made earth....[57]

Notable is not only the accompaniment of an oral poetry with the harp but also the nature of the poem that so enrages Grendel: it appears to be something similar to Cædmon's *Hymn*.

An oral performance is also and not surprisingly mentioned in the poem *Widsith*, which recounts in the first person details from the life of a Germanic minstrel. The character Widsith (= Far-Traveler) describes a performance he has given with the help of someone named Scilling (perhaps a name given to his harp, after the analogy of all the named swords one finds brandished in Germanic poetry):

> When Scilling and I with clear voice raised the song before our victorious lord—loud to the harp the words sounded in harmony—then many men proud in mind, of full knowledge, said they had never heard a better song.[58]

The "harp" itself has since 1970 been identified with the Germanic round lyre, ever since the musical instrument found among the treasures of the Sutton Hoo[59] ship burial was identified as such, but evidence, as I have tried to show elsewhere,[60] leaves the question of its nature open but leans in the direction of the true harp, technically known as a triangular-frame harp. No one, of course, knows what the musical setting for the extant Anglo-Saxon poems sounded like.

More important than these issues of performance practice are those the orality of Anglo-Saxon poetry raise about its composition.

24

INTRODUCTION

In the mid-twentieth century the theory of oral-formulaism was proposed after the analogy of classical Greek epic poetry and based on ethnographical work done by Milman Parry and Albert B. Lord among illiterate twentieth-century Bosnian poets.[61] This theory maintains that a poet, even one performing a lengthy epic, composes as he or she goes along, using stock phrases known as formulae as a mnemonic and compositional aid.

The consequent theory, known as oral-formulaism, is perhaps best known to the general public as an explanation for the repeated phrases we find in Homer—"wine-dark sea," "the crafty Odysseus," and so forth. The theory maintains that the poet composed orally by formulas rather than, say, a modern poet would, who has the private leisure to compose slowly and painstakingly word by word. Early oral formulaists who studied Anglo-Saxon poetry sometimes insisted on a rigorously literal adherence to this method to describe the extant texts;[62] those who choose to discuss this issue in recent years usually temper it by emphasizing the influence of literacy upon orality.[63]

One can easily discern a trace of formulas in the extant written records. *Beowulf maþelode   bearn Ecþeowes* ("Beowulf spoke, son of Edgtheow") is a line generations of graduate students in *Beowulf*-seminars have encountered with a mixture of boredom and relief—boredom because the formula is repeated so often in the poem, relief because it becomes a line they need not thumb their dictionaries to construe. In the religious poetry translated for the volume, frequently used phrases like *ece dryhten* ("eternal Lord") or *halig of heofenum* ("holy out of the heavens") reveal the vestiges, perhaps, of a poetic culture that had its roots in orality.

On a less technical level, what strikes one about Old English religious poetry is its variety. The poets, most of them anonymous, delighted in subjects like retellings of Bible stories, grim warnings about the approach of Judgment Day, stories about the apostles and their missions, dialogues between the soul and the body, poeticizations of liturgical materials, lives of the saints (including those of their own nation), and at least in one very notable example, a mystical vision not dissimilar to that experienced centuries later by Julian of Norwich.

Amid this variety, however, there are underlying unifying factors, especially the apocalyptic elements (for a poem does not have to be about Judgment Day to use it as a controlling motif) and—more than anything—the merger of the heroic ethos inherited from the pagan past with a Christian ethic and metaphysic at first glance inimical to it. I will return to both of these issues when I attempt to define the nature of Anglo-Saxon spirituality below.

Not as much need be said about Old English prose in a volume such as this as about Old English poetry. It shared the same general themes and subjects as did the poetry. In other words, even though the poets had a special diction and a highly technical prosody, they were interested in exactly what the religious prose writers were interested in.

Old English prose was used for a variety of reasons, and monuments of legal writing (some by Wulfstan), scientific writing, translations of important Continental or English texts (like those of Orosius, Gregory, and Bede), and historical chronicle survive. The most important genre, though, is that shared by the sermon and the homily (the first a general exhortation, the second an explication of a biblical text). This is the genre that contributes the prose texts translated for this volume.

The relationship between orality and literacy in the Old English sermon or homily has not been studied as much as that in the poetry, but in many ways it is just as interesting and important. We of course imagine—and accurately—a sermon as an oral genre involving a cleric speaking aloud to a congregation. But often sermons were written by bishops and abbots for the lesser clergy to read aloud. And even more important, the composition of sermons was a highly literate activity, with many of them being loose translations of earlier sermons or pastiches of passages from prior texts, or marbled through with quotations and allusions from prior texts, most notably the Bible and those authored by the church fathers. Thus it is risky to speak of, say, the tenor of Ælfric's thought, when much if not most of what we find in a typical sermon of his are ideas already expounded in earlier texts.

One example should suffice as an explanation of this. The first work of Old English to be printed in the modern era was Ælfric's sermon, "On the Sacrifice of the Eucharist,"[64] included in this volume. It was printed in the sixteenth century as part of the Anglican polemic justifying the Protestant secession from the Roman Church, because it contains passages that argue for a symbolic rather than the real presence of Christ's body and blood in the eucharist—of course, one of the major points of debate between the reformers and counter-reformers in the sixteenth century. What the reformers failed to see, however, is that it also contains passages that argue the contrary. The sermon, in fact, is a synthesis of two ninth-century texts, both with the same title, *De Corpore et Sanguine Domini*, one written by Ratramnus, monk of Corbe, who argued for the symbolic presence, and the other by his own abbot, Paschasius Radbert, who argued for the real presence in what must have amounted to an intramural controversy.[65] Ælfric evidently had both texts available and either sought an uneasy synthesis or did not realize that the two authors were arguing irreconcilable positions. Where is Ælfric's mind among all this? What is his own contribution?

Perhaps the place to locate Ælfric and the other Anglo-Saxon writers of sermons and homilies is in their prose style. Latin "insular" prose style—that is, the Latinity of the British Isles in the early Middle Ages—was often florid, complex, given to elaborate punning and etymological games, often highly alliterative, and sometimes syntactically impenetrable. Aldhelm,[66] counted among the greatest of writers by his contemporaries, has to a large extent gone into eclipse because of what we now perceive to be the excesses of his Latin prose style. At its best, as it is in the writings of, say, Bede, Latin style among the Anglo-Saxons has a beauty and dignity striving toward the simple. Perhaps the most important insight about the prose writers producing vernacular works is that they rarely had to strive for the simple. They achieved it consistently and with ease and almost never attempt the devices of Latin in its most florid forms. Perhaps this is where we may most securely locate the orality of the Old English sermon. The florid Latin prose seems to have been aimed at an erudite and elite readership, while the writers of the vernacular sermons never (or as Gilbert and Sullivan once said, hardly ever) lost sight of their need to communicate aloud to the people.

The prose sermons and homilies translated in this volume are arranged in a rough chronological order that may bespeak the development of English prose during the Anglo-Saxon period. Earlier collections of anonymous sermons and homilies, like those contained in the Vercelli and Blickling books, exhibit a good, serviceable prose of relative short sentences characterized by a direct if sometimes labored simplicity. Ælfric and Wulfstan, educated in the tenth-century Benedictine Reform, begin the second millennium with a highly developed, often poetic prose that still avoids florid excesses yet has a rhetorical energy that is often compelling yet always clear and direct. Ælfric loosely imitated the Old English poetic line when he reached his artistic maturity as a stylist, producing, especially during the later part of his career as a writer, syntactical units of four stresses somewhat more relaxed, less compressed than a poetical line often linked loosely by alliteration.[67] His texts are frequently lineated by modern editors as poetry. Wulfstan, on the other hand, produces, as Dorothy Whitelock puts it, "a forcible, trenchant style, preeminently suited for preaching,"[68] and Dorothy Bethurum lists its characteristics as "alliteration, rhyme, [a] large number of intensifying adjectives, parallelism of word and clause, exclamations and rhetorical questions."[69] J. P. Kinard speaks of his "unsurpassed" variety in creating lists of roughly synonymous nouns and his lack of tropes and similes,[70] while Angus McIntosh establishes his fondness for two-stress rhythmical units coextensive with small grammatical units.[71] Both writers, in other words, write in a polished style that can only be termed artistic. The Bodley collection, copied down in the early Norman years but producing texts dateable to late Anglo-Saxon England, retreats somewhat from this level of art, but it is still graced by a style simple and direct, admirably suited to oral delivery.

Perhaps this comment will serve as a summation of the artistic achievement of Anglo-Saxon literature: The poetry of the period is essentially conservative in nature, preserving an archaic prosody and diction and using it to generally good effect, and sometimes extending to levels only the language's major poets can reach—*Beowulf*, and, among the poems translated in this volume, *The Dream of the Rood*. The prose is much more flexible, forward looking, responsive to the needs (sometimes extreme) of the times—dignified yet often exciting, simple and direct yet sometimes not without great artistry.

Anglo-Saxon Spirituality

Any attempt to define the distinctive nature of Anglo-Saxon spirituality runs, of course, into several fairly serious obstacles. First is the wide time span in which the vernacular literature of the Anglo-Saxons was written—from the late seventh through the late eleventh centuries, a full four hundred years. This is the same span, roughly, that separates us from Shakespeare. It could be argued that ideologies have shifted more rapidly in the past four hundred years than during the age of the Anglo-Saxons, but even granting a more stable outlook among that people than among us, we must still admit that Bede's England in many ways was not Alfred's, Alfred's not Edward the Confessor's. The general ideas that unify Anglo-Saxon spirituality that I offer below are of course meant to be suggestive rather than prescriptive.

Another obstacle—and an even more serious one—is the scarcity of what we now term *mysticism* in Anglo-Saxon England. *Spirituality* is of course a larger term than *mysticism*, and one's spirituality does not have to include it, but there is still a tendency among scholars as well as the general public to conceive of spirituality in individualistic, affective ways largely alien to the Anglo-Saxons. They have, in other words, no treatises delimiting one's struggles to love God, no autobiographical accounts of visions or mystical experiences. The closest one comes to this last is *The Dream of the Rood*, and it is not very close. Nor was the vocabulary of mystical spirituality (the purgative, illuminative, unitive stages; the *via negativa* and the *via positiva*, etc.) available to them.

Another difficulty is perhaps not so obvious. The Anglo-Saxons wrote their vernacular religious literature in certain genres that favored the conventional over the innovative. Their sermons and homilies were often derivative, drawing on previous collections of such materials, often from other cultures. The frequency of Caesarius of Arles in the notes to critical editions of Old English sermonic materials bears witness to this. The poetry—with its alliterative requirements, specialized vocabulary, and roots in orality—was pan-Germanic and secular in origin. This conservatism—both latent and overt—militated against innovative expressions of their own spirituality.

Some generalizations, though, can be made. As a starting point we must take into account not only the Anglo-Saxon Church and doctrine but also the pagan past of the Anglo-Saxons themselves. The converted paganism left its mark on Anglo-Saxon Christianity—a mark that survives almost imperceptibly today in the names of some of the days of the week, the word *Easter*, some moments in the church calendar, and so on, but these details aside, what the church's engagement with the paganism of the past gave to Anglo-Saxon spirituality was an outlook that was at heart eschatological and heroic. In addition, the Roman Church that the Anglo-Saxons adopted with such enthusiasm added a distinctly liturgical characteristic to their spirituality.

The rest of Western Christendom in the early Middle Ages was of course also given to eschatological expectations. As Bernard McGinn writes,

> ...the formation of a distinctive Western European culture was the product of leaders whose hopes were not centered on building a new society but on the expectation of the end of all human effort in the Last Judgment.[72]

Gregory the Great, the pope the Anglo-Saxons considered their apostle, was particularly given to interpreting the troubles of his time, especially the depredations of the Lombards, as signs of the End.[73] The Irish were also interested in the coming Judgment, an interest that helped spark their missionary activities.[74]

What is distinctive, though, about the Anglo-Saxon engagement with eschatology are two things: the vivid imagination that enlivens their treatment of it and the ubiquity of the Judgment and End in their writings, witnessed by not only the frequency with which they approach it as the main topic of a given work but also by its appearance as a secondary or tertiary theme in a work not ostensibly about the End. This dual ubiquity is likewise a witness to the survival of originally pagan pessimism in their eschatological ideology.

INTRODUCTION

As far as it can be reconstructed, primitive Germanic religion was pessimistic in nature, looking forward to an End of the World. The gods were in conflict with the giants, and a last battle was toward. That these concepts are not that different from Christian eschatological expectations should be obvious to all. Pope Gregory's doctrine of building altars in sacred groves worked as well with the abstract as with the concrete. Christ the greater-than-Thor died on Calvary and would at the world's End struggle with the devil, who is more dangerous than the Germanic giants. But Germanic beliefs departed from those of the Christians in that the gods were fighting a losing battle, whereas Christ was, is, and shall be the absolute victor.[75] But Armageddon/Ragnarok was still a merger amenable to the converted pagan's religious outlook. Thus we have both sermons and poems replete with graphic eschatological imagery.

Both Anglo-Saxon poetry and prose take a grim delight in making the reader slow down and take notice of the concrete details of the coming End. As the Vercelli homilist puts it in *The Day of Judgment* translated for this volume:

> Beloved people, the events of the great Day of Judgment will be terrible and fearful for all creation. On that day the flashing lightning will burn up blood-stained middle earth....And on that day the light of the sun will depart.

The visual here dominates: a lightning flash reveals a smear of blood before darkness falls. The vision is terrifying, and the movement toward darkness mimetic of the coming End. In this sermon, moreover, the damned will "slide down into the eternal punishment of Hell and there amongst devils exist in murder and crime, in torment and sorrow, amidst woe and worms"—the first five nouns abstract, the last one uncomfortably concrete. Or, for the poet of *Judgment Day I* (the first of two Old English poems about Judgment Day):

> Then the King of humankind will kindle
> the land with fire. That will not be a little
> gathering to convene! Flame will be fueled
> once fire has grabbed the ends of the earth,
> the burning flame the bright creation.

31

Here the brightness of fire and flame compete with that of "bright creation"—and the fire and flame (at least temporarily) will win, just as do the giants, who will defeat the Germanic gods. The height of this grim delight in the concrete is arguably to be found in the *Soul and Body* poems, where the end of the individual and the End of the World imaginatively merge: "[The Body's] head is split, hands splayed apart,/jaws gaping, gums torn."

Even in works on other subjects, the Judgment Day will surface with all its grim, appalling imagery. An extended look at the Old English *Phoenix* will help define the eschatological aspect of Anglo-Saxon spirituality. *The Phoenix* is a 677–line poem whose first 380 lines are a paraphrase of the Latin poet Lactantius's *De Ave Phoenice*, while the remaining portion is heavily indebted to the part of St. Ambrose's *Hexameron* that offers a Christian allegorical interpretation of the self-regenerating mythical bird.[76] The dominant image of the poem is the Phoenix's paradisal dwelling place, which the poet invests with all the sweetness and freshness he can muster from his stock of Old English poetical words:

> Winsome are those woods. Fruits do not decay there,
> bright blossoms, but the trees ever stand
> green, just as God commands them.
> In winter and summer alike those woods are
> hung with flowers. Leaves never fade
> there under the sky....

Into this sunny world, though, almost like a snake into a garden, comes an eschatological passage chilling and withering in its insistence that the End of the World is near, that violence and destruction are inevitable. In the second portion of the poem, where the poet's agenda is most given to religious allegory, he makes the connection between a human's transitory life and the Phoenix's coming death. Having established this connection, the poet suddenly veers into an excursus on Judgment Day:

> Then many of the kin of men
> will be led to Judgment. The Father of angels,
> the true King of victory, will call a synod,

the Lord of retainers, to judge with righteousness.
Then all people on earth will
rise up as the almighty King will
command, the Captain of angels, with the sound
of trumpets over the wide abyss, the Savior of souls.
Dark death through the Lord's might
will end for all the blessed. The noble will throng,
more in multitudes, when this world
that has done badly will burn up in shame,
ignited in a pyre....

The poem goes on in this manner for the subsequent hundred or so lines, occasionally glancing back at the Phoenix and the poem's main didactic concerns: everyone will be terrified at the Day of Judgment, the fire of Judgment will consume the world's wealth, the dry bones of the dead will be gathered, Christ will sit on the seat of Judgment, the blessed will be purged of sins through fire, and so on.

Where did all this come from? Lactantius was simply interested in a marvelous and legendary bird. Ambrose was of course interested in the religious uses of the legend, but his explication of it is moral rather than eschatological, pertaining, in other words, more to individual ethical matters than the End of the World. Perhaps the *Phoenix*-poet found his inspiration for his eschatological flight from these words of Ambrose:

> Therefore, faith is your nest. Fill it with the good fragrances of your virtue, that is, of chastity, pity and justice. Enter faith's inner sanctuaries which are redolent with the sweet fragrance of excellent deeds. May departure from this life find you clothed in faith, so your bones may put on flesh again and be like a watered garden whose greenery is quickly awakened. Recognize the day of your death, like Paul, who said, "I have fought the good fight; I have finished the race; I have kept the faith. There is a crown of righteousness in store for me" (II Tim.4.7,8). Like the good phoenix he entered his nest and filled it with the excellent fragrance of martyrdom.[77]

There is admittedly a hint of the Judgment Day here, but it is only that—a hint. The Judgment is, moreover, individual and not universal, and the imagery is positive, not destructive: there is no fire, no apocalyptic trumpets as we find in the Old English *Phoenix*. If this passage was the Old English poet's point of departure, what is of interest is the turn his mind took—one into destruction and eschatology.

The presence of Judgment Day and the End of the World is all the more perplexing in this poem when we recognize the obvious— the stark contrast in the nature of time the poet imposes on his material with that inherited from Lactantius. The Latin poet creates a world in which cyclical time governs: every thousand years the Phoenix, now grown old, leaves its paradise and flies to a wood in Syria where it builds a nest on top of the phoenix-tree. The sun sets the nest afire, and out of the ashes comes a renewed fledgling Phoenix. This is a myth that is cyclical at its heart, for the new Phoenix is not resurrected into an eternal state of being as Christ and the believer are in the Old English poet's allegorizing, for it is simply a rejuvenated Phoenix subject to the same laws of its nature as every previous and every coming Phoenix are.

Most critics who comment, always in passing, on the presence of Judgment in this poem explain it as necessary to the poet's allegory of resurrection: the Judgment is, of course, the temporal locus of the general resurrection.[78] This is, of course, a reasonable explanation, and perhaps we need go no further. But I am still troubled by its ease and reason, for the *Phoenix*-poet descants on the Judgment with too much vigor and at too great a length, drifting away from his sources, for this explanation to be compelling. Nor does this explanation treat the other, shorter, eschatological passages in the poem where there is no indication in the sources and no warrant for them. For instance, when near the beginning of the Lactantian portion of the poem, the *Phoenix*-poet gives his sunny portrait of the Phoenix's paradise quoted above, he appends a chilling reminder of the coming End:

> In winter and summer alike those woods are
> hung with flowers. Leaves never fade
> there under the sky. Nor does fire ever scorch
> them forever and ever before that change
> which will come upon the world.

34

The corresponding passage in Lactantius reads:

> The sun's grove is here and, planted with many trees, the
> sacred wood is green in the beauty of perpetual leaves. This
> spot was not violated by Phaethon's flames when he set the sky
> ablaze with fires....[79]

The *Phoenix*-poet subtracts the classical mythology (Phaeton,
whose chariot bears the sun across the sky) but retains the fiery heat
of the sun, which can never scorch the Phoenix's paradise. But then
his mind veers away into a brief eschatological direction, built upon
the sun's fire: the greater fire coming at the End of the World will
finally devour this paradise's pleasant immutability. The association
imposes linear time upon cyclical while reminding us on a very
basic level that we cannot (like Lactantius's Phoenix) escape our
mortality, that we are liable to Judgment.

Just six lines later, the *Phoenix*-poet revisits his micro-apoca-
lypse, perhaps to reaffirm the idea in his reader's mind, perhaps simply because that is the way his own mind works: "Thus will it abide
in bloom until the fire's coming,/God's Judgment, when the graves,/
the dark chambers of champions, will be opened." Again, there is no
warrant for this in Lactantius, who entirely lacks anything that can
be construed a source for this passage.[80] In the intervening six lines,
it seems, the thought of fire has been growing in the *Phoenix*-poet's
mind, and that thought grows increasingly more eschatological. Not
only will there be a fire to mark the end of linear time, but the graves
will also be opened and God will sit in Judgment. We have traveled
along a straight line away from the Phoenix's cycle of generation,
immolation, and regeneration. Instead of emphasizing how the
eschatological imagery arises naturally from the *Phoenix*-poet's allegorizing on the bird and resurrection, we would do well to recognize
how unnatural a connection it was.

The argument still could be made that the Phoenix myth was
not so inimical to linear time and the coming Judgment as I have just
suggested. After all, Lactantius and the *Phoenix*-poet both give a
thousand years as the life span of the Phoenix, and a thousand years
is, of course, the millennium touted in St. John's Apocalypse (see Rv
20:1–3). Ambrose in his *Hexameron*, though, gives five hundred years

as the life span of the Phoenix, as does the Latin *Physiologus*, which also treats the Phoenix legend and which may have influenced the *Phoenix*-poet,[81] and that number, of course, does not figure prominently in the Apocalypse. The Exeter Book, which contains *The Phoenix*, moreover, was copied according to the accepted estimates sometime in the last half of the tenth century, in other words soon before the Anglo-Saxon world confronted the portentous year 1000.

Interestingly, the earliest reference to the Antichrist from the British Isles is an Irish fragment written in Latin, also copied in the tenth century, and it too mentions the Phoenix:

> The phoenix is a bird which builds its nest for seventy-two years. No one can understand such mysteries and the adornment he makes from his feathers, as well as the sound from his singing. A fire comes from heaven and burns that nest and tree and makes ashes on the earth. Rain comes [from] Africa and puts out the fires. From the ash and the rain will be born the girl from whom Antichrist will come. Two young virgin girls will stand there, called Abilia and Lapidia, from whose breasts will pour the milk by which they will nourish him for five years. When five years are completed, he will begin to reign.[82]

What is significant is not so much the connection of the Phoenix myth with such specific details drawn from the apocalyptic speculation as the millennium and Antichrist, but the tendency of the *Phoenix*-poet to run counter to his sources *at the most unlikely of places* and shift into an eschatological mode. He never interprets the thousand-year life span of the Phoenix as the apocalyptic millennium, and he is not interested in the grotesque insertion of the Phoenix's ashes into the genealogy of Antichrist. For him, the Judgment need not be mediated by grotesque apocalyptic symbolism; it is simply a fire destined to burn, and its coming is inevitable. Its presence in his mind—and I think in the mind of Anglo-Saxon writers in general—is always ready to ignite a poem or a sermon into Judgment Day.

In fact, the *Phoenix*-poet's resistance to the apocalyptic myth leads us to another question. Why did the Anglo-Saxons resist such myth, even when the seemingly natural course of their subject would direct them to it? An important distinction must be made here. In the early Middle Ages, apocalypticism could take one of two directions, termed by Bernard McGinn "predictive" and "non-predictive."[83] The former relates the cryptic imagery inherited from the biblical Apocalypse to events in an author's world, the intended effect to demonstrate to the reader how "current events" relate to spiritual events. The latter avoids such expectation, focusing on the End as a means to foster moral betterment. This form of apocalypticism owes much to Augustine, who resisted the effort to contemporize the Apocalypse.[84] Both forms of apocalypticism could exist side-by-side in the same age, nation, or culture. What is distinctive about Anglo-Saxon eschatology, though, is how little Anglo-Saxon writers were interested in the predictive type. It is almost nonexistent. A glance at Bede's *Commentary on the Apocalypse* reveals, for instance, how Augustinian he is in this regard.[85]

Wulfstan's *Sermo Lupi ad Anglos*, of course, is also worth investigating in these terms. Wulfstan was a significant historical figure as well as a writer of note. He lived during the tumultuous time of the second series of Viking invasions, which heralded in the new millennium. His was an age, especially for Anglo-Saxon England, full of wars and rumors of wars—one which eventually saw not the End of the World but the end (at least until the mid-eleventh century) of what in later ages would be termed Home Rule, for the Vikings toppled the Anglo-Saxon dynasty from England's throne in a see-saw campaign in A.D. 1014–1016, when the Dane Cnut emerged as victor and new King of England. Wulfstan, as archbishop of York, was one of King Æþelræd's chief counselors and lawmakers, but he survived the change, still wielding both ecclesiastical and political power. Before the Danish victory he had written sermons calling for the English to repent and emend their ways in hopes that God would favor them and their nation would avoid the final destruction the Vikings had brought so near.

The most celebrated of these sermons is the *Sermo Lupi ad Anglos*. In it Wulfstan alludes to Gildas's *De Excidio Britonum* and in his forceful Old English prose catalogues the sins of his battered nation, most notably the suspicious and treacherous murder of Æþelræd's elder brother Edward. He presents, sometimes in lurid detail, the violence of the Vikings as punishment for the sins of the English, all the while calling for a repentance that could, God willing, gain for his nation a reprieve. The powerful opening of the sermon demonstrates the extent to which Wulfstan cast his ideas in an apocalyptic light. Wulfstan writes:

> Beloved people, know the truth! This world is in haste, and it nears the end, and therefore it is always in the world the longer the worse! And so it must get very worse before the advent of the Antichrist. And certainly it will become terrible and grim then far and wide in the world. Eagerly understand also that the devil has led this nation astray too much now for too many years....

The reference to Antichrist places Wulfstan's sermon squarely in a great medieval apocalyptic tradition: Antichrist would appear at the End of the World, and the violence and trouble attending his advent and reign, foretold in the Bible, would be recognizable signs of the coming End. Wulfstan generates great urgency through his choice of words, particularly the Old English *nealæcð* and *georne:* the End "draws near," and to understand is not enough, for one must understand it "eagerly."

What is noteworthy, though, is not the presence of Antichrist at the opening of this sermon, but his absence throughout, for after this initial passage Wulfstan immediately begins his realistic, non-mythic political agenda: There has been too little loyalty in the land, and we are not seeking a remedy for the evils that increase daily. Laws (says the writer of legal codes) are continuously broken. We have earned the miseries that have come upon us. We do not pay tithes, and churches have been robbed. The poor and infants have been sold as slaves, and alms have diminished. Violence has been widespread. There have been plagues afflicting both people and animals. Taxes are too high. Bad weather has led to crop failure. Our desires have been fashioned for us into a law. The land is full of back-stabbers. Prince Edward was betrayed and murdered. Groups of men buy slave women for sex and then resell them to the Vikings. Serfs flee to the Vikings and return with the enemy to kill or enslave their lords. The Viking berserkers can kill ten Englishmen in battle. And the Vikings rape English women while their husbands and fathers are compelled to look on. We pay huge amounts of tribute-money, but everywhere the Vikings burn, rob, plunder, and enslave. And all this is punishment for our sins of fraud, assault, murder, insults to Churchmen, adultery, incest, fornication, and oath breaking. There are harlots and child-killers, priest-slayers, witches, sorceresses, and thieves. Gildas in the times of the Britons warned his nation of these very crimes, and God allowed an army of English to conquer them. But let us guard ourselves against such things, for we have been worse than the Britons! Let us do what is necessary and follow righteousness and thus atone for our sins. Let us love God and follow his laws.

Thus Wulfstan almost to the end of his sermon. His last sentences, though, read:

> And let us often understand the great Judgment at which we all must appear and protect ourselves eagerly against the raging fire of the torments of hell and earn for ourselves those glories and joys that God has prepared for those who do his will in the world. May God help us. Amen.

Wulfstan reprises the End of the World for the end of his sermon, using some of the same vocabulary as at the beginning. The End becomes a rhetorical envelope for his sermon, with the Last Judgment at its end made, perhaps, inevitable by the appearance of Antichrist at the beginning. What comes in the middle can then be construed mimetically as the apocalyptic tribulations intervening between the advent of Antichrist and the final Judgment. He thus telescopes the present troubles into those of the future.

If Wulfstan does engage in this literary mimesis consciously, his treatment of the End is rather detached. Antichrist disappears, and the focus is entirely on the various sins and crimes of the English and on the consequent scourge of the Vikings. What is missing is a point-by-point connection of the present troubles either directly or through grotesque symbolism. Wulfstan's is, in effect, an apocalypse with a disappearing mythos.

The significance of this should be evident if we recall what some people who were roughly his contemporaries were producing as apocalyptic texts. The Irish fragment, quoted above, that links the Phoenix to Antichrist is of course one example. Its author envisions a myth: the Phoenix's fiery nest produces two virgins whose milk nourishes Antichrist for five years before his apocalyptic career begins. Wulfstan, though, mentions Antichrist but then resists such myth. A similar instance is the Old High German poem *Muspili*.[86] This poem depicts apocalyptic events in which Elijah, traditionally identified with one of the "two witnesses" of Revelation 11:3–13,[87] returns to earth never having suffered death (he was assumed bodily into heaven in Elisha's sight when a chariot took him there) and does battle with Antichrist. In *Muspili* Elijah is defeated, and his blood sets fire to the mountains—a detail as fanciful as the milk from the virgins who emerge from the Phoenix's nest. This will occasion the other apocalyptic cataclysms—the earth's desiccation, the fall of heavenly bodies, earthquakes, and the fire of Judgment. Wulfstan is interested in none of this. For him, it is enough to mention Antichrist before turning his attention to what truly interests him—finding ways to frighten his fellow nationals into paying tithes and following the laws that he and the other lawgivers have compiled. The Apocalypse and the coming Judgment are there, but only as a trace. Similarly Adso's "Letter on the Origin and Time of the Antichrist" from the mid-tenth century speculates about the Last World Emperor, whose righteous and victorious career would immediately precede that of Antichrist;[88] we find no such curiosity in Wulfstan. All this highlights Wulfstan's restraint: Antichrist will come and the age even now hastens to its end, but our job, he declares, is to emend our ways and live righteously, thus perhaps averting the real (not mythic) disasters that have come upon us.

The Germanic heroism the Anglo-Saxons inherited from their pagan past is just as ubiquitous as their fascination with Judgment Day. In the old gods' struggle against the forces of evil, what was important was heroism in a losing fight. This was more than a sentiment; it was for the Germanic tribes a moral imperative. As early as Tacitus in the first century, Germanic ethics was associated with the injunction of a warrior to die with his defeated lord in battle:

> When they have come into battle, it is shameful for the chieftain to be excelled in valor, shameful for the entourage not to

match the valor of the chieftain. Furthermore, it is shocking and disgraceful for all of one's life to have survived one's chieftain and left the battle....[89]

Almost a thousand years later, the poet who wrote the *Battle of Maldon*, a poem describing a losing battle of the Anglo-Saxon alderman Byrhtnoth and his entourage of thanes against the Vikings in 991, we find this same moral injunction firmly in place. After Byrhtnoth is slain and some cowards flee the battle, one by one the loyal thanes proclaim their loyalty to their fallen lord and die besides him. At the end of that poem the old thane Byrhtwold utters the famous lines defining the pessimism at the heart of Germanic heroism: *Hige sceal þe heardra,   heorte þe cenra,/mod sceal þe mare,   þe ure mægen lytlaδ*[90] ("Our minds must be the harder, hearts more keen, courage the greater, as our strength diminishes").

In his *The Coming of Christianity to Anglo-Saxon England*, Henry Mayr-Harting places the native heroic ideology of the Anglo-Saxons centrally in their conversion to Christianity.[91] For him, "the ability of Christianity to come to terms with the values of the Heroic Age was a primary factor in its success among the Anglo-Saxons."[92] The heroic narratives, endemic to that culture, were greatly influential in developing the vocabulary of what the Anglo-Saxons considered exemplary in their religious heroes. Mayr-Harting's prime example is the placing of the Anglo-Saxon saint Guthlac—subject of a Latin Saint's Life by Felix[93] and two Old English poems (one translated for this volume)—somewhere between the traditions of Mediterranean hagiography exemplified by Athanasius's *Life of Antony*[94] and the heroic tradition exemplified by *Beowulf*.[95] For the Anglo-Saxons, Guthlac-as-Antony could merge easily with Guthlac-as-Beowulf. As I have tried to show elsewhere, a similar merger can be seen in the Anglo-Saxon construction of St. Andrew, a saint and a hero whose exploits in rescuing his fellow-apostle Matthew are elaborated in an Old English sermon (translated for this volume) and a long Old English poem, *Andreas*.[96]

Perhaps André Vauchez best sums up the heroic nature of early medieval spirituality when he writes about the monks:

> By presenting religious life primarily as a ceaseless struggle
> against the "Ancient Foe," monastic spirituality awakened
> widespread reverberation within a warlike society whose secu-
> lar ethic…favored related values.[97]

Clinton Albertson goes so far as to name the religion in Anglo-Saxon
England the "Heroic Age of English monasticism" and suggests that it
"makes the heroic cast of Anglo-Saxon literature so much more
understandable."[98] The influence, of course, worked both ways.

The Dream of the Rood is worth analyzing in this context. In this
famous poem, a dreamer has a paradoxical vision of the cross
(= Rood), seeing it alternatively as a rough gallows tree and a bejeweled relic. It speaks to him, recounting in a graphic way the events
of the crucifixion. Christ is no sacrificial victim in this poem; he is a
hero with whom a Germanic warrior could readily identify. (This is
also the case, of course, in the Old Saxon poem *Heliand.*[99]) The
Rood itself speaks and recounts how Christ ascended it to effect
humankind's salvation:

> Then the young hero ungirded himself, he who was God
>   Almighty,
> strong and stern. He ascended the wretched gallows,
> mighty in the sight of many, when he wanted to redeem
>   mankind.

Not only is he a "hero" in this poem, he is also a "powerful king"
and "lord" (= *dryhten* in Old English, originally the designation of a
warlord in charge of a band of warriors). When Christ's disciples (in
the Bible, Nicodemus and Joseph of Aramathia) come to bury him,
they seem to be a numerous band of Germanic retainers. The Rood
refers to them as "troops" and "warriors." Here is the description of
Christ's funeral obsequies:

> Then they began to work him a grave,
> the warriors in the slayer's sight. They carved it from bright
>   stone;
> they set in it the works of victories. Then they began to sing a
>   woeful song,
> wretched in the eventide.

If the slain Beowulf had been interred in a sepulcher rather than burned in a pyre, these lines would not be out of place in the poem celebrating his heroism.

When the Rood explains to the dreamer how it has become a bejeweled relic, it speaks the words of a Germanic retainer who has been rewarded by his *dryhten* for faithful military service: "Then glory's prince honored me/over all trees of the wood...." The dreamer responds to this like a Germanic retainer looking for a *dryhten* to serve:

> It is now my life's hope
> that I will find the victory-wood
> alone more often than other men,
> worship it well. My will for that
> is great in my spirit, and my safety is
> right in that cross. I have few friends
> powerful on earth, since they have departed
> from the world's joys, sought wonder's king,
> and live now with the high Father,
> dwell in glory. And every day
> I look for that time when the Lord's cross
> which I once beheld here on earth
> will fetch me in this fleeting life
> and bring me where the bliss is great,
> joy in Heaven, where the Lord's hosts are
> seated at the banquet.

One thinks of the banqueting scenes in *Beowulf* or of the speaker in the Old English poem *The Wanderer*, who is a thane without a *dryhten*, wishing once more to be a member of a *comitatus*.

The ingrained loyalty, inherited from their converted paganism, transferred to the Roman Church. Their writings reveal a deep love of the church and its liturgy. Perhaps the best example of this is the marvelously beautiful *Advent Lyrics*, translations that apotheocize the O-antiphons from the Advent liturgy. But they also delighted in other liturgical and ecclesiastical matters in their sermons and poems. They translated into Old English poetry important passages from the liturgy, like the Lord's Prayer and the Psalms, and they wrote sermons about and for the dedication of churches. The sermons particularly were dominated by the liturgy, for the important collections were most often organized according to the church calendar. Ælfric and the compiler of the Blickling Homilies, for instance, produced volumes of sermons and homilies that worked their way chronologically through the church year, treating various saints and major festivals or fasts on the appropriate days.[100]

In his *The Spirituality of the Medieval West*, André Vauchez notes the essentially liturgical character of the spirituality of the early Middle Ages, terming, for instance, the Carolingian era (of course contemporaneous with much of Anglo-Saxon times) a "liturgical civilization."[101] He defines this term as a "religion [that] was...identified with the worship rendered to God by the priests who were its ministers."[102] What this meant was a diminishment of the role of the laity and an identification of religion with clerical culture. The strong emphasis placed on the liturgy by the Cluniac monks in the tenth and eleventh centuries is one—albeit extreme—manifestation of such a liturgical culture.[103] Anglo-Saxon England experienced a monastic liturgical reform roughly contemporaneous with that of Cluny,[104] led, as we have seen, by Dunstan, Æþelwold, and Oswald. There might be a direct correlation between this revival and the nature of the extant literature in Old English, for most of the manuscripts that contain it were copied during the years of the monastic reform.

The liturgy—office and mass with their cyclical attention to the church's feasts and commemoration of the saints—formed the very fabric of clerical life.[105] It is an arresting fact that the vast majority of Anglo-Saxon religious texts can somehow be related to the liturgy. Sometimes the relation in obvious: when the Psalms and Lord's Prayer were translated, for instance, their translators were rendering important passages of the liturgy into the vernacular. The various saints' lives found among Old English sermonic literature functioned as homilies for the various saints' days. The longer lives, such as those of Eddius Stephanus of Wilfrid, Felix of Guthlac, Alcuin of Willibrord, and Willibald of Boniface[106] (all written in Latin and thus beyond the scope of this volume) would have served suitably as *lectio divina* for those saints' days. In other instances the connection to the liturgy might not be as obvious, but it is still usually discernible. *The Dream of the Rood* resonates with the feast of the Invention of the Cross (May 3), for instance; the *Judgment Day* poems resonate with certain apocalyptic readings in the lectionaries.

A brief look at one of the pieces translated here that was drawn from the liturgy can give us some flavor for the liturgical orientation of Anglo-Saxon spirituality. The rendering of the Lord's Prayer is as follows:

> Holy Father, you who dwell in Heaven,
> honored be the joy of your glory. May your name be hallowed
> in your works by the sons of the people. You are the savior of
>   men.
> May your spacious kingdom come and your will firm in
>   counsel
> be raised under the roof of Heaven and also on the wide earth.
> Give us for this day just dignity,
> our continued loaf, comforter
> of men, steadfast Savior.
> Do not let us be tossed too much in temptation,
> but, Ruler of the people, give us good deliverance
> from every evil for ever and ever.

The poet, as can be readily seen, sticks fairly close to the Vulgate version of the Lord' Prayer (see Mt 6:9b-13; cf. Lk 11:2b-4).[107] What we notice are certain short expansions of the liturgical texts, ones less like the parallelisms mandated by the conventions of Old English poetry and more like the tropes (expansions of the words of the liturgy) in practice throughout the West at this time.[108] The famous Winchester troper is an example;[109] Winchester was, of course, for a time the capital of Wessex, in whose dialect most works of Old English literature were copied. The way tropes were formed is as follows: a composer of a trope would take a phrase from the liturgy and interpolate or add to the end an originally nonliturgical phrase somehow amplifying or explaining the liturgical phrase. Thus in one well-known instance, in the phrase *Kyrie eleison* we find interpolated the words *fons bonitatis Pater ingenite a quo bona cuncta procedunt*, producing the troped "Lord, source of goodness, Father not born, from whom all good proceeds, have mercy on us."[110] An example of this trope-like expansion from the Old English *Lord's Prayer* is the line, "May your name be hallowed in your works by the sons of the people," for the Bible's simple *sanctificetur nomen tuum*. What is interesting is that this troping is being done in the vernacular.

We have come back to the words of King Alfred, who, in his letter of preface to his translation of Gregory's *Pastoral Care*[111] addressed to Bishop Wærferð of Worcester, spoke about the mechanisms of translation: "...among many and various cares of this kingdom I translated into English the book called *Pastoralis* in Latin and *Shepherd Book* in English sometimes word by word, sometimes *meaning by meaning*" (translation and emphasis my own). Meaning by meaning: what we see among the translators and adapters among the Old English poets and homilists is an effort to transport the values of the liturgy to the people in their own language. But this transportation occurred at a level beyond the lexical and syntactical, transcending the linguistic altogether. By baptizing, as it were, the heroism and eschatology of the Anglo-Saxons, they were translating for their readers their spirituality on a level truly meaningful.

Authors, Manuscripts, Texts

Most works of Old English literature, including most of those translated here, are anonymous. There are only two poets whose names come down to us that can be associated for certain with extant poetry—Cædmon and Cynewulf—while Ælfric and Wulfstan tower over a sea of anonymous sermons and homilies. Each of these four authors is included in this volume among a larger group of anonymous poems, sermons, and homilies. Since one of the conventions among Anglo-Saxonists is to treat works of Old English literature in groupings according to the manuscripts in which the work is found, I here offer a brief treatment of each of the four named authors included in this volume followed by discussion of the major manuscripts represented in this book.

Cædmon: Bede provides the little we know of Cædmon. His story, at least the first half, is so well known that we need not repeat

46

it except by way of a brief summary. Cædmon lived in the mid-seventh century, was a herdsman by trade, and worked for (perhaps as a lay brother) Hild's monastery of Streanaeshalch, later known as Whitby, where the synod was convened in 661 to debate the differences between the Celtic and Roman Churches, especially the dating of Easter. It is possible that Cædmon was a herdsman there at the time of the synod. A few years later, sometime close to the year 670, the miracle that initiated English poetry occurred to him. At a feast, a harp was passed around so each person there could in turn sing a song by way of mutual entertainment. This may be, incidentally, strong evidence for oral-formulaism, since Cædmon (with presumably others there) was said to be illiterate. But Cædmon left before it was his turn, for he had no skills at poetry. At watch among the animals that night he had a vision in which an angel appeared and demanded of him the song he had failed to produce earlier. After some protest, he complied, offering the nine-line creation-hymn (actually a poetical paraphrase of the first verse in the book of Genesis). This is the earliest recorded poem in the English language.

The next morning he sang it before the doubtless amazed reeve, his superior, who brought him to Hild, who, responsive to the miracle, elevated Cædmon to the status of choir monk (thereby conferring on him a sort of honorary literacy) and enjoined him to continue his poetic efforts. Bede recounts his methods. A literate monk would read him a passage from the Bible; he would ruminate over it like a cow chewing the cud (Bede's metaphor—taken from the Bible, of course, but also some sort of reference to Cædmon's former employment), and then the next morning he would offer up a poem. Bede gives a short resume of Cædmon's publications, as we would now call it, including poetical versions of the books of Genesis and Exodus and a poem on Judgment Day. That poems survive in Old English that have exactly these subjects caused earlier Anglo-Saxonists to ascribe them to Cædmon, but his nine-line *Hymn* is the only poem safely ascribable to him. It exists in English in some seventeen manuscripts of Bede's *Ecclesiastical History*, including four in Cædmon's native Northumbrian dialect.

Cædmon lived for some years in his monastery, continuing his poetical efforts, and he died there a saintly, tranquil, and humble death, with Bede claiming for him premonitions of his demise—sure indication in hagiographical writings of sanctity.

Cynewulf: Many more lines of poetry can be safely ascribed to Cynewulf, yet much less is known of his life than that of Cædmon. In fact, he is nothing more than a name—but that statement is not as devoid of interest as it would be applied to others, since Cynewulf made so much of his name by spelling it differently anagrammatically in runes and using it as a means of signing his poetry. This is the only way we know so much poetry is his.

Runes were the angular symbols representing sounds that were usually used for inscriptions in stone and wood among the early Germanic peoples. Each rune had a name as well as a sound associated with it: "thorn" (what pricks your finger if you grasp the wrong plant) for þ, Ash, the ash-tree for æ, etc. Cynewulf wrote four surviving poems and near the end of each interwove the words for the runes in anagrammatical order, indicating them as his signature. In two he spells his name as given above, while in the other two he spells it "Cynwulf."

The name was a fairly common one, and various Cynwulfs or Cynewulfs have at times been proposed as the poet—an early ninth-century priest from Dunwich, the late eighth-century bishop of Lindisfarne, and the late tenth-century abbot of Peterborough. The poems themselves on somewhat shaky linguistic grounds could be dated to the ninth century, perhaps in the West Mercian sub-dialect of Anglian.[112]

The poems he wrote are the 731–line *Juliana* contained in the Exeter Book, a poetical saint's life of a virgin martyr from the early fourth century; the 1321–line *Elene* from the Vercelli Book, the story of how St. Helena, the Emperor Constantine's mother, found the True Cross; *Christ II* (427 lines) from the Exeter Book, a poem about the Ascension; and the 122–line *Fates of the Apostles*, translated for this volume. It is contained in the Vercelli Book, immediately following the longer poem *Andreas*, about the apostle Andrew's adventures in the country of the cannibals. *Fates* tells in verse something of the evangelistic career of each of the apostles.

INTRODUCTION

Ælfric: A prolific prose writer, Ælfric is the literary giant of the later Anglo-Saxon era. He lived from about A.D. 955 to about A.D. 1012 and was first a monk at the Abbey of Cerne and later abbot of Eynsham. A product of the Benedictine Reform of the tenth century led by Archbishop Dunstan, Ælfric was likely the pupil of Æþelwold, bishop of Winchester. Ælfric lived what amounted to a fairly quiet literary life during his troubled times of renewed Viking invasions. He wrote school books of Latin-acquisition, translated Bede's *De Temporibus Anni*, began a remarkable effort of biblical translation by rendering its first seven books into English (the *Heptateuch*), and produced several cycles of sermons and homilies. For them he translated various works of earlier homilists, sometimes piecing more than one sermon, homily, or treatise into a coherent whole. He also wrote a number of letters, including two to Archbishop Wulfstan, one of which, like the works mentioned above, is in English.

His homiletic corpus comprises three cycles—two termed *Catholic Homilies* and the third *Lives of the Saints*. This latter is not, as its title may indicate, pure hagiography; instead, it is a series of sermons on the saints arranged according to their feast days in the calendar. The *Catholic Homilies* contain more of these sermonic lives, in addition to other, more general topics pertaining the liturgical year. Each series contains about forty sermons, and all or part of them are contained in a number of manuscripts. In addition, he wrote a fair number of sermons not collected in these three cycles. They exist scattered about in various manuscripts among the anonymous pieces and have been collected into two volumes in the Early English Text Society *Homilies of Ælfric: A Supplementary Collection*.[113]

The sermons translated here are as follows: *St. John the Apostle* is a hagiographical sermon about that important biblical and legendary figure. It is taken from the first series of *Catholic Homilies*, written about the year 989. Its main source is the apocryphal *Acts of John*, and thus it belongs to the same sub-genre as the Blickling Homily on St. Andrew as well as the important Old English poem *Andreas*. This last comment also applies to his homily on *St. Denis and His Companions*, also translated for this volume. Its ultimate source is Abbot Hilduin's *Life of St. Denis*, the legendary descant on the biblical figure of the

Athenian philosopher Dionysius the Areopagite, whom St. Paul converts in Acts 17. Denis for Hilduin, Ælfric, and indeed most medieval people was a conflation of the biblical figure, the legendary evangelist of France, and the important writer of mystical treatises known to us as Pseudo-Dionysius. The sermon on St. Oswald shows the interest Ælfric shared with other Anglo-Saxon writers in native sanctity. The main source for the Oswald material is Bede's *Ecclesiastical History*, Book III. The fourth and last of Ælfric's sermons translated here is his important *On the Sacrifice of Easter*, mentioned earlier as the first work of Old English to be printed in modern times. Its sources are the eucharistic treatises of both Ratramnus and Radbert and the work Ælfric himself mentions, the *Lives of the Fathers*, a compendium of sayings of and anecdotes about the early Egyptian monks and hermits.

Wulfstan: The life of Ælfric's exact contemporary and correspondent Wulfstan, bishop of Worcester and archbishop of York (c. 960–1023) was, it seems, the more eventful of the two. Like Ælfric a Benedictine monk (whose house, however, is unknown), Wulfstan first came to prominence during the dark years following Alderman Byrhtnoth's defeat at the hands of the Vikings in 991. By 996 he was bishop of London, by 1002 simultaneously bishop of Worcester and archbishop of York (the pluralism explained by the deteriorated state of the living of York's see in the wake of Viking violence). He died in 1023 as archbishop, having relinquished Worcester to a suffragan in 1016, the year the Viking Cnut came to the throne of England.

Wulfstan was a political figure of major importance. He became a close counselor to Æþelræd Unræd in 1008 and produced major law codes for him—the *Canons of Edgar, The Peace of Edward and Guthrum*, and *The Institutes of Polity I* and *II*. Though someone who cast the invading Vikings in the bleakest of moral colors, he survived politically intact into the reign of Cnut, producing the new monarch's first two law codes, *Cnut I* and *Cnut II*.

Wulfstan wrote fewer sermons than Ælfric, who not only corresponded with him but also provided some materials Wulfstan used when writing both legal works and sermons. Among the sermons translated for this volume are the famous *Sermo Lupi ad Anglos*, treated above, a jeremiad against the sins of the English that depicts the

Vikings as God's scourges. Its source, as mentioned above, is Gildas's similar jeremiad, but the topical details and compelling rhetoric come straight from Wulfstan. The *Sermon on the False Gods*, noteworthy for its euhemeristic[114] interpretation of the classical gods' origins and the equation of certain deities from the Greek and Roman pantheon with the gods of Germanic (particularly Viking) mythology, has as its source Ælfric's sermon of the same name. Wulfstan reworked it, condensing it and tightening its prose. Ælfric's main source, in turn, is Martin of Braga's *De Correctione Rusticorum*. Wulfstan's sermon on *The Sevenfold Spirit* is a sermon more about the evil gifts of the devil that attempt to pervert the traditional gifts of the Holy Spirit. Like the *Sermo Lupi*, it has strident apocalyptic elements.

Blickling Book: The Blickling Book, formerly from the library at Blickling Hall in Norfolk and now part of the William H. Scheide Collection at Firestone Library, Princeton, contains nineteen sermons. A passage from the sermon *On Holy Thursday* gives the date of the manuscript's compilation, A.D. 971, so it was produced during the years of the tenth-century Benedictine Reform. The anonymous sermons themselves are likely somewhat earlier, perhaps from the late ninth century.

Translated for this volume are four sermons, given here in their order in the manuscript. *The End of the World* draws its imagery from the common stock of Old English eschatology. *The Birth of John the Baptist* elaborates the gospel account in Luke 1. *The Dedication of St. Michael's Church* is a folktale whose heart is the story of a bull who wished to be a hermit and lived apart from its flock. This sermon is famous because its concluding passage, a summary of some grim imagery in the apocryphal *Visio Sancti Pauli*,[115] has demonstrable connections with the description of Grendel's mere in *Beowulf*, also dependent on the *Visio*. The sermon on *St. Andrew* is ultimately a translation of the Greek hagiographical romance, the *Praxeis Andreou* (through a possible Latin intermediary), which recounts the apostle Andrew's rescue of St. Matthew (Mathias in the Greek) from the country of the cannibals and his close brush with death and subsequent devouring there before he effects that country's conversion. Another version of this same sermon is contained in MS Cambridge Corpus Christi College 198; both are prose renderings of the elaborate and lengthy Old English poem *Andreas* from the Vercelli Book.

Vercelli Book: The Vercelli Book is an anthology of religious works, both sermons and homilies and also poetry, dating probably from the last half of the tenth century (the time of the Benedictine Reform), possibly in Canterbury. Its present location in the cathedral library in Vercelli has been a puzzle over the years; I have suggested elsewhere that internal and external evidence suggest that it was brought there by the English delegation to the Council of Vercelli in A.D. 1050.[116]

The book contains six poems and twenty-three homilies, as they are usually termed, though most are properly sermons. The poems are *Andreas*, Cynewulf's *Fates of the Apostles* (translated for this volume and mentioned above in the section on Cynewulf), *Soul and Body I*, *Homiletic Fragment I*, *The Dream of the Rood* (translated for this volume and analyzed in the section of the Introduction entitled "Anglo-Saxon Spirituality"), and Cynewulf's *Elene*. Three of the sermons are translated for this volume. *The Day of Judgment*, like its companion piece in the Blickling Book, is one of the many Old English treatments of eschatological matters. There is no identifiable source, though a longer version of it exists in a manuscript housed in Cambridge, Corpus Christi College. Part of it was originally an Old English poem, as is indicated by the alliterative scheme. The sermon for *Christmas Day* is a rendering of passages from the apocryphal *Evangelium Pseudo-Matthaei*. The *Rogation Day* sermon (one of two in the book) is an explanation of the customs of rogation time and has no identifiable source.

Bodley 343: Oxford Bodleian Library MS Bodley 343 is a large collection of sermons and homilies copied in the latter half of the twelfth century. There are eighty-five items included, most in Old English. Item #5, according to its editors' numbering, actually comprises sixty-seven short Latin sermons. Some of the Old English sermons appear in no other collection, four by

Ælfric; the three non-Ælfrician pieces unique to Bodley 343 are translated here.

The manuscript's date, of course, removes it by a century from the Anglo-Saxon period. Yet their sermons and homilies date from that period, most to the late tenth or early eleventh centuries. The manuscript attests to a surviving interest in Anglo-Saxon literature and spirituality well into the Norman period. The language of the manuscript shows scribal struggles with what would have appeared as an archaic form of English. There are consequently early Middle English syntactical forms. *The Temptation of Christ* is a homiletic excursus on Matthew 4:1–11. Its main source (and that of Blickling Homily II and Ælfric's *Catholic Homily I*, also treatments of Christ's temptation) is likely Gregory's *Homilia in Evangelia xvi*. The *Transfiguration of Christ* is a homily on the account of the transfiguration in Matthew 17, whose main source is Bede's homily *In Quadragesima*. *The Transience of Earthly Delights* is a rather gripping sermon with affinities to the Judgment Day and also the soul and body themes in Old English literature, whose main source is Caesarius of Arles's sermon *De Elemosinis*.

The Exeter Book: The Exeter Book is a large Old English manuscript bequeathed by Bishop Leofwine in 1072 to the cathedral library of his see of Exeter. Unlike the Vercelli Book, it originally contained only poetry, and much of it is secular in nature. The religious poetry, though, is prominent, with the initial poem the composite *Christ*, whose first section, the *Advent Lyrics*, is translated for this volume. The Exeter Book was probably copied as what we would now call a poetry anthology in the second half of the tenth century; perhaps the impetus for it, not withstanding the secular pieces, was also the Benedictine Reform. A number of the poems translated for this volume are taken from the Exeter Book.

The *Advent Lyrics* is a poem as it stands of 439 lines, most of whose twelve sections are loose translations and elaborations of the liturgical O-antiphons for Advent. The original opening lines are lost because the folio on which they doubtless were written became separated from the rest of the manuscript. They are the initial lines of the antiphon *O Rex gentium*. One of the poem's sections, the seventh, is a remarkable dialogue between Joseph and the Virgin Mary, which some have termed the first drama in English.

Guthlac A, the poem immediately following the composite *Christ*, is a saint's life of 818 lines, recounting the struggles of Guthlac of Crowland (d. circa 715), a nobleman and a contemporary of Bede who left his worldly life to become a hermit after the pattern of the Egyptian Father Anthony. It is largely a dialogue between the saint and the devils who tempt him in their unwillingness to relinquish their habitations in the wilderness to him. Its conclusion, in which Guthlac is transported by the apostle St. Bartholomew back from Hell Mouth, where the devils have lately been tormenting him, to his hermitage, where he is welcomed by the wild birds he has been feeding with his own hand, is charming and moving, worth the ticket for the whole show. The poem is followed by a related poem, not translated for this volume, *Guthlac B*, about the saint's pious death. The main source for the latter poem is Felix's Latin *Life of Guthlac* and, though debated, possibly *Guthlac A* as well.

The 677–line *Phoenix*, a translation and expansion of Lactantius's Latin poem of the name, is a description of the legendary bird who lives unique of its species for a thousand years, immolates itself, and then rises young again from the ashes of its own pyre. Its spirituality is a function of its allegory; roughly the second half of the poem is the author's explanation that the Phoenix represents believers who can choose a good life and be resurrected into heaven and also Christ himself in the resurrection that effected humankind's salvation. The description of the earthly paradise (home to the big bird), its rejuvenated plumage, and the host of birds who desperately try to fly as a retinue for the returning Phoenix but cannot keep up is vivid and lively.

Soul and Body II is just as vivid, but in a grim sense. It is a darkly fanciful explanation about how the soul of a damned person must visit its decayed, entombed body every seventh night and complain about how it caused their mutual damnation. The poem is essentially the same as the first part of the Vercelli Book's 166–line *Soul and Body I;* what that poem adds is the body's response. I have chosen the Exeter Book's monologue over the Vercelli Book's dialogue for the grim effect of the end, when we realize that the body cannot hear the soul, for it has decayed entirely away—an artistic success I find greater than the squabble the Vercelli poem becomes.

Judgment Day I is a 119–line poem, treated above, which describes the End of the World and the coming to Judgment in graphic detail to inspire in the reader holy dread. It should not be confused with *Judgment Day II*, an Old English version of the Latin poem often ascribed to Bede.

The Lord's Prayer I, the last poem translated from the Exeter Book, is, as mentioned above, a poetical rendering of that most famous of prayers. There are two other Old English versions of it.

The Junius Manuscript: The Junius Manuscript, copied about the year 1000 and named after its seventeenth-century editor, the Dutchman Franciscus Junius, is now in the Bodleian Library, Oxford. It contains four rather long poems, each except the last verse paraphrases of portions of the Bible. They are *Genesis* (including both *Genesis A* and *Genesis B*), *Exodus, Daniel,* and *Christ and Satan.* Junius thought the manuscript contained poems written by Cædmon, a not completely implausible assumption, given the manuscript's correlation with the list of Cædmon's work supplied by Bede (mentioned above), but there is no evidence that any, in fact, are. For this volume I have translated two important sections of *Genesis,* "Abraham and Isaac" from *Genesis A* and "Satan in Hell" from *Genesis B.* Each is a highly imaginative descant on the biblical material.

Although the manuscript presents them as one poem, *Genesis A* and *Genesis B* are in fact separate poems, with *B* interpolated into the appropriate place in *A. Genesis A* narrates the events of the first book of the Bible through its twenty-second chapter, the story of the sacrifice of Isaac, translated for this volume. Thus it omits treatment of more than half of the chapters of Genesis, the portion devoted to the stories of Jacob and Joseph. *Genesis B* comprises lines 235–851 of the composite poem. About half of *Genesis B* is translated for this volume. It is a lengthy treatment of the devil's rage and despair in hell as he formulates the plan to tempt Adam and Eve. *Genesis B* has a large proportion of hypermetric lines and, more important, many loaned words from Old Saxon, a close Continental cognate with Old English. These facts led Eduard Sievers in 1875 to posit an Old Saxon original for the part he identified as *Genesis B*, suggesting that it was added to the larger poem at the appropriate place. In 1894 a portion of that original was discovered in the Vatican Library.

Genesis A is a spirited narrative featuring in its latter part Abraham as a Germanic warrior leading his thanes to battle. The story of his near sacrifice of his son is vigorous, not without poignancy. *Genesis B*, though, is truly remarkable, largely because of the access the Old Saxon poet and his Anglo-Saxon translator give into Satan's distorted mind. Readers are immediately taken by its striking similarities to the first two books of Milton's *Paradise Lost*, and some have even suggested that Milton's genesis for his greatest poem was an encounter with the edition of the poems of the Junius Manuscript published by Junius in 1654—a suggestion not without some merit.

The Nowell Codex: MS Cotton Vitellius A.xv, or the Nowell Codex, a manuscript of the early eleventh century now housed in the British Museum, is one of the most famous of all medieval manuscripts, for it contains the greatest of all Old English poems, *Beowulf*. *Judith*, translated for this volume, immediately follows that great poem; the manuscript contains as well some twelfth-century copies of Old English works, originally a separate manuscript, bound together with the eleventh-century material probably in the late sixteenth century by its antiquarian owner, Robert Cotton. The eleventh-century portion contains some prose pieces as well—a fragmentary *Legend of St. Christopher*, *The Wonders of the East*, and *The Letter of Alexander to Aristotle*.

Damaged like *Beowulf* in the 1731 fire that destroyed so much of the vast Cotton library, *Judith* was originally copied as a fragment in the original manuscript. It begins near the end of its ninth fitt (a term referring to something equivalent to a chapter designation) and continues through the twelfth. The poem as it stands, moreover, begins in mid-sentence. If there were originally all the early fitts, the poem would have run to about 1300 lines. As it stands now, it is 349 lines long. The material that the scribe chose to include, though, is the important part of Judith's story, which, of course, is presented in the Vulgate Bible. The maiden Judith has just arrived in the Assyrian camp as the fragment begins. Then her murder of the warlord Holofernes, who in a drunken stupor has brought her to his bed, and the subsequent rout of the Assyrian army are related with all the heroic vigor one finds in Old English secular battle poetry. A good guess is that the scribe or an earlier compiler chose to copy only the climax, as it were, of a longer poem.

This volume contains two other poems. The Old English translation of Psalm 121 is taken from the Paris Psalter, a manuscript preserved in the Bibliothéque Nationale containing versions and Old English translations of the Psalms and other liturgical texts. It is included here not only as an example of the liturgical focus of Anglo-Saxon spirituality, but also as a demonstration of how an Old English poet, already given by his own traditions to a verse form rich in parallelism, rendered a poem originally in Hebrew, whose own tradition likewise was based on parallelism. The Old English poet's response is to expand the parallel structure.

Finally, *Maxims II*, the gnomic poem that concludes this volume, is contained in a copy of the *Anglo-Saxon Chronicle* in MS Cotton Tiberius B.i, now in the British Museum, another survivor of the Cottonian fire of 1731. It presents in its homely aphoristic style an Anglo-Saxon world in harmony with itself, where the beasts of the wild, the rivers, the stars, inanimate objects, and the kings all live in peace because God, like them, inhabits his proper place in the cosmos:

> In the country a wood
> must bloom with blossoms. On the earth a hill
> must stand green. God must be in the heavens,
> the Judge of deeds. A door must be in the hall,
> the wide building's mouth. A boss must be on a shield,
> fast defense of fingers. A bird must sport
> above in the air.

With that irenic vision—one the turmoil of the Anglo-Saxon world largely belied, but one perhaps its poets and homilists in their efforts to depict the life of the spirit as they knew it occasionally experienced—this volume and this Introduction concludes.

THE TEXTS

BLICKLING HOMILY X

The End of the World

Most beloved people, listen! Now will I remind all of you and teach you—both men and women, both young and old, both wise and unwise, both rich and poor[1]—that each of you should behold and examine himself and, according to the great or small sins he has done, quickly turn toward the better and toward the true remedy. Then we will gain for ourselves the almighty and merciful God, because the Lord wills that all people be whole and sound and turn toward true knowledge. As David says,[2] God never scorns or rejects the humble of heart and the fearful and those who tremble and quake and dread their creator. But he hears their prayers when they call to him and ask him for grace.

Let us now see and acknowledge and zealously perceive that the end of this world is very near and that many perils have appeared[3] and the evil deeds and wrongdoings of the people have multiplied. And from one day to the next we hear of unnatural torments and unnatural deaths that have come upon people throughout the nation. And we often see nation arise against nation[4] and disastrous battle arise in wicked deeds. And very often we hear recounted the death of a worldly man whose life was dear to his people, whose life was thought fair and bright and joyous. Likewise we also hear about various plagues and growing hunger in many places of middle earth. And we hear about many an evil here in this life growing common and even flourishing, with no abiding good and every worldly thing very sinful. And too much does the love

61

cool[5] that we should have for our Savior, and we leave behind the good works that we should perform for our soul's health.[6] Such are the signs that just now I have mentioned of the troubles and dangers of this world. Thus Christ himself told his disciples that all these things would happen before the end of this world.[7]

Let us now hasten with all the strength of good works and be eager for God's mercy, now that we can see that the End of the World is approaching. Therefore I exhort and admonish everyone to consider deeply his own deeds so that he might live righteously here in the world before God and in the sight of the highest King.

Let us be generous to the needy and eager to help the poor, since God himself commanded us that we truly keep the peace and have concord between us. And let those who have children teach them righteous conduct and show them the way of life and the right road to heaven. And if they live unjustly in any part of their life, let them immediately be separated from their sins and turn from their wrongs so that we might be pleasing to God through all of this. As it is commanded to all faithful people and is necessary and profitable to all, they should keep well their baptism and place in life, not only those who are subjected to God in various orders—bishops and kings and priests and archdeacons—but also truly subdeacons and monks.

Nor should people be too proud in their thoughts here in this life nor too strong in their bodies nor too eager for wickedness nor too bold for malice nor too full of deceits nor too fond of guile. Let them neither weave slanders nor set snares. Nor can they expect that their bodies might or may atone for the burdens of sin in the grave. But there they molder in the ground and there await fate, until God the almighty wishes to work an end for this world. And when he draws his burning sword[8] and smites through all the world and pierces our bodies and cleaves asunder this middle earth and the dead stand up, then our bodies will be made clear as glass and then nothing unrighteous can be concealed.

Therefore we have need no longer to follow works of guile, since we must earn for ourselves the peaceful covenants of God and men and the right faith established firmly in our hearts so that he can and will dwell there and grow and blossom there. And we should confess the true faith in God and our Lord Jesus Christ, his only begotten Son, and in the Holy Ghost, who is co-eternal with the Father and the Son. And we should place our hopes in God's holy and catholic church. And we should believe in the forgiveness of sins and the resurrection of the body[9] on Judgment Day. And we should believe in eternal life and in the heavenly kingdom that is promised to all who are now God's servants. This is the righteous faith that is proper for everyone to hold and practice well, because no servant can do a good work before God without love and faith. And it is very necessary that we remember and consider ourselves— and most eagerly when we hear God's books recited and read before us and the gospel recited and his heavenly glories made known to all. Let us then eagerly strive accordingly to be better and better because of the teaching we have often heard.

Alas, beloved people, listen! We should be careful not to love too much what we will have to forsake, lest indeed we forsake too much what we should possess eternally. Let us now understand very clearly that no one in the world has so much wealth or such proud treasure here in the world that he will not after a little time come to his end, that he will not forsake all that delighted him here in the world and was most precious for him to have and hold.[10] And one is never so dear to his family and friends and they never love him so much that they will not immediately shun him when his body and spirit are separated and think his company hateful and foul. This is no wonder. Lo, what else is someone but flesh after the best part, which is the soul, departs? Lo, what else is the remains but food for worms?

Where then are his riches and feasts? Where then are his glory and splendor? Where then are his worthless clothes? Where then are those ornaments and those expensive garments with which he once adorned his body? To what have his desires and lusts that he had here in the world come? Lo then, he must with his soul alone pay the price to almighty God for all that he did sinfully here in this world.

Let us now hear a story about a certain rich and powerful man. He owned in this world great wealth and many and various proud treasures and lived in joy. Then it happened that his life came to an end—and a sudden end came upon him of this transitory life. There was a certain man among his family and friends who loved him more than anyone else. Then because of grief and sorrow for the other's death he did not wish to live long in his country. So, sad at heart, he departed from his homeland and from his dwelling and lived away from that land for many years. But his grief never subsided, and it greatly oppressed and afflicted him. Then he began to long again for his homeland, because he wanted to see it again and look at the tomb of the one whom he had often seen among the living fair of face and figure.

Then those dead bones called out to him and said, "Why have you come here to look at us? Now all you can see here is a piece of earth and the leavings of the worms, where earlier you saw fine cloth adorned with gold. Now look at the dust and dry bones where you once saw limbs that were, according to the nature of flesh, fair to look at. Alas, my friend and kinsman, remember this and look to yourself, since you now are what I once was. And after a little while you will be as I now am.[11] Remember this and understand that the wealth that I once had has all gone and perished and my dwellings are withered and decayed. But turn toward yourself and turn your heart toward this advice: make sure your prayers are acceptable to almighty God!"

Then he departed so sorrowfully and in such grief from this vision of dust that he turned from all the worship of this world and began to learn the praise of God and teach it and love his spiritual kindred. And through this he earned for himself the gifts of the Holy Spirit and also rescued the soul of the other from its punishments and released it from its torments.

May we now, dearest people, have this in mind and establish this example in our hearts, that we must not love too much the ornaments of the world or this middle earth, because this world is all undone and dead and corrupt and ruined. And this world will all fade away.

Let us then eagerly think about the beginning of this world. When it was first created, it was all full of fairness and was blossoming on its own with very many delights. And in that time it was pleasant for people on the earth, and there was on the earth healthful and whole serenity and abundant peace and noble children. And in that time this middle earth was so fair and delightful that it drew people to itself and away from the almighty God through its beauty and through its fairness and delight. And when it was so fair and delightful it withered in the hearts of Christ's saints, and now that it is fading and ending it still blossoms in our hearts—as is not fitting.

Now there is clamor and weeping everywhere. Now everywhere there is wailing and loss of peace. Now there is evil and slaughter everywhere. And everywhere this middle earth flees from us with much bitterness. And we follow it while it flees and love it while it falls to ruins. Listen, in this we can see that this world is ending and passing away.

Let us then consider this while we can and may, that we ought to follow God zealously. Let us eagerly obey our Lord and give him thanks for all his gifts and all his mercies and all the kindness and benefits that he has ever shown us, this heavenly king who lives and reigns forever and ever without end. Amen.

BLICKLING HOMILY XIV

The Birth of John the Baptist

Dearest people, we are admonished and reminded in this book and in these holy scriptures about the worship of this holy time that now today[12] we must honor and celebrate—the famous birth of St. John the Baptist.[13] About this we can know and understand that this day he is greatly to be honored and worshiped, because we heard when the holy gospel was read that the churches do not honor the birth of any of God's saints[14]—neither the patriarchs nor the prophets nor the apostles—except Christ himself and this John. There were many holy and faithful prophets before John who were great and famous and sanctified by God himself and so enlightened and sanctified by the gifts of the Holy Spirit that they all prophesied beforehand what was about to happen and made it known to all. And they were in God's counsel for all his secret judgments, and they stood against kings and evil and powerful earls. And they bridled the heavens with their might, and they shone in all their marvels with many godly strengths. And they told the truth and spoke signs, those that the Lord himself had given. But nevertheless it is not and cannot be said about any of them what the Lord Jesus said about this John, that never was there born of woman one more famous or better.[15]

And the evangelist right at the beginning of his gospel wrote about this John's birth and said, "In the days of Herod the king there was a very great religious whose name was Zachariah, and his

wife's name was Elizabeth, who was from the daughters of the patriarch Aaron." And the holy evangelist wrote about him and said,
"They were very faithful before God, and they walked without
blame in all the commandments of God. Lo, how very blessed were
those noble parents of St. John, whom no guilt of this harmful
world harmed. Nor did any sin wound them. Nor did evil witness
cloud them. Nor did any vice disturb them. But they were mindful
of all of God's commandments, and in every way they were very
obedient to the divine law. And now their youth and their middle
age remained without any sin. How can we reckon that the old age
and end of their life would not be like the beginning? Elizabeth was
not then unfruitful of godly virtues, although she was late with
respect to children. Yet she was not late in bearing a child when it is
understood about her that her giving birth happened when she was
old, for a great while before this holy event the house [of her soul]
had to be cleansed. The hospice for Christ's harbinger, the shelter
for the guest, Christ's messenger, and the hall of the Holy Spirit—
such a temple altogether worthy for God—had to be found in
which the wisdom of the Holy Spirit could dwell.

And when every human sin was stilled in the parents of the
blessed St. John and they stood blameless in all their life, then
immediately their infertility fled from them and immediately their
age was enlivened and their belief and purity conceived. Then the
man St. John was begotten, he who was greater and better than anyone else. He was like God's angels, and he was a trumpet, Christ's
herald in this middle earth. And he was the spokesman for God's
Son and the standard bearer of the supreme King, the forgiveness
of sins, and the setting right of heathen nations.

And I say that the evangelist was the fusion of both the old and
new laws, because he wrote beforehand of the divine strength of his
father and mother so that by the deeds of the parents the worth of
the child should be understood by all these other people, because by
his birth alone she surpassed all human law. And now at Christ's
birth's arising, St. John, the new day-star, the beam of the true Son
of God himself, will come. Let the herald give voice! And now
because the Judge is the Lord Christ, the trumpet is St. John. And
now he will come with God himself into this middle earth. Let the

messenger St. John go before him! And since it is everyone's duty to tell the merits of St. John's life, because he was praised and honored by the voice of truth, the Lord himself said about him in his gospel, "Why did you go into the wilderness? To seek a prophet? I say he is greater and better than any prophet."[16] Thus no human tongue is sufficient to relate the divine power of this begotten messenger.

Also, the archangel St. Gabriel spoke and said to Zachariah his father, "Be not afraid, Zachariah! All your prayer has been heard by God, and your wife Elizabeth will bear you a son, and you will call his name John, and you will then have hope and joy, and many will rejoice at his birth. He will be exceedingly great before God. He will drink neither wine nor ale, but he will be filled with the Holy Spirit in his mother's womb. And he will turn many children of Israel toward their Lord, and he will go before God filled with the Holy Spirit and with the power of the prophet Elijah to win a people fit for the Lord."[17]

Let us then, dearest people, hear how very marvelously St. John was filled with the power of the Holy Spirit when he was resting in his mother's womb and how he came to heaven before he touched earth and there received the Holy Spirit before he had a human spirit and received divine gifts before he had human life. And he began to live before God before he himself might live, just as St. Paul the apostle said, "I do not live, but Christ lives."[18]

Moreover, in the sixth month after St. John was conceived the Son of glory entered this middle earth and the heavenly honor filled the virgin womb of St. Mary. And when she went to the holy Elizabeth[19] her cousin, immediately the child leapt and began to exalt his Lord and from his mother's womb hailed and greeted him who was in the Virgin's womb and strove to speak and make him known to people before he himself lived and saw human light. O dearest people, what an enthusiastic spokesman he was and an impatient general, he who wanted to tell about the Savior who was about to come into the world before he himself received the secret formation of natural birth! And he first came to the King and grasped a weapon with which to fight before he possessed the limbs of his body. And he first sought a battle before he saw the light. And thus in his birth he overcame all the law of our human birth.

THE BIRTH OF JOHN THE BAPTIST

Let us examine the high deeds of St. John, who awoke in his mother's womb to God's Son, whose own birth was set apart from natural birth. And though St. John was late in bodily birth, nevertheless he fulfilled the service of an evangelist in the spirit alone. And as soon as he was begotten and born, he gave speech to the Father and loosened his tongue, when the archangel had bound his father with the bonds of silence because he had not believed his words. Great then is the honor of holy St. John's birth, and all orthodox people ought to rejoice in his arrival and bless him, because scripture so spoke about him that many ought to rejoice at his birth. Great is the holiness and the honor of St. John, of whose greatness the Lord Jesus himself gave sign. And it is known that among those born of women there will not be a greater person than John the Baptist [except the Lord Jesus Christ][20] himself, who was without a human father, begotten in a Virgin's womb.

St. John then goes before all other prophets, and he excels the virtues of all other patriarchs in apostolic authority, and he overcomes in the honors of his virtue the glory of all other martyrs of God. And among all God's saints he is most triumphant and elect. And all natural birth is eclipsed by St. John.

Listen, we heard when Isaiah the prophet was read, that the Holy Spirit spoke thus through him about St. John: "I will send my angel before your face, who will prepare the way before you."[21] That was indeed a very high name with which St. John was called: "angel."[22] And so that his life was ordered like his name, he here on earth lived an angelic life. When did he [sin in his food, since he subsisted][23] on roots and the honey of the woods? Or where was he ever guilty in his clothing, he who was clothed with a single garment woven of camel's hair? Or how could anyone ever be greater than the one who always loved God in all his life and who never left the wilderness? Or when did the guilt of talkativeness defile him who was separated so far from everyone? Or how did the sin of silence harm him who so strongly rebuked the Jews who came to him to hear his teaching? For he said, "You generation of snakes, who told you to flee from the coming wrath of God?"[24] And when the crowds asked him how they could escape God's wrath, he then taught and admonished them with these words and said to them,

"He who has two tunics, let him give the second to the one who has none. He who has food, [let him give some to the one who has none][25]...and be thankful to the Savior for your nourishment."[26]

Let us then follow the teaching of our high and famous guardian that we might obey the pure sayings of our Lord that he will say to the people on the terrible Day of Judgment, to those who now do not show mercy to the poor, "Truly I say to you that as long as you did this to one of those who believe in me, though he were the least and most wretched, it was as if you had done it to me myself."[27]

What more shall I say about St. John, says the one who made this book, except that he first walked before Christ before he might himself walk? And the same Holy Spirit filled the hearts of father, mother, and son with his gifts, to whom be always glory and honor forever and ever. Amen.

BLICKLING HOMILY XVII

The Dedication of St. Michael's Church

Dearest people, the honor and the blessedness of this high and holy archangel's feast[28] admonishes us and reminds us that we should say something in blessed memory about him who is everywhere to be honored and glorified in his church, consecrated both by his own work and in his own name. And thus it first appeared and was made known to all. It by no means shines by the beauty of gold and silver, but it stands glorified in various honors through godly power. It is also in outward appearance of evil color, but inside it is made holy by eternal virtue. Thus can it easily be that the holy archangel should come from heaven and be mindful of the people's frailty, so that he humbled himself to establish and build it with his own hands. By this he desired that mortal people might there yearn for that higher citizenship and for eternal companionship.

This is Michael's holy church,[29] established on the high knoll of a certain mountain. It appeared in the likeness of a cave. Thus the church is famous in the land of Campania. Then there is a very famous city nearby between the inlets of the sea named the Adriatic built on the mountain of Garganus that is named Sepontus. From the walls of the city there are twelve miles up to the high knoll, which I mentioned earlier, of the archangel's church. And it stands there with joy and growing bliss. The same book that was found and discovered in that church first revealed that church and made it known. It says in it that there was a certain man, powerful and successful before the world, whose name was Garganus, in that city. That wealthy man gave the mountain the same name by which he himself was called. This man possessed great wealth. The wealthy man's endless herds and unnumbered flocks of cattle and various animals grew and flourished there until his flocks spread out and covered all the mountain's field. Then it happened that a certain bull scorned the fellowship of the other animals and lived as a hermit out in the wilderness, and then at last turned away from the other cattle and the animals and their place. The bull then scorned the driving of the herdsmen and lived in that wilderness at the mouth of a certain cave. When the lord found out that the bull had gone in pride out into the wilderness, he then became angry, because it seemed to him that the bull who had gone out there beyond the massive mountain was mad. Then he gathered a great host together of his people and headed out along the path even beyond the woods and searched for the proud bull.

Then he at last encountered it on the knoll of the mountain and saw that it stood alone by some cave's mouth. Then he was greatly stirred up with anger because it had gone so mad and traveled about so proudly. Then he took his bow and bent it and then with a poisoned arrow began to shoot at where he saw the bull standing. Then as soon as he let the arrow fly there came a very great blast of wind against it, and the arrow immediately was turned about and hit the same wealthy person from whom it first came, so that he immediately died.

When the townsfolk saw this, they became very frightened because of the marvel, for they had never seen such a wonder. And then they did not dare get near to the place where they saw the bull standing.

In that same time there was a holy bishop in their town named Sepontus. They then sought him out and told him about that wonder and he counseled them what to do about this. Then he taught them and gave them advice to fast for three days and do this in honor of St. Michael and desire that God make known what was hidden and concealed from the people. When they had done this both in fasting and in psalm singing and in alms, then in the night the high and holy archangel Michael was revealed to that same bishop and he spoke to him humbly and lovingly and said this:

"You did worthily and wisely when you sought from God in heaven what was hidden from the people on earth. Know also that the man who was hit there by his own arrow was hit by my own will, and my name is Michael.[30] I am the archangel of the King of heaven, and I always stand in his sight. I tell you now also that I especially love this place here on earth and I have chosen it over all others and also will make known in many signs that take place here that I am the creator and herdsman of this place in all ways."

When this was spoken and made known, the townspeople went to that place with their holy bishop very glad and rejoicing, and according to their custom prayed there mightily to the living God and to the holy archangel Michael and humbly offered gifts there to God.

And they then saw two doors in that church. There was the south door, somewhat larger in form. And still they could not go up to the cave, which was so high there, before they broadened and worked the path upward. But outside every day they devoutly said their prayers.

At that time their neighbors the Neapolitans still followed pagan customs and obeyed devils. They then commanded the citizens of Benevento and Sepontus that the two countries begin a war and scorned their land as a reproach and gave them no alternative except proud battle and threats. Then their holy bishop taught them and gave them counsel to fast for three days and give much in the way of alms and sing holy songs of praise to the archangel Michael as to the most faithful protector for help and comfort so that they could deceive and vanquish the deceit of their enemies.

Then at the same time the pagans shamefully and sinfully asked their false gods with various idols to help them. And the blessed archangel Michael appeared to their bishop in a vision and promised them the coming victory[31] and said to him that their prayers had been heard by God. And he told them to marshal themselves against their enemy at the third hour in the morning. And he also promised them that he would himself see their acts and be there to help them. Then they were very happy in the morning and went rejoicing against the pagans. And they knew by the angel's words both about their victory and also about the flight of the pagan men and their downfall.

And then immediately in the beginning of the battle, Mt. Garganus on which they had to fight was all oppressed with great terror and dread, and a wild storm arose from the mountain, and the mountain's peak was all covered with a dark mist.[32] Then lightning flew like fire arrows toward the pagan people so thickly that they by no means could look toward it because of the burning of the flames. Then what the prophet foretold was fulfilled. And he praised the Lord, saying thus: *Qui facit angelos suos spiritus et ministros suos ignem urentem*, "Sometimes the same God sends the spirit of his angels as avengers; sometimes he sends them through the flame of fire."[33]

Then the pagan people fled as if the fire killed them, as if the Christians crushed and oppressed them with their weapons, until they roughly overcame the pagan nation of the Neapolitans, those who lived half-alive in their city, and attacked those who escaped the harm and danger. Then God's angel who came there for our help and comfort was revealed to us Christian people. And then he bowed humbly to the King of kings, to Christ himself, and the pagan people all went into his hand and lived according to Christian doctrine and accepted baptism, and they devoutly perceived that God's angel had come for the help and comfort of the Christian people.

And then while the Christian people were well considering these things, they saw and counted up that there were also six hundred people killed by the fire alone and with the arrows of fire apart from those whom they had killed and slain with their weapons. Then they went home so victory-bright and so crowned with bliss that immediately they humbly and lovingly thanked the almighty God and the archangel Michael in their holy church for the victory they had gained.

Then they also found before the north door of that church on the marble something like human footprints as if some person had stood there. And the footprints were plain and visible on the stone, as if they were made in wax. Then they devoutly perceived that the blessed Michael had been present with them for their help while they were at the battle, and he himself had ordered the miracle of victory and made it known in a profound sleep. Immediately they rebuilt the church there on the stone, and there fashioned and adorned beautifully an altar inside of it, and with great joy afterward they consecrated and honored that place. Then they had great love for and belief in that church.

And there was a great terror also among the people, and there was a great concern and doubt in their spirits about what to do about the door-stone, whether they should consecrate it in the new church or what God's will for it was and for the holy worker who had made it with his hand. Then they first took counsel to raise a church along the east side of that place and consecrate it there in the name of St. Peter, Christ's holy servant. And they built two altars in it and consecrated one in the name of St. Mary, Christ's mother, and the other to St. John the Baptist, Christ's godfather. Then their worthy bishop blessedly and healthfully brought forth for them a plan and counseled them to send quickly to Rome to the pope and inquire and ask of the pope and curia what they counseled about this, whether they dare consecrate that church in another manner.

The blessed pope then sent this message and gave this word: "If it be proper for humans to consecrate the church there, it is most fitting for it to be consecrated on the day of the victory. If its holy guardian thinks otherwise about that place and prefers something else, then it is by far the best to seek for what his will is about that day. And when the time draws near, let us both fast with our citizens for four days[34] and devoutly ask the Holy Trinity for the gift of showing, making manifest, and bringing forth through the archangel a wondrous sign to the people so that he may make it known to the people what to do."

Then they all did as their noble bishop advised and fasted for four days. Then on the night in which they completed their fast, St. Michael was shown in a vision to the bishop and said to him, "There is no need for you with respect to this matter to consecrate the church, because I have already fashioned it and consecrated it. You now must go inside of it and wait for me, and devoutly believe in the protector of that place and draw near to it in your prayers. It is your duty to sing a mass inside of it tomorrow and afterward serve this people there at the eucharist. It is my duty to appear in a venerable miracle and make it known through myself and consecrate it and bless it."

Immediately in the morning, rejoicing greatly on account of that answer with much agreement in prayers and with gifts of holy songs of praise, they came there and all went into the church. Out of the portico's doors on the threshold, it was seen that the footsteps which I mentioned before that had been encountered in the marble had begun to go outward. The church with this portico could receive and hold about five hundred people. Then something appeared in the middle, against the south wall of that worthy altar. It was all covered and overspread with purple tapestry. That same house was also planned with corners, by no means according to the custom of the people's work, so that the walls were squared off, but it rather seemed to be in the likeness of a cave. And often the stones stuck out as if from a steep cliff. The roof was also of various heights; in some places it was as if one might nearly touch it with the hands, but in others one could easily touch it with the head. I thus believe that the archangel of our Lord sought out—and loved—the purity of heart more than the adornment of stone.

The knoll was then as it now is known to be, with the mountain great on the outside. And it is overgrown here and there with frosty woods; sometimes it is overspread with green fields. And then after the holy songs of praise and masses were completed, they turned back to their houses with great joy and bliss and with the angel's blessing. Then the bishop established good singers and mass priests and many church servants there who afterward would worship daily with the proper succession of services. There was nevertheless no one who dare come into the church after sunset. But at daybreak, after the first light, they would gather inside for their songs of praise.

Then there was also a very pleasant and clear spring[35] that ran out of that same stone of the church's roof on the northern side of the altar, which the inhabitants of that place used. There was a glass vessel next to this stream, hanging by a silver chain, that received this pleasant water. It was the custom there of that people when they had gone to the eucharist to go up to that glass vessel along a ladder and there receive and taste that heavenly liquid. It was then pleasant to taste and healthful to the innards. This is also a miracle, that many people with fever and various other diseases would immediately be healed through the taste of this liquid. Likewise in other ways countless diseases of the people were often and frequently healed there, and manifold wonders similar to this to which their might was fitting and worthy were and yet are revealed and made known there, but most often on the day of his feast and commemoration.

Then from the surrounding region the people often came. Then it must be believed and readily known that many and various diseases of the people were healed, and the angel's might and his wonder were there worshiped, and most often manifested on that day, as St. Paul said, *Qui ad ministrum summis*, "Angels are spirits for ministering from God sent here into the world"[36] for those who with spirit and with strength earn for God the eternal homeland, so that they are a help to those who must always fight against the corrupt spirits.

But let us now pray to the archangel St. Michael and the nine orders[37] of the holy angels that they may be our help against the fiends of hell. They were the holy ones for the receiving of human souls. As St. Paul was looking toward the northern part of this middle earth, from where all waters descend, he saw over the water a certain gray stone.[38] And north of that stone a frosty wood had grown up, and there were dark mists there, and under the stone was the dwelling of monsters and outlaws. And he saw hanging on that cliff in the icy woods many black souls bound by their hands. And the fiends there in the likeness of monsters were grasping them like greedy wolves. And the water below under the cliff was black. And between the cliff and the water were something like twelve miles, and when the twigs broke apart the souls who hung on the twigs fell down and the monsters grabbed them. These then were the souls who sinned here in the world with unrighteousness and would not stop before the end of the lives.

But let us now devoutly pray to St. Michael that he lead our souls into joy where they may rejoice in eternity without end. Amen.

BLICKLING HOMILY XIX

St. Andrew

Here[39] it is said that after the Lord Jesus Christ ascended to heaven, the apostles were together, and they cast lots among themselves, where they should travel to teach. It is said that the blessed Matthew's lot fell to the city of Mermedonia; it is then said that the men who were in that city did not eat bread or drink water but ate the bodies of men and drank their blood. And each person who came a stranger to that city, it is said that they immediately took him and cast out his eyes and gave him poison to drink that was mixed with great magic. And when they drank this drink, immediately their heart was loosened and their mind changed.

Then the blessed Matthew went into that city, and they immediately seized him and cast out his eyes and gave him poison to drink and sent him into prison, and they commanded him to eat the poison, but he would not eat it.[40] Therefore his heart was not dissolved and his spirit[41] was not changed, but he was always praying to the Lord with great weeping, and said to him, "My Lord Jesus Christ, since we left all our kin and followed you, and you are the help of all of us who believe in you, behold now and see what these people do to your servant. And I ask you, Lord, to give me the light of my eyes, that I may see those in this city who begin to do the worst torments; and do not forsake me, my Lord Jesus Christ, nor give me over to the most bitter death."[42]

When the blessed Matthew had prayed and said this, a great and very bright light lit up the prison, and the voice of the Lord materialized for him[43] in the light, saying, "Matthew, my beloved, behold me." The blessed Matthew then looked and saw the Lord Christ, and again the Lord said, "Matthew, be strengthened and do not fear, for I will never forsake you, but I will deliver you and all your brothers from all danger, and all those who believe in me in every age forever. But stay here twenty-seven nights; after that I will send to you your brother Andrew, to lead you out of this prison and all those who are with you." And when he had said this, the Lord spoke to him again, "Peace be with you, Matthew." He then continued in prayers and was singing the Lord's praises in the prison.[44] And then the unjust men came into the prison to bring out the men and eat them. Then the blessed Matthew shut his eyes, lest the killers should see that his eyes were restored, and they said among themselves, "Three days now are left until we want to kill him and make him into our food."

The blessed Matthew then fulfilled the thirty days. The Lord Jesus Christ spoke to the holy Andrew his apostle, when he was in the land of Achaia and there taught his disciples. He said, "Go into the city of Mermedonia and lead your brother Matthew out of the prison, for there are yet three days left until they intend to kill him and turn him into food." The holy Andrew answered him and said, "My Lord Jesus Christ, how may I travel there in three days? I suspect it is better that you send your angel who may travel there more quickly, for, my Lord, you know that I am a fleshly[45] man, and I may not travel there more quickly, for, my Lord, the journey there is too long and I do not know the way." The Lord Christ said to him, "Hear me, Andrew, for I made you and I have established and ordained this journey for you. Go to the shore of the sea with your disciples, and there you will find a ship on the shore. And ascend into it with your disciples."

When he had said this, the Lord Jesus still spoke and said, "Peace with you and with all your disciples." And he ascended into heaven. [Then St. Andrew arose in the morning and went to the sea with his disciples and saw a boat along the shore and sitting inside of it three men.][46] The holy Andrew then arose in the morning, and he went to the sea with his disciples, and he saw a ship on the shore and three men sitting in it. And he rejoiced with great joy and said to him,[47] "Brother, where do you intend to travel with this small ship?" The Lord Jesus Christ was in the ship as the helmsman, and his two angels with him were changed into the likeness of men.[48] The Lord Christ then said to him, "To the city of Mermedonia." The holy Andrew answered him and said, "Brother, take us with you on the ship and bring us into that city." The Lord said to him, "All men flee from that city; why do you want to go there?" The holy Andrew answered him and said, "We have a small errand there, and we have need to complete it there." The Lord Jesus Christ said to him, "Ascend to us into this ship and give us our travel money."

The holy Andrew answered him, "Listen brother, we do not have the fare, but we are disciples of the Lord Jesus Christ whom he chose. And he gave us this commandment and said, 'When you go to preach the gospel, do not take with you bread or money or two cloaks.' If you then will do us mercy, tell us quickly. If you will not, at least tell us the way." The Lord said to him, "If this commandment was given to you from your Lord, ascend here with joy into my ship."

The holy Andrew then ascended into the ship with his disciples, and he sat by the helmsman of the ship, who was the Lord Jesus Christ. The Lord Jesus Christ said to him, "I see that these brothers are tired of the choppiness of the sea. Ask them whether they want to disembark and await you there, until you fulfill the service for which you are sent and come again to them." The holy Andrew said to them, "My children, do you want to disembark and await me there?" His disciples answered and said, "If we leave you, then we will be exiles from all the good things that you have prepared for us, so we will be with you wherever you travel."

The Lord Jesus Christ spoke to him about them. "If you are truly his disciple who is called Christ, speak to your disciples[49] about the miracles your teacher did, so that their hearts might be cheered and they might forget the terror of the sea." The holy Andrew then said to his disciples, "One time when we were with our Lord, we embarked with him in a ship, and he appeared to us as if he were sleeping in order to tempt us and caused a great choppiness upon the sea from the wind, so that the waves themselves were heaved over the ship. We were very afraid and called to him, the Lord Jesus Christ, and he then arose and commanded the wind to be still. Then a great calmness came upon the sea, and all who saw his work were afraid. Now then, my children, do not be afraid, because our God will not forsake us." And when he said this, the holy Andrew set his head upon one of his disciples and slept.[50]

The Lord Jesus Christ then knew that the holy Andrew was asleep. He said to his angels, "Take Andrew and his disciples and set them before the city of Mermedonia, and when you set them there, come back to me." The angels then did as they were commanded, and he ascended into heaven.[51]

Then morning came to the city of Mermedonia and his disciples were there sleeping with him.[52] And he woke them and said, "Arise, my children, and see God's mercy, which has now happened to us. Know that our Lord was with us in the ship and we did not perceive him.[53] He humbled himself as a helmsman, and he appeared to us as a man to tempt us." The holy Andrew then looked into heaven and said, "My Lord Jesus Christ, I know that you are not far from your servants, and I beheld you on the ship, and I spoke to you as to a man. Now then, Lord, I ask you that you reveal yourself to me in this place."

When this was said, the Lord showed his face to him in the likeness of a fair child and said to him, "Andrew, rejoice with your disciples." The holy Andrew then prayed and said, "Forgive me, Lord, that I spoke to you as to a man; I expect I have sinned, because I did not recognize you." The Lord then said to him, "Andrew, you did not in the least sin, but because you said that you could not travel here in three days, I therefore appeared like this, because I am mighty [enough] to do all this with a word and appear to each just as I please. Now then, arise and go into the city to your brother Matthew and then lead him and all who are with him out of the city. Only I let you know, Andrew, that they will bring upon you many tortures and drag your body through the streets of this city, so that your blood will flow over the earth like water. They will want to lead you to death, but they may not. Yet they may bring many afflictions upon you, but nevertheless endure all, Andrew, and do not act according to their disbelief. Remember how I suffered many afflictions from the Jews: they scourged me, and they spat on my face. But I endured it all that I might show you in what way you should endure. Listen to me, Andrew, and endure these sufferings, because there are many in this city who should believe in my name."

When he had said this, the Lord Jesus Christ ascended[54] into heaven. The holy Andrew then went into the city with his disciples, and no one could see him. When they came to the door of the prison, they met there seven guards standing. The holy Andrew then prayed in his heart, and quickly they were dead. The holy Andrew then went to the door of the prison, and he made the sign of Christ's cross. And the doors were quickly opened, and he went into that prison with his disciples, and he then saw the blessed Matthew sitting alone, singing.[55] Then the blessed Matthew and the holy Andrew kissed each other.[56] The holy Andrew said to him, "What is it, brother? How did you come to be here? Now there are [only] three days left before they kill you and turn you into food!" The holy Matthew answered him and said, "Brother Andrew, did you not hear the Lord saying, 'I will thus send you as sheep among wolves?'[57] It then happened that when they sent me into this prison that I prayed to our Lord to appear, and he quickly showed himself to me and said, 'Wait here twenty-seven days, and after that I will send you your brother Andrew, and he will release you and all those with you out of this prison.' I now see it just as the Lord said to me. Brother, what shall we do now?"

Then the holy Andrew and the holy Matthew prayed to the Lord, and after the prayer the holy Andrew placed his hand[58] on those people's eyes who were blind,[59] and they received sight. And again he lay his hand on their hearts, and their understanding returned to them. The holy Andrew said to him, "Go to the lower parts of the city, and you will find there a great fig tree. Sit under it, and eat of its fruit until I come back to you." They said to the holy Andrew, "Come now with us, for you are our leader, lest perhaps they take us again and they bring us to the worst torments." The holy Andrew said to them, "Go there, because nothing at all will injure you or distress you."

Then they all went quickly, just as the holy Andrew com-manded them. And in the prison there were two hundred and forty-eight men and forty-nine women whom the holy Andrew released. And then he made the blessed Matthew go east with his disciples, and the holy Andrew set [him][60] on the hill where the blessed Peter the apostle was.[61] And there he stayed with him.

The holy Andrew then left the prison and began to go out through the middle of the city, and he came to a certain place and there he saw a pillar standing and upon the pillar a brass image. And he sat by the pillar awaiting what should befall him.

Then the unrighteous people went to lead out the people[62] and turn them into food. And they found the doors of the prison open and the seven guards lying dead. When they saw that, they turned back to their leaders and they said, "We have found your prison open, and we went in and found no one there." When the leaders of the priests heard this, they said[63] among themselves, "What can this be? Perhaps some wonder has entered the prison and killed the guards and suddenly [released] those who were locked up there."

After this the Devil appeared to them in the likeness of a child and said to them, "Listen to me and seek out here a certain foreign man whose name is Andrew and kill him. He is the one who released the prisoners from the prison, and now he is in this city. You now know him; hurry, my children, and kill him."

The holy Andrew then said to the Devil, "O you arrow hardened to every unrighteousness, you who always fight against mankind, my Lord Jesus Christ has lowered you into hell!" When the Devil heard this, he said to him, "I hear your voice, but I do not know where you are." The holy Andrew said to him, "Since you are blind you do not see any of God's saints."

Then the Devil said to the people, "Behold and see him, because he is the one who spoke against me." The citizens then ran, and they shut the gates of the city, and they sought the holy Andrew so they might take him.

Then the Lord Jesus appeared to the holy Andrew and said to him, "Arise, Andrew, and reveal yourself so that they might know that my power is in you." The holy Andrew then arose in the sight of the people, and he said, "I am the Andrew whom you seek." The people then ran, and they took him and said, "Because you did this to us, we will pay you back for it!" And they considered how they might kill him.

Then the Devil went among them and said to the people, "If you want to, put a rope about his neck and drag him through the streets of this city, and let us do this until he dies.[64] And when he is dead, let us divide his body among our citizens." And then all the people who heard this liked it, and they quickly put a rope about his neck, and they dragged him about the streets of the city. And while the blessed Andrew was drawn his body was mixed into the earth so that the blood flowed over the earth as water.

When it became evening they put him into the prison and they bound his hands behind him and they forsook him.[65] And all his body was disjointed.

Likewise on the next day they did the same. The holy Andrew then cried, and he said, "My Lord Jesus Christ, come and see what they do to me, your servant. And I suffer it all for the commandment you gave me when you said, 'Do not do according to their unbelief.' Behold, Lord, and see what they do to me." When he had said this, the Devil said to the people, "Strike him on his mouth so he does not speak this way." Then it happened that they again shut him in the prison.

Then the Devil took seven other devils with him whom the holy Andrew cast out of there, and going into the prison they stood in the sight of the blessed Andrew. And they mocked him greatly[66] and said, "What is it that you have found here? Who will free you from our power? Where are your boast and your brag?" The Devil then said to the other devils, "My children, why have you not killed him?" They answered him and said, "We could not because we saw the sign of Christ's cross on his face and were afraid. We know that before he came into this hardship he was our master. If you can, you kill him. We will not obey you in this, lest perhaps God free him and send us into worse torment." The holy Andrew said to them, "Even if you kill me, I will not do your will, but I will do the will of my Lord Jesus Christ." And thus they heard him and fled away.

In the morning it happened that they dragged the holy Andrew again, and he cried with a great moan to the Lord and said, "My Lord Jesus Christ, these torments are enough for me, for I am tired. My Lord Jesus Christ, once on the cross you suffered and said, 'Father, why have you forsaken me?'[67] Now it has been three days since I was [first] dragged through the streets of the city. You know, Lord, man's frailty: I call on you to receive my spirit. Where are your works, Lord, with which you strengthened us,[68] saying, 'If you obey me and follow me, not one lock of your hair will perish'? Behold, Lord, and see, for my body and the hairs of my head are mingled with this earth. It is only three days since I [first] was dragged into these worst of torments, and you did not appear to me. My Lord Jesus Christ, strengthen my heart." While he thus was praying, the Lord's voice came to the holy Andrew in Hebrew, saying, "My Andrew, heaven and earth may pass; my words never pass.[69] Look behind you and see your body and the hairs of your head, what they have become." The holy Andrew then looked and saw a flourishing tree bearing fruit. And he said, "Now I know, Lord, that you have not forsaken me."

Then it happened in the evening that they shut him up in the prison and said among themselves, "Therefore he will die this night." The Lord Jesus Christ appeared to him in the prison, and he stretched out his hand and took him and said, "Andrew, arise!" When he heard that he quickly arose whole and prayed to him and said, "I give you thanks, my Lord Jesus Christ."

The holy Andrew then looked and saw a pillar standing in the middle of the prison and on top of the pillar an image of stone. And he stretched out his hand and said to it, "Fear the Lord and the sign of his cross before whom heaven and earth are afraid! Now then, image, do what I command you in the name of my Lord Jesus Christ. Send a great water through your mouth so that all those who are in this city might be destroyed."

When he had said this, the blessed Andrew,[70] quickly the stone image sent a great water through its mouth like saltwater, and it ate at men's bodies and it killed their children and beasts. And they all wanted to flee from their city.

The holy Andrew said, "My Lord Jesus Christ, do not forsake me, but send me your angel from heaven on a fiery cloud to encircle all this city so they may not go on account of the fire."[71] And when he said this, a fiery cloud descended from heaven, and it circled all the city. When the blessed Andrew saw that, he blessed the Lord.

The water rose up to a man's throat and ate at their bodies intensely. And they all cried and said, "Woe on us, because all this has come upon us on account of this foreigner whom we have shut up in the prison! What should we do?" Some of them said, "If you wish, let us go into the prison and lead him out lest perhaps we perish evilly, and let us all cry and say, 'Since we believe in the Lord of this foreign man, then he will free us from these troubles!'"

When the blessed Andrew perceived that they had turned to the Lord, he said to the stone likeness, "Stop now through the might of our Lord and send no more water out of your mouth!" And this said, the water stopped, and no more came out of its mouth. The holy Andrew then went out of the prison, and that same water did him service before his feet.[72] And the survivors came to the door of the prison, and they said, "God, have mercy on us[73] and do not do to us as we have done to this foreigner."[74] The holy Andrew then prayed in the people's sight, and the earth opened and swallowed the water with the [dead] men.

Then the men who saw that were greatly frightened, and they said, "Woe to us, for this death is from God, and he will kill us for this tribulation that we have given to this man. Truly he has been sent from God and he is God's servant."

The holy Andrew said to them, "My children, do not make yourselves afraid, for those who are in this water will live again! And this has happened so that you might believe in my Lord Jesus Christ." The holy Andrew then prayed to the Lord and said, "My Lord Jesus Christ, send your Holy Spirit to wake all those who are in this water that they might believe in your name." The Lord then commanded all who were in the water to arise.

After this the holy Andrew commanded a church to be built on the place where the pillar stood. And he gave them the commandments of the Lord Jesus Christ. "And love him, for great is his power," [he said]. And he appointed one of the leaders bishop, and he baptized them and said, "Now then, I am ready to go to my disciples." They all appealed to him and said, "Stay with us a little while, so that you might do us a kindness, for we are newly converted to this belief."

The holy Andrew then would not listen to them, but he saluted them, and so he left. A great crowd of the people followed him, weeping and crying. And then a light shone above their heads, and as the holy Andrew was traveling away from there, the Lord Jesus Christ appeared to him in the road in the likeness of a fair child and said to him, "Andrew, why do you go like this without the fruit of your labors and forsake those who appealed to you and were not merciful to their children who followed you weeping? Their cry and lamentation has ascended to me in heaven. Now turn around again to this city and stay there seven days until you strengthen their hearts in my belief. Go then to the city with our disciples and believe in my faith!" When he had said this, the Lord Jesus Christ ascended into heaven.

The holy Andrew then turned again to the city of Mermedonia, and he said, "I bless you, my Lord Jesus Christ, you who convert[75] all souls, because you did not allow me to leave with my hot heart out of this city." And they[76] rejoiced with great joy, and he stayed with them seven days, teaching and strengthening their hearts in the faith of our Lord Jesus Christ.

When the seven days were fulfilled, just as the Lord had commanded him, he left the city of Mermedonia, hastening to his disciples. And all the people led him [out] with joy, and they said, "The Lord God is one:[77] he is Jesus Christ and the Holy Spirit to whom be wonder and power in the Holy Trinity forever and ever, truly without end!"

VERCELLI HOMILY II

The Day of Judgment

Beloved people, the events of the great Day of Judgment will be terrible and fearful for all creation. On that day the flashing lightning will burn up blood-stained middle earth and those who are now in great boasts and in useless display of gold and silver and fine cloth and false treasure. Yet we are now most like the one who was overconfident that it by no means would come upon us!

And on that day the light of the sun will depart together with the light of the moon and the lights of all the stars.[78] And on that day Christ's cross will shed blood between the clouds, and on that day the Lord's face will be very terrible and fearsome and in the shape in which he was when the Jews beat him and hung him and spat on him with their spit. On that day the sinful will cry and weep, because they earlier did not want to atone for their sins, but they will sorrowfully feel ashamed and will fall down into torment.

On that day the trumpet will be blowing[79] from the four corners of this middle earth, and then all will arise[80]—whomever the earth swallowed and fire burned up and sea drowned and wild animals ate and birds bore away—all of them will arise on that day. On that day our Lord will sit in his, the great majesty. And his face and his body will appear. Then the wounds will be seen by all the sinful,[81] yet by the faithful he will be seen whole. And then the Jews may see the one whom they earlier killed and hanged. And the true Judge then will judge all people, all according to their own works.

Listen, then it will seem to the sinful that nothing—neither cold nor heat, hard nor soft, what is loved nor what is hated—will take away from the Lord's love and separate them from his will. And now you do not want to do his will, now that we easily can!

Lo, listen! That is beyond all capacity to examine or consider, that the wretched sinners must sorrowfully feel ashamed at the face of our Lord and his saints and the glory of the heavenly kingdom. And then they will depart into the torment of the eternal hell![82] Alas, listen! The hearts of humans will be wretchedly darkened so that they must ever abandon the deadly devil. In useless cunning they lead them astray so that they commit sins and do not do the will of him who created them on the earth and quickened their souls and gave them eternal life.

Lo, listen! People absolutely do not fear him. How the Devil will accuse them before the multitude at the great Judgment of all the unrighteous works that will be done here! Lo, listen! People do not fear that great devil Antichrist[83] with his punishments in hell and with his miseries and the grievous torments which will be paid to them as reward for their sins. Lo, listen! We do not fear the coming terror of the Day of Judgment, which is a day of miseries and a day of troubles, and a day of unhappiness and a day of crying and a day of lamentation and a day of grief and a day of sorrow and a day of darkness.

On that day[84] the open heaven will be revealed[85] to us and the glory of angels and destruction of all creation and the sin of the earth, faithless strife and the fall of angels, the cry of thunder and the storm of darkness and the flash of flames and groaning creation and the fight of spirits and the grim revelation and the divine power and the hot shower and the joy of hell's inhabitants and the song of trumpets and widespread burning and the bitter day and the separating of souls, and the mortal dragon[86] and the destruction of devils and the narrow pit and black death and the burning abyss and the bloody stream and the great fear of fiends and the fiery rain and the heathens' groaning and the fall of hosts, the multitude of heaven-dwellers and the might of their Lord and that great assembly and the fierce cross and the judgment of the righteous and the indict-ment of fiends and the pale faces and the terrible word and the weeping of the people and the shameful host and the burning hell and the terror of worms.

And then to each of us will such terrors be revealed. There the sinful may wish that they had never lived, born of father and mother or that each of them be turned into dumb beasts. Lo, it would be better for them all than all middle earth with its treasures, which heaven arches over.

Lo, listen! We do not fear what we see daily with our own eyes. Now we do not believe in the other! Our neighbor dies, and then a hateful bier is prepared for the body; it decays in the cold earth, and the transitory body rots there in filth and as food for the corpse-ripping worms.

Lo, listen! It then will be a grievous sorrow and a wretched separation of the body and the soul if the wretched inner man, that is, the weary soul that is wicked and neglectful of God's com-mandments here, will after that separation slide down into the eternal punishment of hell and there amongst devils exist in mur-der and crime, in torment and sorrow, amidst woe and worms, between the dead and the devils, and in fire and in bitterness and in filth and in all the punishments that devils have prepared from the beginning for which they were created and which they them-selves have earned.

But let us now be mindful of the needs of our souls and do good in the day to which we may be committed and forsake murder and crime and pride and envy and idle boasting and unrighteousness and adultery, gluttony and drunkenness, foolishness and sorcery, greed and avarice, deceit and hypocrisy, slander and deception, strife and scheming and miserliness and all the habits that the devils exemplify in themselves.

But let us love our Lord with all our spirit and strength and all our heart and mind, with all truth and wisdom. Let us love our neighbors as ourselves and be merciful to the poor and the foreign-ers and the sick so that through this our Lord may be merciful to us.

And if nevertheless any one of us has a sin committed against him by another in word or in deed, let him forebear it mercifully,

90

lest God punish him for that anger. Just as he himself said, "Dimittite et dimittetur vobis,"[87] ["Forgive as you are forgiven"]. Let us suffer for our Lord's love all that is done to us here in the world to trouble us. Listen! We need to remember how much he suffered for us after he took on a human body for the eternal salvation of humanity and through that saved us from the Devil's slavery and gave us reaccess to the eternal life that we earlier had forfeited—if we desire to earn it. Thus the prophet says, "Then the Lord saves and puts in the kingdom of heaven those who are humble before God and man here in the world."[88]

Listen! We hear that they are blessed and prosperous before God who are humble and gentle in the world.[89] Listen! We then understand with the prophets that they are wretched and wicked before God who are proud and envious here in the world. Of all sins this is the one most hateful and displeasing to God, because humankind was first pushed down into hell through envy. But then through mercy and humility they were released from there out of the Devil's slavery. Lo, listen! It is necessary for us to open our ears and hearts to the teaching of the gospel, which is often read to us and our teachers preach and narrate to us. Listen! Now we adorn ourselves in idle boasting with gold and with jewels and bless ourselves and are glad, since we expect that we will never give them up and too seldom remember our Lord and the need of our souls, which must enter eternity after this life, with souls and with bodies in whatever state as we deserve here and now. May we have good repentance from our sins! Even if it happens that one of us sins against another in word or in deed, remedy is then best for it, because one is never so sinful that remedy is not always allowed for him.

Therefore let us now hasten to God before death seizes us—for it is approaching very near! And let us be wise and truthful and merciful and generous and righteous and charitable and pure and kind and God-fearing and studious and willing to serve and obedient to God and our lords and patient with God's will. And he will then give us as a reward that eternal kingdom that was prepared for us from the beginning. Let us now hasten to him as long as we still may determine our course in life. There they never divide what is loved or multiply what is hated. Nor does day follow day or night follow night, but eternal light is there[90] and bliss and eternal glory and eternal joy with our Lord, the savior of middle earth, who is ever the same God who lives and reigns with the Father and with the Son and with the Holy Spirit, to whom be glory and honor forever and ever, world without end. Amen.

VERCELLI HOMILY VI

Christmas Day

Here begins the story of the miracles that happened
before the advent of our Savior, the Lord Jesus Christ.

It says here about the famous event that happened on this day
that the almighty Lord himself sought out this world and was born
into this world through a spotless woman so he could redeem all
humankind from the torments of those in hell and bring them to
the glory of the heavenly kingdom. And on this day, which is the
almighty Lord's birthday, he filled all of this middle earth with the
new light of his coming. And from the beginning of the world all of
God's saints have spoken about this event that we honor today and
sung about it in books and in holy songs. And even though they all
spoke and preached about it, nevertheless one of God's saints sang
most clearly about the glory of this day and said, "This is the day
the LORD has made. Let us rejoice and be glad in it!"[91] Because on
this day the King of all kings and the Ruler of all rulers for the love
of us sought this middle earth from the high kingdom of heaven,
because the heavenly things serve him gloriously with the earthly
and with this lowly creation.

When then the blessed time approached in which the Lord
desired to be born bodily, a very majestic sign went before him. It first
happened on the day in which he was born that no man could fight
with weapons. But as soon as they wanted to fight with weapons, their
arms weakened and their hands deceived them, and they softened

93

themselves for peace and could fight no more. Likewise it also happened that seven nights before Christ was born the sun began to shine at midnight just as if it shined the hottest and brightest in summer. That signified that he sent the earthly sun as a hostage shining at night before him. Likewise it also happened that for a few nights before Christ was born three wells sprung up, and out of one of them oil flowed from morning until evening, and everyone who came to it was allowed to take as much as he wanted. Likewise many other miracles happened there before the time in which he was born that no one may now scarcely count, let alone relate.

Then it happened on the same day (which was yesterday) on which the Lord was born at night before the morning star arose, that the emperor traveled with all his retinue to Bethlehem, the city in which the Lord was born. When it was the third hour of the day (which was yesterday), he looked in the air near the sun and saw, together with all his host that was with him, that the sun shone brighter than it ever had shone before, and it was all circled about with a threefold golden ring. When Augustus[92] the Emperor saw this, he called out to all the host and said, "It is evident that this is the sign of the King of heaven, which he has sent before him, and I know that the time has arrived that he wishes to seek us out in this world. Therefore from the beginning of middle earth it has been said, besides other miracles of his birth that were spoken about, that this was the last of the signs that had to be given before he was born in this middle earth. It is fitting for us to honor the glorious King who sent us his sign before him so clearly."

And then he quickly proclaimed that it be sent to every region which belonged to his kingdom and proclaimed that everyone in prison be set free[93] and that those set in chains be released and that those who were condemned to die for their crimes be granted their lives and that to the guilty their guilts be forgiven.

And then[94] in that same night before the morning star arose, the Lord was born into this middle earth and angels accepted him when he was born and prayed to him and sang to him wonderful praise and spoke thus: "Glory to God in the highest and on earth peace to people of good will."[95]

When Herod the king found out that Christ had been born in Bethlehem, a city of Judah, he commanded him to be sought through all the tribes so he might be killed. One day before Herod[96] the king commanded that the child be killed, the angel of the Lord appeared to Joseph in a dream and said, "Take Mary and the child Jesus and journey through the desert to Egypt." Joseph did this just as he had been commanded. And as they were journeying, they came to a certain cave, and they wanted to rest in it. Then Mary got off the beast, holding the child Jesus at her breast. There were three servants with Joseph, and one woman journeying together with Mary.

Then suddenly out of the cave there came many dragons, [who when they saw the child, cried out loudly in fear....Then, behold, they looked about them and saw the mountains and cities][97] of Egypt, and they rejoiced greatly. And when they came to the city, they had no acquaintances with whom they might lodge. They turned to the temple of the gods and went in, with Mary holding the child Jesus at her breast. All the idols fell before Mary's feet,[98] and they shrank in size. When this was related to Afradisius the duke, he came there with all his host, and he went into the temple and saw all the idols lying on the ground. He went to the woman Mary and he prayed to the child Jesus and he spoke to all his host and said, "Unless God were here, our gods would by no means have fallen on their faces. And therefore it is necessary for us to do just as our gods have done, lest his wrath and the danger of death come upon us."

Then afterward the angel of the Lord appeared to Joseph and Mary and said to them, "Go back again to the land of Judea. All those who sought to kill the child are dead."

Then Jesus grew and was strengthened in spirit and strength and wisdom.[99] He became perfect among God and among the people. To him alone be glory and honor for ever and ever.

Listen, we have now heard told a small part of the story of our Lord's birth, also about the miracles he performed in his childhood. Let us now earnestly strive to be better while we hear such examples of our Lord related and read before us. Let us now have peace and love among us, so God will pay us an eternal wage at our end.

VERCELLI HOMILY XI

Rogation Day

Beloved people,[100] these are the days holy and healthful and medicinal for our souls, and it is fitting for us that we observe them well with fasting and with prayer and with visits to relics and with our going about humbly. For St. Peter[101] the head apostle first appointed us to keep these days and to observe them on account of the errors of the heathens, because they worshiped their idols and devils on these days, and now because of these matters we must honor and worship these days with the appointed goods that are appropriate to these days.

According to the book they are now appointed for us so that throughout them we should learn the eternal counsel for ourselves. Likewise our Lord has kindled for us many spiritual lanterns[102] that we must light up for ourselves with heavenly piety and holy doctrine, so that no one will remain in the darkness of heresy who wishes to see the light of truth. What are these lanterns that our Lord has given to us to enlighten the dimness of humankind's infidelity? They are the patriarchs, the prophets, the apostles, the bishops, the priests, and the many other divine teachers of God's church. And we have great need to observe the right doctrine and the holy examples and obey the holy gospel with fear and fasten it firmly in our hearts.

Let us now remember how in his gospel the eternal Lord taught us, saying, "*Non qui ceperit, sed qui perseveraverit usque in finem salvus erit,*" "It is not the one who begins a good deed and then forsakes it but the one who endures in good deeds who will be made whole."[103] And just as daily sins do not diminish, so also daily medicines[104] will not diminish.

There are two times here in this world that are always fulfilled in order. *"Tempus flendi et tempus ridendi,"*[105] that is, a time of weeping and another time of laughter. We cannot always have laughter. And I well know that everyone desires to see true joy in middle earth. But it is not, was not, nor ever will be. But we should seek true joy where it is, that is, in Christ himself in the height of the kingdom of heaven. As he, the Lord himself, says, he who thus prophesied the strife and the comfort of the faithful in his gospel: *"In hoc mundo pressuram habebitis. Mundus hic gaudebit; vos autem tristes eritis, sed tristitia vestra convertitur in gaudium,"* "You will have oppression in this middle earth, and middle earth will rejoice in this and you will be sad. But you will be free from sighing, for it will turn again for you into joy."[106]

So then, beloved people, we should strive in this present life even if it is not easy, with God helping us, so that we always do what is good and through that virtue gather fruit with joy and with happiness in the world to come, just as it is written in the psalm: *"Qui seminant in lacrimis, in gaudio metent,"* "They who sow in tears will once more reap in joy."[107]

For the sin of the first man, Adam, we were expelled from the homeland of paradise and sent into this world of exile, and thus we live in this middle earth as if we have no homeland here. The apostle Paul spoke about this: *"Dum sumus in corpore peregrinamur a domino."* St. Paul said, "While we are here in the body we are exiled from God."[108] From here we may earn for ourselves that eternal homeland and that true joy. We may not have either of them here in the world, but we will possess in the future what is kept for us in our homeland.

Why must we seek in this middle earth the transmigration of joy in heaven? Let us from now on strive to earn it that we may arrive blessedly in the eternal and best homeland, where our kin wish to see us and our ancestors, who are the patriarchs and prophets and apostles, may rejoice, where our fellow citizens the angels and archangels await us and where the glorious city of Jerusalem[109] is, where our Lord Jesus Christ waits with outstretched arms.

Lo, we consider ourselves spiritual merchants. We must purchase with these earthly things the heavenly hoards of gold and with these transitory things eternal and everlasting wealth. When they come home with sound profits, merchants should be prosperous. Likewise we should be very thoughtful and very sorrowful as long as we are here in our efforts at earning eternal life so that we may again rejoice in the heavenly home of the celestial kingdom. Nor should we ever consider the labor and trouble here in the world too long, because it comes to an end. But the rewards never come to an end that are gilded for us on behalf of those troubles.

Therefore, beloved people, let us forsake unnecessary laughter and joy. We have great need to weep and make amends once more with tears and wailing, because the Lord said thus in his gospel: "*Ve vobis qui ridetis nunc quia lugebitis et flebitis.*" He said, "Woe to you who now laugh, because you will moreover wail and weep."[110] Even so, he openly said, "Those people who exalt here in the world with the greatest joy and greatest wealth and greatest bliss will receive and endure moreover the greatest unhappiness without end and the greatest sorrow without any bliss."

Therefore, beloved people, while we are here living, let us ask mercy of God, so that he might send us out thus in the love of eternal life that we might the more love the eternal homeland than this present life and always think the more about the life to come than about the one we lead here. These are days of toil and labor as we ourselves may understand in the manifold torments that daily fall on humankind in tempests because of our deeds.

May we now understand, beloved people, that the end of us all approaches us in many ways. God's churches are now robbed and the altars overturned through the plundering and robbery of the heathens,[111] and the walls are broken and breached, and the holy orders have deteriorated because of their own works and merits. And by no means are God's servants alone but also likewise kings and bishops and aldermen—those who are the councilors of this nation—they have plundered the holy orders and the people of God and robbed them with false charges and corrupt bribes. And thus we suffer now for all our deeds these terrible and dreadful things here in the world.

Therefore we have a great and surpassing need to consider all these things that we have spoken about for a while. Let us more eagerly love these holy days by which we may stir up in our souls much good. Let us thank our Lord with words and deeds in this gathering[112] so we might endure this holy time. Let us now strive to observe fittingly with spiritual virtues what is appointed for us there. May God aid us in this, he who lives and rules over us all. Amen.

ÆLFRIC

St. John the Apostle

John the Evangelist, Christ's beloved, was taken on this day[113] to the kingdom of heaven by God's visitation. He was Christ's aunt's son, and he loved him specially, not so much for this kinship but for the purity of his intact virginity. He was chosen for God in virginity, and he always persisted in undefiled virginity. It can be read in history books that he wanted to take a wife, and Christ was invited to his wedding.[114] Then it happened that the wine ran out for his wedding. The Savior then commanded the servers to fill six stone jars with pure water. And he turned that water into wine with his blessing. This was the first sign that he did openly in his humanity.

Then John was so inspired by that sign that he immediately abandoned his bride in her virginity and always afterward followed the Lord. And he became inwardly loved by him because he drew himself away from fleshly lusts. Indeed the Savior entrusted his mother to this beloved disciple when he redeemed humankind on the cross, so that his pure life took care of the pure Virgin Mary and she then lived with him by means of the service of her sister's son.[115]

Later, after Christ's ascension into heaven, there ruled a certain cruel emperor in the kingdom of Rome after Nero. His name was Domitian, the persecutor of the Christian people. He ordered a tub to be filled with boiling oil, and they thrust the famous evangelist into it. But through God's protection he emerged from that hot bath undefiled. Then again, when the cruel one could not suppress the preaching of that blessed apostle, he sent him into exile to an island that is called Patmos[116] so that he might be killed by hunger's sting.

But the almighty Savior did not carelessly forsake his beloved apostle but showed to him in that exile the revelation of things about to happen about which he wrote that book that is called the Apocalypse. And the cruel Domitian was killed in that same year by the hands of his senators. And they all unanimously advised that all his decrees be abrogated. Then Nerva, a very honorable man, was chosen emperor. By his assent the apostle returned again with great honor, he who was sent into exile with insult. Men and women ran to meet him rejoicing and saying, "Blessed is he who comes in God's name!"[117]

When the apostle John went into the city of Ephesus, a widow's body was being carried out toward him for burial. Her name had been Drusiana. She had been very faithful and charitable, and the poor whom she had entirely fed through her generous spirit followed her body mournfully with weeping. Then the apostle commanded the bier to be put down and said, "My Lord Jesus Christ, raise Drusiana! Arise and return home and prepare for us a meal in your house!"[118] Drusiana then arose just as if she had awakened from sleep, and, mindful of the apostle's command, went home.

On the next day the apostle was walking along a street when he saw where a certain philosopher led two brothers who had exchanged all the treasure of their parents for precious gems and then wanted to crush them all to pieces in the sight of all the people for a spectacle, as if in contempt for worldly possessions. It was customary at that time for those who wanted to learn worldly wisdom with zeal to convert their wealth into gems and then to crush them or lump them into some golden lump and throw it into the sea, lest the thought of those possessions hinder them at their lessons.

Then the apostle clasped the philosopher Graton to himself and said, "It is foolish that anyone despise worldly success for the praise of men and be condemned in the judgment of God. Useless is the medicine that cannot heal the sick. So also is learning empty that does not heal the crimes and vices of the soul. Truly my teacher Christ taught a certain young man who desired the word of eternal life that he ought to sell all his wealth and apportion the value among the poor if he wanted to be perfect and afterward have his treasure in heaven and eternal life as well."[119]

The philosopher Graton answered him, "Those gems have been crushed on account of an idle boast. But if your teacher is the true God, join the pieces together into wholeness so that their worth might help the poor." Then John gathered the pieces of those gems and looked into the heavens, saying thus: "Lord Jesus, nothing is difficult for you to do. You have restored this shattered middle earth in your believers through the sign of the holy cross. Restore now these valuable gems through the hands of your angels so that these ignorant people might perceive your might and believe in you." Lo, then those gems suddenly became as if whole, so that no sign of the formerly crushed pieces was seen.

Then the philosopher Graton, together with those young men, fell at John's feet believing in God. The apostle baptized him with all his household, and he began to preach God's faith openly. The two brothers Atticus and Eugenius sold their gems and all their possessions and divided them among beggars and followed the apostle. And a great multitude of believers joined them.

Then on a certain occasion[120] the apostle arrived at the city of Pergamon, where the aforesaid young men had earlier lived. And they saw their servants adorned with fine clothes and shining in worldly glory. Then they were pierced by the devil's arrow and became sorrowful in spirit that they had traveled begging in poor garments while their servants were shining in worldly glory.

Then the apostle perceived this devilish crime and said, "I see that your spirit and your face have turned because you divided your goods among the poor and followed the teaching of my Lord. Therefore go now to the woods and cut yourselves a load of twigs and bring them to me." And they did this according to his command, and in God's name he blessed those green twigs, and they were turned into red gold. Again the apostle John said, "Go to the seashore and bring me back some pebbles." And they did so. And then John blessed them in God's glorious might, and they were turned into valuable gems. Then the apostle said, "Go to the smith and test this gold and these gems." Then they went and came back again, saying thus: "All the goldsmiths say that they have never before seen gold so pure or so red. The jewelers also say that they have never before encountered such precious gems." Then the apostle said to them, "Take this gold and these gems and go and buy estates for yourselves, because you have lost your heavenly wealth. Buy yourselves rich coats so you may shine for a little while like a rose. Flower[121] for a while since you will quickly wither; be rich since you will beg eternally. Listen, the almighty Ruler cannot bring it about to make his servants powerful before the world, abounding in wealth and incomparably shining. Instead he has ordained battle for the faithful souls so that they might believe themselves created for eternal wealth, those who for his name's sake despise transitory goods. You have healed the sick in the Savior's name, put devils to flight, restored sight to the blind, and healed every disease. Indeed this gift is now taken away from you, and you have become poor. You who were great and strong—so much did devils fear you that by your command they left those oppressed by madness—now you fear devils yourselves! The heavenly possessions are common to us all. We were born naked,[122] and naked will we die. The brightness of the sun and the light of the moon and all the stars are common to both rich and poor. Rain showers and church doors and baptism and the forgiveness of sins, the eucharist, and God's visitation are common to all—wretched and blessed. But the unhappy miser wishes to have more than what abounds, though he does not enjoy his abundance without sorrow. The miser has but one body yet various garments. He has but one stomach yet food for a thousand. Indeed, what for cheap greed he cannot give to others, he hoards and knows not for whom, just as the prophet says. In vain is everyone troubled who hoards and does not know for whom he gathers it. Indeed he is not the lord of those possessions when he cannot give them away, but he is the servant of those possessions when he entirely serves them. In addition, sickness grows in his body so he may enjoy neither food nor water. He worries day and night that his goods are safe. He greedily looks after his income, his taxes, his buildings. He robs the poor; he devotes himself to his lusts and his games. Then suddenly he departs out of this world naked and guilty, carrying only sins along with him. Therefore he must suffer eternal punishment."

Just as the apostle was giving this sermon, a certain widow bore the body of her son to burial. He had taken a wife thirty days before. The sorrowing mother then, together with the pall bearers, was wailing and fell at the feet of the apostle, praying that her son might be raised in God's name, just as he did the widow Drusiana.

Then John took pity on the mother and the sadness of those pall bearers and stretched out his body on the earth in a long prayer and then soon arose and again with upraised hand prayed a long while. When he had done this three times, he commanded the young man's body to be unbound and said, "Alas, young man, who through the lust of your flesh quickly lost your soul, alas, young man, you do not know your Creator! You do not know the people's Savior! You do not know the true friend! And for this you run to the worst enemy! Now I shed my tears and eagerly pray for your ignorance, so that you might arise from death and tell these two brothers Atticus and Eugenius how great a glory they have lost and what torment they have earned."

With this the young man Stacteus arose and fell at John's feet and began to rebuke the brothers who were going astray, saying thus: "I see the angels who sorrowfully look after you weak ones and those cursed demons rejoicing in your destruction. The heavenly kingdom was prepared for you and shining buildings filled with feasts and with eternal light. You have lost these things through your folly. And you have obtained for yourself dark dwellings filled with dragons and with roaring flames, filled with unspeakable torments and with horrible smells in which groaning and howling do not cease day or night. Pray therefore with your inward heart to this apostle of God, your teacher, that he raise you up from the eternal destruction just as he raised me from death and he lead your souls that are now blotted out from the Book of Life once more to God's grace and mercy."

Then the young man Stacteus, who had arisen from death, together with those brothers fell before John's feet and the people along with them, all praying with one accord that he intercede with God. The apostle then commanded the two brothers to offer penance for thirty days, making atonement to God, and in that space of time they eagerly prayed that the golden twigs be turned back again to their natural state and those gems to their worthlessness. After thirty day's time, when by their prayers they could not change that gold and those gems back to their natural states, then they came with weeping to the apostle, saying thus:

"You always taught compassion and that one should have compassion on others. And if one has compassion on others, how much more does God desire to have compassion and pardon people, the work of his hand? That which with greedy eyes we committed as a sin, now with weeping eyes we repent."

And the apostle answered, "Carry the twigs to the woods and the stones to the seashore. They will be changed back to their natural states." When they had done this, then they once more received God's grace, so that they cast out devils and healed the blind and sick and did many miracles in the Lord's name, just as they did before.

The apostle then converted to God all the land of Asia, which is reckoned as half the size of middle earth. And then he wrote the fourth book about Christ. It is mostly concerned with Christ's divinity. The other three evangelists—Matthew, Mark, and Luke—wrote earlier about Christ's humanity.[123] Then heretics sprang up in God's church and said that Christ did not exist before he was born of Mary. Then all the bishops of the people asked the holy apostle to compose the fourth book, and he extinguished the presumption of those heretics.

John then commanded a common fast of three days, and after the fast he was so filled with the spirit of God that he surpassed all God's angels and all creatures with an exalted spirit, and with these words began the writing of the gospel, "*In principio erat verbum, et verbum erat apud Deum, et Deus erat verbum,*" etc. This is in English, "In the beginning was the Word, and the Word was with God, and the Word was God. This was in the beginning with God. All things were created through him, and nothing was created without him,"[124] and so forth in all the writing of the gospel. He made much known about Christ's divinity—how he is eternally without beginning begotten of his Father and reigns with him in unity of the Holy Spirit forever. He wrote few things about his humanity, because those three other evangelists wrote abundantly about those things in their books.

On a certain occasion it happened that those devil worshipers who were still unbelieving said that they wanted to force the apostle to their paganism. Then the apostle said to the idolaters, "Go all together to God's church and cry out to your gods so that the church might fall down through your power. Then I will bow to your paganism! If then the might of your gods cannot cast down the holy church, I will cast down your temple through the power of the almighty God. And I will smash your idol. And it will justly be thought that you have given up your heresy and have believed in the true God who alone is almighty."

The idolaters agreed with this statement, and with gentle words John persuaded that people to go further away from the Devil's temple. And he cried out before them all with a clear voice, "In the name of God, this temple must collapse with all the idolatry that dwells therein so that this multitude might know that this paganism is the Devil's worship."

Lo, then suddenly the temple collapsed from its foundation, with all its idols turned to dust. On that same day twelve thousand pagans were converted to Christ's faith and sanctified with baptism. Then the chief idolater still refused with great obstinacy and said that he did not want to believe unless John drank poison and overcame the fatal drink through God's might.

Then the apostle said, "Even if you give me poison, through God's name it will not harm me."[125] Then the idolater Aristodemus said, "You must first watch another drink and immediately die, so that indeed your heart will be thus strengthened for that fatal drink." John answered him, "If you wish to believe in God, I will receive this drink without fear."

Then this Aristodemus hurried to the proconsul and took two thieves from his prison and gave them the poison before all the people and in John's sight, and they died immediately after that drink. The idolater later gave the poisonous drink to the apostle, and he armed his mouth and all his body with the sign of the cross and blessed the poison in God's name and afterward drank it all with a confident spirit. Then Aristodemus and that people kept watch on the apostle for three days and saw that he had a joyous countenance without pallor and fear. And they all cried out, "There is one true God, the one whom John worships!"

Then the idolater said to the apostle, "I still doubt. But if you raise these dead criminals in the name of your God then my heart will be cleansed from every doubt." Then John said, "Aristodemus, take my tunic and place it before the bodies of the dead men and say, 'The apostle of the savior Christ has sent me to you so that you might arise from death in his name and everyone might acknowledge that death and life serve my Savior.'"

Then according to the apostle's command he carried his tunic and placed it upon the two dead men and immediately they arose whole. When the idolater saw this he prostrated himself at John's feet and later went to the proconsul and made these miracles known with a loud voice. Then they both sought the apostle out asking for his grace.

Then the apostle commanded that they fast for seven nights, and afterward he baptized them. And then after baptism they cast down all their idols and with the help of their kin and with every skill raised up for God a great church in honor of the apostle.

Then, when the apostle was ninety-nine years old,[126] the Lord Christ appeared to him with the other apostles whom he had taken out of this life and said, "John, come to me. The time has come for you to feast with your brothers at my banquet."[127]

Then John arose and went toward the Savior, but he said to him, "Now you will come to me on Sunday, the day of my resurrection." And after these words the Lord returned to heaven. The apostle greatly rejoiced in this promise. And on the Sunday at dawn, an early riser, he came to the church and taught the people God's law from cock-crow until dawn and sang mass for them and said that the Savior had invited him to heaven on that day. Then he commanded his grave be dug near the altar and the earth be carried out, and he went alive and healthy to his burial. And he stretched out his hands to God and cried out, "Lord Christ, I thank you that you have invited me to your feast. You know that I desire you with my whole heart. Often have I prayed that I might journey to you, but you said I should wait so that I might gain the more people. You held my body against every defilement, and you always illuminated my soul and never forsook me. You placed your true word in my mouth, and I have written down the doctrine that I have heard from your mouth and the miracles that I have seen you do. Now I commend to you, Lord, your children, those whom your church, maiden and mother, has gained for you through water and the Holy Spirit. Receive me to my brothers with whom you have come and invited me. Open for me the gate of life that the princes of darkness may not meet me. You are Christ, the Son of the living God, you who by your Father's command sustain middle earth and send us the Holy Spirit. We praise you and thank you for all the various goods throughout the ages. Amen."

After this prayer a heavenly light appeared for a time above the apostle inside the grave, shining so brightly that no one's vision could behold a ray of that light. And with that light he gave up his spirit to the Lord who had invited him to his kingdom. He thus departed free from death's pain out of this present life, just as he was exempt from bodily corruption.

Truly afterward was his grave found filled with manna. Heavenly food was called manna; it fed for forty years the Israelite people in the desert.[128] Now this food was found in John's grave, and nothing else, and the food is growing in it until this present day. Many signs are shown there, and the sick are healed and released from all danger through the apostle's intercession. The Lord Christ grants him this, to whom be honor and glory with the Father and Holy Spirit forever. Amen.

ÆLFRIC

St. Dionysius

Paul, teacher of the nations, when he traveled throughout the land preaching the faith just as the Savior had commanded him, arrived on a certain day in a certain famous city named Athens,[129] high and famous, the capital of the Greeks living then in paganism. Dionysius the beloved martyr was there, a teacher of the pagans in their unbelief until Paul converted him from error to right.

Along with some other philosophers, this Dionysius had seen how in the land of Egypt where they were students the sun became dark as black night from midday until the ninth hour when our Lord was suffering for the redemption of humankind.[130] And they marveled greatly at this. Then Dionysius said, "This dark night signifies a great light coming into middle earth, which God himself will truly show to humankind." He was a young man when this happened, and that light afterward came to him through Paul's teaching, just as we declare here in this true reading.

Paul wisely went and looked at their gods all in order and also the altars until he found one altar on which stood this inscription: "*Deo ignoto,*" that is in English, "To an unknown God[131] is this altar consecrated." Then Paul turned around to Dionysius the Lord's man and said, "What is this unknown God whom you honor thus?" Then Dionysius said, "He is yet hidden from the people but will come into the world and rule all things—the heavens and the earth. And his reign will last without end." Then Paul answered, "What do

109

you think about that god? Will he be spirit or a person?" Dionysius answered the worthy Paul thus: "He will be truly God and truly man, and he himself will renew this old middle earth. But he is yet unknown, because he dwells living with God in heaven." Then the holy Paul said, "That God do I preach to you, the one whom you name 'Unknown.' He is born of Mary the famous Virgin, and he voluntarily suffered death for people and arose from death through his lordly might. He also ascended to heaven to his holy Father and sits on his right hand, true God and true man, through whom all things in the world are made. And he will come to judge each according to his deeds at the end of this world with his glorious angels."

After Paul preached the faith there all day long, Dionysius believed in the living God and confessed that his gods were fearful devils.[132] He then eagerly asked Paul to pray for him to the merciful Lord that he might become his disciple.

The next day Paul walked along the street and encountered a blind man who was born that way. He shamelessly asked the famous Paul to heal him in the Savior's name. And the blessed apostle signed his eyes with the holy cross, asking the Savior to give him sight. And immediately he received sight, he who was born blind. And Paul commanded him thus: "Go to Dionysius now that God has enlightened you, and tell him to hasten, as he earlier promised, to be baptized from his former sins."[133]

Then, obedient to the apostle, the one who had been healed went and announced his message boldly to Dionysius. Astonished, Dionysius then asked the messenger, "Are you not the one born blind?" And he immediately answered the worthy man, "I am the same one about whom you speak who was born blind, and the bright sun has not shined upon my eyes until the present day. But the blessed Paul opened my eyes through the might of his Lord, about whom he preaches to the people." Dionysius then arose and hastened quickly to Paul with all his household to holy baptism and became baptized. And he followed Paul for three years together wherever he journeyed and received the Lord's teaching deeply from him until the holy apostle consecrated him bishop of the Athenian city where he was born and commanded him to preach boldly the faith and the holy gospel to that pagan nation.

Then Dionysius, deeply learned, dwelled in that foresaid city at his episcopal see and eagerly preached God's doctrine to the people of that land, of whom he formerly was a teacher in their unbelief. He then converted those citizens to God and the largest part of the people to belief. And he composed many books[134] about the true faith and about the orders of angels with marvelous intelligence. And he sent these books to other bishops whom Paul and the holy John had consecrated. One of these was named Titus, another Timothy, another Polycarp, and some others. He also sent writings to the worthy evangelist John when he was an exile on the Island of Patmos, when the wicked Emperor Domitian exiled him there. Dionysius then comforted him with prophesy and said that he knew it surely from God that John would journey off that island back to the land of Asia, just as it later happened, and there write a gospel, just as it afterward happened.

Then Dionysius traveled everywhere throughout many cities and throughout the countryside boldly preaching the faith. And he converted many people to God and healed the sick in the Savior's name until he found out that the worthy apostles Peter and Paul were in prison in the city of the Romans under that cruel Nero.

Then, if it might be, Dionysius wanted to suffer martyrdom with the apostles and then returned home with wondrous haste, immediately gave up his episcopal see to another bishop, and traveled with companions from Greece to Rome over a long road, always preaching the faith. Then because of his long journey it happened that, just as the Savior willed, the holy apostles were martyred[135] by that wicked Nero before Dionysius could arrive in Rome.

At last he arrived after the Emperor Nero had ended his life with a wretched death and Clement was then pope on Peter's seat. He received with honor the noble bishop and held him with love for his noble service. Then the bishop dwelled openly within Rome with Pope Clement for some while until Clement said to him, just as Christ had directed him, "Do you see, my dear brother, how many lands yet remain pagan? And our Savior's harvest is manifold among humankind, and there are few workers for it. And you are learned in the faith through God and adorned with many virtues. Travel now in God's name to the kingdom of the Franks just as a warrior of Christ with sharp faith. And let it be given to you to bind and to loose, just as I have received from my predecessor the holy Peter, just as the Savior gave him. I say that you will receive all the kingdom of the Franks into your preaching. And may Christ himself be with you wherever you turn, just as he truly was with the blessed Peter and Paul in life. Do not hesitate at all because of that savage people. The harder one works, the better reward does one receive."

He found himself companions, and, emboldened by the Holy Spirit, he traveled about preaching Christianity and baptism to the pagans until he came to a city named Paris in the middle of the pagans in the kingdom of the Franks. And the Savior helped him with signs and wonders so that he gained control of the pagans and quickly converted its citizens to the faith. He then bought land from a believer and there quickly raised up a church by his skill and consecrated God's servants who might serve the heavenly God in the monastic order.

Listen, Dionysius then daily converted many to the faith by his beautiful preaching and joined to his Lord those whom he rescued from the Devil. And people very much sought out that church with faith. The almighty God did so many miracles through that holy man that the miracles converted the perverse pagans to the Savior's faith just as much as his preaching, as books tell us. He sent some of his companions to Spain and to other lands to sow God's doctrine, and he himself dwelled unafraid among the Franks, who mostly wandered in the Devil's cults.

Often the idolaters who were most hostile there assembled their comrades and stirred up strife and came with warfare to the worthy man. But as soon as they saw his face shining with heavenly light, the pagans lay their weapons down and fell down before the holy bishop with wonder, praying for forgiveness. Or if any one of them would not believe even then, then he became afraid and fled away.

It is a marvelous gift of God that these savages with weapons could not withstand that weaponless man, but the Franks and the remote Northmen[136] bowed down to him and to the joyful yoke of glory's King. Then throughout all that land the temples and icons of the pagan gods were broken apart by the hands of those people who had cast them, and God's congregation grew in faith very much.

The old Devil, who is filled with jealousy, had great anger against that man of God because of the people's conversion from his foul cults, and he considered how he could in some way quench with his wiles this great Christianity. Then at last the savage idolaters were stirred up with malice just as the Devil pushed them, and they sent to Domitian, the devilish emperor, who oppressed the Christians after Nero, announcing in writings about the holy man, how through his teaching the rural folk and all the citizenry were converted to Christ's observances and asked him secretly to get some advice from his worthy gods so that their minds would not be speedily destroyed through Dionysius's teaching.

Then this writing came to that emperor in Rome, and he immediately became madly angered so that he commanded all the Christians be killed whom he could discover in all lands. He wanted no one to be left Christian. He also immediately sent a certain high official named Sisinnius, a very hostile devil, to that kingdom of the Franks with many companions to kill Dionysius, the Lord's thane, with their weapons if he would not bow to the disgraceful gods.

Listen, then Sisinnius traveled with great tumult till he came to the city where the bishop was zealously instructing the lay people in the faith. Then the savage one commanded the holy man be bound together with hard knots along with a priest whom he found with him named Rusticus and a certain archdeacon named Eleutherius.[137] These holy men always lived with the bishop until they all traveled together to God.

Then with a great threat Sisinnius immediately asked the holy man what god he worshiped. Then all three of them spoke as if with one voice, "We confess with the mouth and believe in the heart in the Holy Trinity who is the heavenly God, that is, Father, Son, and the comforting Spirit, and we preach to the people the redemption of middle earth through the holy Son whom the heavenly Father sent to be slain for us of his own will."

Then Sisinnius said, "Say if you desire to obey the emperor and believe in his gods. If you do not wish this, then I do not wish to make his commandments known to you for long with words but with hard blows." Then he commanded that the holy bishop be unclothed and beaten without mercy. But he sang his prayers among those tortures, worshiping his Lord, who easily could have rescued him from those savages. But in these short tortures the holy one had to imitate[138] his Lord and suffer death for him just as Christ himself did, who gave himself for us.

Then afterward Sisinnius commanded that Dionysius's companions, the priest and deacon, be beaten. And he commanded that for their belief they be led together in chains to the darkest prison. He again commanded that they be beaten and afterward the bishop be stretched on a bed of iron and burning coals be put under his naked body as was done to Lawrence.[139] But on that bed the holy one prayed to God.

Then the savage one commanded that he be thrown to beasts who were hungry so that they might gnaw the holy man. But as soon as they came to him, those fierce beasts lay at his feet as if they were afraid.[140]

Then the judge commanded that the Lord's thane be thrown into a burning oven,[141] but his prayers put out all the flame, and he was left there whole. Then again the savage judge commanded a gallows be made and the bishop hung on it as an insult. And thus hanging, he preached the Savior to all bystanders, just as Andrew[142] did.

Then afterward the judge commanded he be taken from the gallows and all three be led to a lightless prison and many other Christians to the house of torture. Listen, then the bishop happily drew those Christians in the prison to God with his teaching, and he celebrated mass with them all. While he was breaking the holy host, a heavenly light like they had never before seen came there over all that crowd. The Savior came there also with the heavenly light together with many angels, where the people were looking on and took that host that was consecrated there and said to the bishop with a happy countenance, "Accept this, my beloved, and with my Father I will fill with perfection these mysteries, because with me is a great reward for yourself and health in my kingdom for those who obey you. Now begin with strength, and your memory will stand in praise. The love and good will that dwell in your breast, for whomsoever they plead, they will always be granted them." And after these words he turned back to heaven.

Sisinnius again commanded in the morning that the saints immediately be brought out of that foul prison and commanded them to offer their gift to those lifeless gods if they valued their life or were sensible. The saints then remained in the faith of the Savior, and the mad judge yet wanted to find out if he could turn them away from the worship of God. Then he commanded them all to be beaten again sorely with rods and afterward to be beheaded on account of the Savior's faith.

Then those pagans led the saints to the slaughter, and Dionysius thanked his Lord with praise for all the miracles he had done through him. And they were beheaded with sharp axes, just as that savage one commanded.

And God revealed a very great miracle there through that famous bishop. There came a great light toward the bodies of those martyrs. And the body of the bishop arose with that light, and he took his own head that had been cut off up onto that hill and went with it away from there for over two miles, with the people looking on, praising his Lord with holy songs of praise. And a host of angels also sang there sweetly until the body arrived where it wished to lie with its head and all. And the holy angels continuously sang, just as the book tells us.

Listen, then the pagans who heard that song and saw that wonder cast over their worship and believed in Christ together with some of the murderers. And none of them there refused to believe, and they turned away, afraid on account of that miracle. That was a choice miracle—that the trustworthy martyr was able to walk without a head, praising almighty God, and also run with a host of angels. But God wanted to manifest through that choice sign that his soul lived even though his body was slain. And he wanted to show to the people how great a faith that holy man had in the Savior in his life.

Sisinnius, that unblessed judge, nevertheless would not believe in Christ, but he commanded that all who believed in God through Dionysius's teaching be killed very savagely with various torments. And their souls departed to the true life.

The bodies of that holy priest and that faithful deacon, Rusticus and Eleutherius, lay upon that hill where they had been beheaded with the holy bishop, when his body walked away, just as we have written earlier. Then those pagan murderers bore the bodies of those saints immediately to a ship. They wanted to sink them into the flood. But the almighty Creator opposed that bad counsel.

There was a certain noblewoman who knew of their bad plan, and she invited the murderers to her, as if for kinship's sake. And she got them drunk with wine and commanded some people go secretly in the meanwhile to the ship and steal the bodies. And she held them in honor until that persecution ended and Christianity came back to life after that ruin.

Again, after a space of time, the Christian people took and built a famous monastery over the bodies of those martyrs. There all three lie in special honor. Frequently many miracles are done there through those holy martyrs for the comfort of the people. There the blind receive sight through their prayers and the dead hearing and the crippled motion. And the mad there become sensible through them. And countless miracles are done there very often for the praise of almighty God who lives forever and ever. Amen.

ÆLFRIC

St. Oswald

After Augustine arrived in the land of the Angles,[143] there was a certain noble king named Oswald[144] in Northumbria who believed strongly in God. In his youth he traveled away from his friends and kin by sea to Scotland[145] and immediately was baptized there, together with his companions who had traveled there together with him. Meanwhile his uncle Eadwine, the Northumbrian king, who believed in Christ, was slain by the British king named Cadwallon, and then two of his successors[146] within two years. And this Cadwallon killed and shamefully treated the Northumbrian people after their lord's death, until blessed Oswald washed away his evil.

Oswald came against him and keenly fought him with a small army, but his faith strengthened him and Christ helped him in slaying his enemies. Then Oswald immediately raised up a cross[147] for God's worship before he came to the battle and called to his companions: "Let us fall before the cross and pray the Almighty that he rescue us from the bold enemy who would kill us. God himself knows well that we struggle righteously against this cruel king to save our people!" Then they all fell with Oswald into prayers and afterward on the next day went to the fight and there won victory, just as the Wielder granted them because of Oswald's faith. And they lay their enemy down—that bold Cadwallon with his great army, he who thought that no army could withstand him.

Afterward, that same cross that Oswald raised stood there for worship, and many sick people were healed—and also likewise beasts—through that same cross, as Bede relates to us. One man fell on the ice so that his arm broke and then lay on his bed badly afflicted until someone brought him some of the moss from that same cross, which had grown about it, and the sick man immediately was healed in his sleep on that same night through Oswald's merits. That place is called Heavenfield in English, by the long wall that the Romans built, there where Oswald overcame the savage king. And afterward there was built there a very big church for the worship of God, who ever dwells in eternity.

Lo, then Oswald began to consider God's will as soon as he held the kingdom, and wanted to convert his people to faith and to the living God. Then he sent to Scotland, where the faith then was, and commanded the chieftains to grant his request and send some teacher who could win his people over to God. And this was granted him. They immediately sent to the blessed king a certain reverend bishop named Aidan. He was a man of famous life in the habit of a monk, and he had thrown from his heart all worldly cares, desiring nothing except God's will, so that whatever he received by the gift of the king or powerful men, that he quickly gave with a benevolent spirit to the needy and beggars.

Lo, then King Oswald rejoiced in his arrival and received him with honor for his people's benefit, so that their faith once more would be turned toward God from the apostasy toward which they had turned. Then it happened thus that the faithful king explained to his counselors in their own language the bishop's preaching with a happy spirit and was his interpreter, for he knew Scottish well and the bishop, Aidan, could not bend his speech to the Northumbrian language as yet quickly enough. The bishop then traveled throughout all Northumbria preaching faith and baptism, and that people bent toward God's faith and he always set a good example for them with his works and always himself lived just as he taught others. He loved temperance and divine reading, and he eagerly instructed young men with doctrine so that all his companions who went with him had to learn psalms or some reading, wherever they traveled preaching to the folk. Seldom would he ride but journeyed on his feet and lived as a monk among laypeople with much discretion and true virtues.

Then King Oswald became very eager to give alms and was humble in his habits and generous in all things. And throughout all his kingdom churches were raised and monasteries founded with great eagerness.

On a certain occasion it happened that they sat together, Oswald and Aidan, on the holy day of Easter. Then a royal meal was borne to the king in a silver dish, and immediately there came in one of the king's thanes who was in charge of his alms and said that many needy people were sitting about in the street, each having come for the king's alms. Then the king immediately sent that silver dish to the needy with victuals for all and commanded the dish be cut up and given to the needy, a portion for each. And just so was it done. Then the noble bishop, Aidan, took the king's right hand with great joy and called out with faith, speaking thus to him: "May this blessed right hand never decay in corruption!"[148] And it also happened to him, just as Aidan commanded for him, that his right hand is whole until this day.

Oswald's kingdom then became so large that four nations accepted him as lord[149]—the Picts and the British, the Irish and the Angles, just as the almighty God united them to that extent, for Oswald's merits that afterward honored him. In York he completed that peerless monastery[150] that his kinsman Eadwine had begun earlier, and he labored for the heavenly kingdom with continuous prayers more than he thought how he held in the world the temporary dignity that he loved but little. After matins most often he wished to pray and stand in church in various prayers from the rising of the sun with great remorse. And wherever he was he ever worshiped God with upturned palms toward heaven's guardian.[151]

At that same time also a certain bishop came from Rome, named Birinus, to the king of Wessex, named Cynegils. He was yet a heathen as also was all Wessex. Indeed Birinus turned from Rome by the counsel of the pope who was in Rome and promised that he would do God's will and preach to the heathens in a distant land about the name of Jesus and the true faith. Then he arrived in Wessex, which was still heathen, and converted that King Cynegils to

God and all his people with him to the faith. Then it happened thus that the faithful Oswald, king of Northumbria, came to Cynegils and sponsored him in baptism, happy for his conversion. Then those kings, Cynegils and Oswald, gave to the holy Birinus the city of Dorchester for his episcopal see, and he dwelled therein, raising God's praise and directing that folk with doctrine toward the faith for a long while, until he journeyed blessed to Christ. And his body was buried in that same city until Bishop Hædde once more translated his bones to Winchester and lay them with honor inside the Old Minster, where one may yet honor him.

Lo! Then King Oswald held his kingdom gloriously before the world with great faith and honored his Lord in all his deeds until he was slain in defense of his folk in the ninth year he held his kingdom, when he himself was thirty-eight years old. It happened accordingly that Penda,[152] the king of Mercia, made war against him, he who at his kinsman's death earlier, King Eadwine, aided Cadwallon. And that Penda knew nothing about Christ, and all the Mercian folk was still unbaptized.

Then they both came to the battle at Maplefield and joined battle together until the Christians fell there and the heathens approached the holy Oswald. Then he saw his life's end approach and prayed for his folk who fell and died there and committed their souls and himself to God and thus cried out at his death: "God, have mercy on our souls!" Then the heathen king commanded that his head be struck off together with his right arm and they be set up as trophies.

Then after the killing of Oswald his brother Oswiu[153] succeeded to the kingdom of Northumbria and rode with a host to where his brother's head stood fastened to a stake and took that head and his right hand and carried them with honor to the church at Lindisfarne. Then was fulfilled what we earlier said, that his right hand remained whole in its flesh without any corruption, just as the bishop said. The arm was placed with honor in a shrine made of silver in St. Peter's monastery inside Bamborough by the seashore. And it lies there as uncorrupted as it was when he was slain.

Subsequently his brother's daughter became queen in Mercia and asked for his bones and brought them to Lindsay, to Bardney Monastery, which she greatly loved. But the monks would not, for human errors, take the saint. So a tent was pitched over the holy bones within their hearse. Then, lo, God showed that he was a holy saint, since the light of heaven stood up to the heavens over that stretched-out tent together with a high sunbeam all through the night. And the people beheld it throughout that shire, marveling very much. Then the monks became very afraid and prayed about this in the morning, that they could accept with honor the saint whom they earlier had forsaken. Then the holy bones were washed and borne into that church with honor, and they placed them up in a shrine. And many sick people were healed there through his holy merits from various diseases. The water with which his bones were washed inside the church was poured out in some corner, and afterward the earth that received the water became a remedy for many; with that dust devils were cast out from people who earlier were afflicted with madness.

Also where he fell, slain on the battlefield, they took the earth to sick people and gave it in water for the ill to drink, and they were healed through that holy man. A certain wayfaring man was going toward that field when his horse was taken ill and immediately fell there, rolling all around that ground as if it were mad. When it had rolled throughout that wide field, it came after a long while to the place where Oswald the king fell in that battle, just as we said earlier, and it immediately arose when it touched that place, whole in all its limbs. And its lord was glad to see that. The rider then went forth on his way to where he had intended to go. Then there was a maiden lying in paralysis, afflicted for a long time. He [the rider] then began to relate what had happened to him, and they carried that maiden to the aforesaid place. She went to sleep and soon awoke again, whole in all her limbs from that frightful affliction. Then she bound her head and cheerfully went home, walking on her feet as she had never done before.

Afterward again a certain rider rode on an errand by that same place and bound some of the dust of that precious place in a cloth and brought away with him what he found there. Then he met some cheerful drinking companions back home and hung that dust on a high post and sat with his buddies rejoicing together. A great fire was started in the midst of the beer drinkers and sparks flew against that roof very much until that house suddenly caught all on fire and then the beer drinkers fled away afraid. That house was all burnt down except for that one post on which the holy dust was hung. The post alone remained standing whole—with the dust— and they marveled greatly over the holy man's merits, that the fire could not burn up the earth. And many people afterward sought out that place, fetching its cure for each of their friends.

Then his fame spread far and wide throughout those lands and also likewise to Ireland and also south to France, just as a certain priest relates about a certain man. This priest said that there was a learned man in Ireland who did not pay heed to his learning or his Creator's commands but spent his life in foolish works until he sickened and was brought to his end. Then he called that priest, who has revealed it again thus, and immediately said to him with a sorrowful voice: "Now must I die a miserable death and go to hell for my wicked deeds. Now if I survive I want to pray and turn toward God and to good habits and submit my life all to God's will. And I know that I am not deserving of this reprieve unless some holy person intercede for me to Christ the savior. Now it has been told us that a certain holy king is in our country named Oswald. Now if you have anything of that saint's relics, give it to me, I pray you." Then the priest said to him: "I have a piece of the stake on which his head stood, and if you wish to believe, you will immediately become whole." Lo, then the priest took pity on the man and placed some of the holy wood in holy water and gave it to the sick man to drink. And he immediately recovered and afterward lived a long while in the world and turned to God with his whole heart and with holy works, and wherever he went he revealed these wonders. Therefore no one should repudiate what he voluntarily promises to almighty God when he is sick, lest he lose himself if he denies God.

Now the holy Bede, who wrote this book, says that it is no wonder that the holy king heals sickness now that he lives in heaven, because when he was here alive he wanted to help the needy and the ill and give them food. Now he has honor in the eternal world with the almighty God because of his goodness. Afterward the holy Cuthbert, when he was yet a child, saw how God's angel carried Aidan's soul, the holy bishop, cheerfully to heaven, to the eternal glory he earned while in the world.

Holy Oswald's bones were brought again after many years to the land of the Mercians into Gloucester, and there God often revealed many wonders through that holy man. For that be glory to the Almighty, forever and ever. Amen.

ÆLFRIC

On the Sacrifice of Easter

Beloved people, it is often explained to you about our Savior's resurrection, how he on this very day after his passion[154] mightily arose from death. Now we will explain through the gift of God about the holy eucharist[155] that you are about to receive and enlighten your understanding about these secrets according to both the Old Testament and the New, lest any doubt assail you about this life-giving feast.

The almighty God commanded the general Moses in the land of Egypt to command the people of Israel to take from each household a yearling lamb in the night in which they traveled out of the country into the promised land and offer that lamb to God and afterward kill it and fashion the sign of the cross on their door posts and lintels with the lamb's blood.[156] Afterward they ate of the lamb's flesh and unleavened bread with the lettuce of the field.

God said to Moses, "Do not eat any part of the lamb raw or boiled in water but roasted in the fire instead. Eat its head and its feet and its innards. Do not leave any of it until morning. If any is left, burn it up. Partake of it in this manner; gird up your loins and wear your shoes. Have your staff in your hands and eat it quickly. This event is God's Passover."[157]

And in that night throughout Pharaoh's kingdom the first-begotten child was killed in each house. And God's people Israel was spared from this sudden death through the offering of that

124

lamb and the marking of its blood.[158] And then God said to Moses, "Hold this day in your memory and celebrate it famously among your kindred with eternal service and eat only unleavened bread for seven days during this festival."[159]

After this event God led the people of Israel over the Red Sea with dry feet and drowned Pharaoh in it with all his army, he who had pursued him.[160] And afterward he fed the people of Israel for forty days with heavenly nourishment and gave them water out of hard rock until they came into the promised land.[161]

I have treated some of this story in another place. Now I want to open up some more that pertains to the sanctified host. Christians may not now keep the old law bodily, but it is fitting for them to know what it betokens spiritually. The innocent lamb that the old Israel then sacrificed signified according to spiritual understanding Christ's suffering, he who, innocent, shed his holy blood for our redemption.[162] God's servants sing about him at each mass: "*Agnus dei, qui tollit peccata mundi, miserere nobis.*"[163] In our tongue this is, "You Lamb of God, who takes away middle earth's sins, have mercy on us."

The people of Israel were set free from this sudden death and from Pharaoh's servitude through the lamb's offering that bore the sign of Christ's suffering. Through this we are released from eternal death and the savage Devil's control if we rightly believe in the true redeemer of all middle earth, Jesus Christ.

The lamb was offered in the evening, and our Savior suffered in the sixth age of this world. That age is reckoned the evening of this weary middle earth. They made the mark of a "tau," that is, the sign of a cross, on their doors and lintels with the lamb's blood and were thus shielded from the angel who killed the firstborn child of those Egyptians. And we have to mark our foreheads and our bodies with the sign of Christ's cross so that we may be set free from ruin when we are marked either on the forehead or in the heart with the blood of that lordly suffering. The people of Israel ate the lamb's flesh in their eastertide when they were set free, and we now spiritually[164] eat Christ's body and drink his blood when we partake of the sanctified host with true belief.

They kept for themselves the time of eastertide for seven days with great honor, during which they were set free from Pharaoh and traveled out of his land. So we Christians also should keep Christ's resurrection for ourselves as an eastertide for those seven days, because through his suffering and resurrection we are redeemed. And we are purified through the holy eucharist, just as Christ himself said in his gospel: "Truly, truly I say to you, you have no life in yourselves unless you eat my flesh and drink my blood. The one who eats my flesh and drinks my blood dwells in me and I in him, and he will obtain eternal life, and I will raise him up on the last day. I am the bread of life that has descended from heaven, by no means that which your forefathers ate, the heavenly food in the desert, and afterward died. The one who eats this bread lives forever."[165] He sanctified bread before his suffering and distributed it among his disciples, saying, "Eat the bread. It is my body, and do this in memory of me." Again he blessed the wine in a chalice and said, "Drink of this, all of you. This is my blood, which is shed for many for the forgiveness of sins."[166]

The apostles did just as Christ commanded, so that they later consecrated bread and wine for the eucharist in his remembrance. So also should all who come after them and all priests according to Christ's command consecrate bread and wine as eucharist in his name with the apostolic blessing.

Some people now have often and frequently questioned how the bread, which is made from wheat and baked by the fire's heat, can be turned into Christ's body or the wine, which is pressed out of many grapes, be turned through a single blessing into the Lord's blood. Now I say to such people that some things are said about Christ as a token, others as the real thing. This thing is true and real, that Christ was born of a virgin and suffered death of his own will and was buried and rose from death on this day. He is spoken of as bread and lamb and lion and whatever else as a token. He is called bread because he is our life and that of the angels. He is called lamb for his innocence, lion for the strength through which he overcame the strong Devil. But nevertheless Christ is neither bread nor lamb nor lion according to true nature.[167]

Why is then the consecrated host called Christ's body or his blood if truly it is not that which it is called? Truly, the bread and the wine that are consecrated by the priests' mass seem to be one thing to the human understanding without, yet call out another thing within to the believing spirit. Without, they appear to be bread and wine either in shape or in taste. But they are so truly after the consecration of Christ's body and his blood through spiritual mystery. A pagan child may be baptized, but it by no means transforms its outer shape, even though it is inwardly changed. It is brought sinful through Adam's transgression to the font, but it is inwardly cleansed from all sins although outwardly it does not change its shape. Also likewise the holy water of the font, which is called life's wellspring, is like other waters in form and is subject to decay, but the might of the Holy Spirit draws near to the decaying water through the blessing of priests and it may wash body and soul from all sins through spiritual might. Likewise now we see two things in this one creation according to its true nature. The water is a decaying liquid and after the spiritual mystery it has healing power.

Thus also if we see the consecrated host according to bodily understanding, we see that it is a creation, decaying and changeable. If we understand the spiritual power in it, then we perceive that there is life in it and it gives immortality to the one who partakes of it with faith. Great is the difference between the unseen might of the consecrated host and the visible shape of its own nature. It is by nature decaying bread and decaying wine, and it is according to the might of the divine word truly Christ's body and his blood, by no means bodily but spiritually.

Great is the difference between the body in which Christ suffered and the body that is consecrated as eucharist. Truly the body in which Christ suffered was born of Mary's flesh with blood and with bones, with skin and with sinews in human limbs made alive by a rational soul. And his spiritual body, which we have as host, consists of many grains without blood and bone, limbless and soulless, and it can be considered bodily in no way but is considered all this spiritually. Whatever it is in the host that gives us the substance of life, it is from its spiritual might and unseen effect. Thus the consecrated host is called a mystery, because one thing is seen in it and another perceived. That which is seen has bodily form, and that which we understand by it has spiritual might.

Indeed Christ's body, which suffered death and rose from death, nevermore dies but is eternal and impassable. The host is temporal, by no means eternal, corruptible and is distributed in pieces, ground between teeth and sent into the belly. But is it nevertheless according to spiritual might complete in every portion. Many partake of the holy body, yet it is nevertheless complete in every portion according to the spiritual mystery. Although a smaller part may be given to someone, nevertheless there is not greater might in the larger part than in the smaller, because it is whole in each person according to its unseen might.

This mystery is a down payment and a symbol. Christ's body is truth. We accept this down payment in a mystery until we arrive at the truth, and then the down payment is ended. Truly it is, as I said earlier, Christ's body and blood not bodily but spiritually. Nor should you question how this can be, but accept it in your faith that it is done like this.

We read in the book that is called the *Lives of the Fathers*[168] that two monks prayed to God for some revelation concerning the consecrated host and after the prayer assisted at mass. Then they saw a child lying on the altar at which the priest was celebrating mass, and God's angel stood with a knife, waiting for the priest to break the host. Then the angel dismembered the child in the dish and poured its blood into the cup. Afterward, when they went to the host, it was changed into bread and wine, and they partook of it, thanking God for the revelation.

Also St. Gregory prayed to Christ that he might show a doubting woman a great affirmation of this mystery. She went to the eucharist with a doubting mind, and Gregory immediately received from God that the piece of the host that she would partake of should appear to them both as if a finger lay there in the dish all bloodied. And the woman's doubt was then answered.

Let us now hear the apostle's word about this mystery. The apostle Paul spoke about the people of Israel of old, writing thus in his letter to all the faithful:[169] "All our forebears were baptized in a cloud and in the sea, and they all ate the same spiritual food and they all drank the same spiritual drink. They truly drank from the rock that followed after them, and that rock was Christ. The rock out of which the water flowed was not Christ bodily, but it betokened Christ, who called out thus to all believers: 'Whoever is thirsty, come to me and drink, and out of his innards will flow life-giving water.'[170] He said this about the Holy Spirit, whom those received who believed in him.

The apostle Paul said that the people of Israel ate the same spiritual food and drank the same spiritual drink because the heavenly food that fed them for forty years and the water that flowed from the rock had the symbolism of Christ's body and his blood, which are now offered daily in God's church. They were the same that we now offer—not bodily but spiritually.

I said to you somewhat earlier that Christ consecrated bread and wine before his suffering into a host and said, "This is my body and my blood."[171] He had not suffered yet, but still he changed the bread through unseen might into his own body and the wine into his blood, just as he earlier did in the desert before he was born as a man, when he changed the heavenly food into his flesh and the water flowing out of the rock into his own blood.

Many people ate of the heavenly food in the desert and drank of the spiritual drink and nevertheless died, just as Christ said. Christ did not mean that death that no one can avoid, but he meant the eternal death that some of the people earned for their apostasy. Moses and Aaron and many others of that people who were pleasing to God ate that heavenly bread, but they did not die the eternal death. Nevertheless, they passed away in the general death. They saw that the heavenly food was visible and corruptible, but they understood spiritually about these spiritual things and partook of it spiritually. The Savior said, "He who eats my flesh and drinks my blood has eternal life."[172] He did not command they eat the body in which he was housed or drink the blood that he shed for us. But he intended with these words the consecrated host, which is his body and blood spiritually. And he who tastes it with a believing heart has eternal life.

In the old law believers offered to God different gifts that had future tokening of Christ's body that he himself offered afterward for our sins as a sacrifice to his heavenly Father. Indeed this host that now will be consecrated at God's altar is the memorial of

Christ's body, which he offered for us, and his blood, which he shed for us, just as he himself commanded, "Do this in my memory." Christ suffered one time through himself, but nevertheless his suffering is daily renewed through the mystery of the consecrated host at the holy mass. Thus the holy mass accomplishes much both for the living and for those who have passed away, just as it has often been shown.

We must also consider that the consecrated host is both Christ's body and also that of all believing people, according to the spiritual mystery. Thus the wise man Augustine says about this: "If you want to understand about Christ's body, listen to the apostle Paul saying thus, 'Truly you are Christ's body and members.'"[173] Now the mystery is laid out for you on God's table, and you will receive your mystery, into which you yourselves are evolving. Become that which you see on the altar and receive that which you yourselves are. Again the apostle Paul spoke about this: "We many are one bread and one body."[174]

Understand now and bless this: many are one bread and one body in Christ. He is our head, and we are his members. Bread does not consist of one grain but of many and wine not of one grape but of many. Thus we must have unity in our Lord, just as it is written about the faithful host, that they were in as great a unity as if they were all one soul and one heart.

Christ consecrated on his table these mysteries: our peace and our unity. He who receives the mystery of this unity but does not keep the requirement of true peace does not receive this mystery for himself at all but instead an accusation against himself. It will be much good for Christians to go eagerly to the eucharist, if they carry to the altar innocence in their hearts, if they are not beset by vices. For the evil person it does no good but leads to destruction if he tastes the consecrated host unworthily.[175]

Holy books command us to mix water with the wine at the eucharist because the water betokens the people just as the wine Christ's blood. And therefore neither shall be offered without the other in the holy mass so that Christ will be with us and we with Christ, the head with the members and the members with the head.

Earlier I wanted to treat the lamb that Israel of old offered at eastertide, but I wanted first to tell you about this mystery and afterward about how one must partake of it. The symbolic lamb was offered at their eastertide, and the apostle Paul said in the epistle for this day that Christ is our eastertide, he who was offered for us and on this day rose from death.[176] Israel partook of the lamb's flesh just as God commanded with unleavened bread and the lettuce of the field. And we must partake of the consecrated host of Christ's body and his blood without the yeast of evil and wickedness.[177] Just as yeast changes things in their nature, so also do vices change human nature from innocence to guiltiness. The apostle taught that we must by no means feast on the yeast of evil but on the unleavened substance of purity and truth. Lettuce is the name of the plant that we must eat with the unleavened bread. It is bitter to the taste. And we must purify our hearts with the bitterness of true repentance if we want to partake of Christ's body.

By no means were the people of Israel used to raw meat, though God commanded them not to eat it raw or boiled in water but roasted in a fire. He wants to partake of God's body raw who without discrimination thinks that Christ was only a man like us and was not God. And he who according to human wisdom wants to question the mystery of Christ's taking on flesh, does it as if boiling the lamb's flesh in water, because the water betokens in this case human understanding. But we should know that all these mysteries of Christ's humanity were arranged through the might of the Holy Spirit. We then partake of his body roasted in a fire because the Holy Spirit came in the shape of fire to the apostles in various tongues.[178]

Israel had to eat of the lamb's head and feet and innards and had to leave there nothing overnight. If anything were left over there, they had to burn it up in a fire and not break its bones. According to spiritual understanding we eat of the lamb's head when we receive Christ's divinity into our faith. Again, when we receive his humanity with love, we eat of the lamb's feet, because Christ is the beginning and the end. God was before all worlds and became man at the ending of this world. What are the lamb's innards but Christ's secret commandments? We eat them when we receive the word of life with greediness. Nothing may be left of this lamb until morning because God's sayings are to be meditated upon with great care so that all his commands and works might be contemplated with the understanding in the night of this present life before the last day of the general resurrection might appear. If we cannot meditate on all the mysteries of Christ's incarnation, then we must commend the remainder with true humility to the Holy Spirit and by no means too boldly question these deep secrets beyond the scope of our understanding.

They ate the lamb with girded loins. The wantonness of the body is in the loins, and he who wishes to partake of the host must bind up this wantonness and receive with purity the consecrated meal. They were also shod. What are shoes except the skins of dead beasts? We will be truly shod if we imitate with our conduct and deeds these people who have passed away, they who prospered in God by the keeping of his commandments.

They had their staves in their hands at their meal. The staff betokens leadership and pastoral care. Those who know better and can do better must rule over other people and support them with their help. It was commanded to the partakers that they should eat quickly because God shuns those who are slack among his thanes and he loves those who seek the joy of eternal life with God's quickness.

It is written, "Do not delay submitting to God, lest the time be lost through slack delay." Those partakers could not break the lamb's bones. Neither could the soldiers who hung Christ break his holy bones as they did to the two thieves who hung on his either side.[179] But the Lord arose from death whole without corruption. And they will have to see him at the great Judgment whom they had wounded savagely on the cross."

In the Hebrew tongue this time is called Pascha, that is in Latin, "Transitus," and in English Passover, because on this day God's folk passed from the land of Egypt over the Red Sea from slavery into the promised land. Our Lord also passed over in this season, as the evangelist John said, from this middle earth to his heavenly Father. We must follow our Head and pass over from the Devil to Christ, from this unstable world to his secure kingdom. But first we must pass over in our present life from vices to holy virtues, from bad habits to good habits, if, after this transitory life, we want to pass over to the eternal and after our rising to Jesus Christ. May he lead us to his loving Father, he who gave him over to death for our sins. To him be glory and praise for this kindness forever and ever. Amen.

WULFSTAN

On the False Gods

Alas, it is of old that many things went amiss through the Devil and that humankind disobeyed God too much and that paganism did its damage—and still does—all too far and wide. We nevertheless do not read anywhere in books that any idol was raised up anywhere in the world in the time before Noah's Flood. But afterward it happened that Nimrod and the giants built that marvelous steeple[180] after Noah's Flood and, as the book says, among them arose as many languages as there were workers. Then afterward they traveled about in the spacious lands and then humankind immediately increased very much. And then at last they were seduced by that old Devil who earlier had deceived Adam, and they wrongly and foolishly fashioned for themselves pagan gods and neglected the true God, their own Creator, who created them and fashioned them into humans.

They then also through the Devil's teaching took it for wisdom to worship as gods the sun and the moon on account of their shining brightness and at last through the Devil's teaching offered them gifts and forsook their Lord who created them and made them. Certain people also said that the shining stars were gods and began to worship them eagerly. And some also believed in fire on account of its sudden burning, and some also in water, and some believed in the earth because it feeds all things. But they could have easily known, if they knew the distinction that he is true God who created all things for the enjoyment and use of us people on account of the great goodness that he granted to humankind. These creatures also all do just as is appointed for them by their own Creator and can do nothing except by our Lord's permission, because there is no other Creator except the only true God in whom we believe. And we love and worship him alone over all other things with sure belief, confessing with our mouths and with the spirit's sincerity that he alone is true God who created and fashioned all things.

Yet those pagans would not be content with as few gods as they earlier had, but at last accepted for worship various giants and violent worldly people who became mighty in worldly power and were terrible while they lived and foully fulfilled their own lusts.[181]

One of them lived in the old days on the island named Crete. He was named Saturn, and he was so savage that he did away with his own children, all but one, and unlike a father caused them to lose their lives immediately in their infancy.[182] He nevertheless uneasily left one alive, though he did away with all his brothers. And this one was named Jove, and he became his hated enemy. He exiled his own father from that foresaid same island named Crete and wanted very much to destroy him if he could. And this Jove became so very lustful that he took as his wife his own sister. She was named Juno, and she became a very high goddess according to the pagan reckoning.

Her two daughters were Minerva and Venus. These sinful people whom we have spoken about were reckoned the most famous gods in those days, and the pagans worshiped them very much through the Devil's teaching. But the son nevertheless was worshiped among the pagans much more than was the father, and he is also accounted the most worthy of all the gods whom in those days the pagans took for gods in their heresy. And he has as another name, Thor,[183] among some peoples. The Danish nation loves him most and in their folly worship him most eagerly. His son is named Mars. He ever caused and fashioned strife and often stirred up conflict and revenge. After his death the pagans also worshiped this wretch as a high god, and as often as they would make war or go to battle, they would offer him gifts beforehand in worship of this idol, and they believed that he could aid them with great might in the battle because in life he loved battle and strife.

There was also a certain person who was named Mercury in life, who was very deceitful and, though very glib, false in deeds and in trickery. The pagans also caused him to be a famous god for themselves according to their reckoning and offered him gifts at crossroads frequently and often through the Devil's teaching and often brought him various worship offerings on high hills. This idol was also worshiped among all the pagans in those days, and he is named Odin in his other name in the Danish custom.

Now some of those Danish people say in their heresy that this Jove, whom they call Thor, was the son of Mercury, whom they name Odin, but they do not have it right, because we read in books, both pagan and Christian, that this hateful Jove truly is Saturn's son. And a certain woman named Venus was Jove's daughter, and she was so foul and so vile in lust that her own brother mated with her, as is said, through the Devil's teaching. And the pagans also worship this evil one as a high woman.

Many other pagan gods also were variously established and also likewise pagan goddesses were worshiped very much throughout middle earth for the destruction of humankind, but these are the foremost according to the pagan reckoning, though they lived foully in the world. And the tricky Devil, who always is deceptive around humankind, brought those pagans into the most wretched heresy, so that they chose for themselves as gods such foul people, who established their foul lust as their law and lived all their life in uncleanness as long as they existed. But he is blessed who despises all such things and loves and worships the true God who created and fashioned all things. One in three persons is almighty God, who is Father, Son, and Holy Spirit. All these three names enclose one divine might and are one eternal God, ruler and creator of all creatures. To him always be praise and honor forever and ever without end. Amen.

WULFSTAN

On the Sevenfold Gifts of the Spirit

Isaiah the prophet wrote about the sevenfold gift of God in his prophesy about the Holy Spirit and about his sevenfold gifts.[184] The sevenfold gifts are named thus: *sapientia* in Latin, that is wisdom in English; *intellectus* in Latin, that is understanding in English; *consilium* in Latin, that is counsel in English; *fortitudo* in Latin, strength of spirit in English; *scientia* in Latin, good sense in English; *pietas* in Latin, piety in English; *timor Domini* in Latin, the fear of God in English.[185] These sevenfold[186] gifts truly were in our Lord in perfection, and the Holy Spirit still daily distributes them to Christians, each according to his desire and his spirit's eagerness, just as bishops in confirmation eagerly long for God himself.

And indeed that person has wisdom through the gift of God who lives wisely and always considers how he might please God. And he has good sense through God's gift who always turns it toward his Lord's will with good works. And he has good counsel through God's gift who ever guides himself about what is to be done and what to be left undone. And he has strength of spirit through God's gift who can forebear and endure much and ever be patient in every humility and again in good occurrences not forsake his diligence but be always discreet in every way so that he be not too glad in joy or too despondent in woe. And he has good sense through God's gift who loves goodness and innocence and is better within than he is thought without and knows for himself the difference between truth and untruth. And he has piety through God's gift who is devout and shows respect to other people, to his peers and also to his subordinates and does not want to despise or shame the other with words or deeds. And then the fear of God is the seventh gift of these spiritual gifts, and this gift is the beginning of all wisdom.[187] And he who has the fear of God fully by no means forsakes many of the things that are necessary for his soul to have and to hold. And the person who is deprived of all these seven gifts is by no means dear to God or belongs to God, nor is he ever pleasing to God unless he earlier earn his end so that he improves and works God's will through something.

Now the evil spirit and the invisible enemy has contrariwise sevenfold ungifts that are the ruin of many people, and these are in every way opposed to all of these good gifts of God that we spoke about earlier. And he distributes them daily to the people who unhappily obey him and neither care for God's gifts nor have the fear of God nor keep God's law but follow their desire and idle will. And the evil ungifts of the wicked Devil are thus named in the Latin language: *insipientia*, that is unwisdom; *stultitia*, that is folly; *inprovidentia*, that is recklessness; *ignaria*, that is weakness; *ignorantia*, that is ignorance; *impietas*, that is wickedness; *temeritas*, that is insolence.

Every right wisdom comes from God, because God himself is true wisdom, and every person is happy and blessed who has that wisdom which comes from God's own gift and through that arranges his own life with wisdom. This wisdom, as we said before, is the gift of the Holy Spirit, and the Devil sows against it unwisdom and deceit and so works through it that the unhappy person does not care for wisdom or order his life wisely and, yet more, does what is wicked, so that he reckons himself nevertheless for a while cautious and wise and is also very often such a deceiver disguised as if he were wise yet nevertheless is more often thinking about deception than about wisdom.

And against that understanding that comes from God's own gift the Devil sows lack of understanding and also does what is even worse, that the person through deceiving appearance acts as if he were understanding, who understands little of reason and of good in any degree.

And against the wise counsel that comes from God's own gift the perverse Devil sows recklessness and also does what is worse, so that the person through a false appearance acts as if he were well counseled, who does not care for counsel with any amount of reason.

And against the steadfastness of spirit and strength of spirit that come of God's own gift the sinful Devil sends weakness and wicked cowardice, so that the person fails in every need and also, what is worse, nevertheless causes the person sometimes to show himself mighty and unafraid who has no boldness in his heart.

And against that good sense and sagacity which come from God's own gift, the hateful Devil sows and sends ignorance and, what is worse, causes the person nevertheless to appear to himself as if he had deep insight, who by no means has any measure of discernment.

And against that piety which comes of God's own gift, the Devil sows and sends wickedness and skill, so that the unhappy person never honors what is fitting for him to honor and also does not give respect either to his servants or to his peers and yet also teaches what is worse, that he nevertheless deceitfully appear as if he were pious of spirit and under this deceitful appearance do the greatest damage.

And against that unique fear of God which comes of God's own gift the savage Devil teaches insolence and brings reckless people into instability in word and deed and sometimes also in what is yet worse, and causes certain people to be like hypocrites, as if they had the fear of God, while all their thoughts are filled with wickedness.

There was never a worse evil or a thing more hateful to God than that hypocritical evil,[188] because the Devil himself arranges it and makes that thing appear to him as if it most often seems very good at first but later becomes very evil and then full bitter in the end. And too many people nevertheless are led astray by the Devil with such tricks so that they speak and appear entirely differently than they think. And they are downright hypocrites who are accustomed to this.

And with these vices indeed is the wretched person Antichrist[189] all filled. His words and deeds are thought good by foolish people, but they are all evil and deceitful. But the arch-hypocrite nevertheless fabricates it so that the least person knows how he must accuse himself before the archfiend because he neither becomes in the world any more worldly-wise nor more eloquent in words nor worse in heart nor more crafty in deceit than he is. And there are now also too many people in this deceitful world who likewise speak or think falsely through hypocrisy and regard as prudence that with which they may so falsely deceive others. But all this comes from the Devil, although they never suspect it, and they do harm with such clever deeds first to themselves and afterward to many. And such clever deceivers who in this way deceive others most often agreeably in unrighteousness and through that do harm before God and before the world are forerunners and servants of Antichrist who make his way wide—though they do not suspect it.

Christ almighty zealously taught truthfulness and concord and that everyone should firmly resist the desire to sin. And Antichrist teaches untruthfulness and deceit and that everyone should zealously fulfill his desires, and with such bad teaching he perverts and misleads all too many. And so also do the arch-liars who reckon as prudent false deception of another, vanquishing another with "untruthful truth" and allowing another to live ignorantly in his lust, [suggesting] he should by no means regard very excessively what the books command or have restraint over bodily lusts! But he gives word to what is most faithful and wise in his thoughts, he who can most readily think elsewise and speak most often of some unfaithful thing. He also gives word to those things that are stupid, so that he holds great self restraint as little. But that food was fashioned for men for one thing only, that men should enjoy it (and also women for fornication!) for the one who desires it.

And true is what I say, with all such teachings Antichrist pleases and hatefully leads astray all too many. Therefore there is never any worse law in the world than when one follows all his lusts and sets up his lust for himself as a law. And ever as we near the end of this world, so wantonness and sinful deeds become ever the more and more common among the people through the Devil's hurts and his bad teaching. But he is blessed who indeed warns himself to any extent. God be our help! May the name of the Lord be blessed, etc.

WULFSTAN

Sermo Lupi ad Anglos[190]

Beloved people, know the truth! This world is in haste, and
it nears the end, and therefore it is always in the world the longer
the worse! And so it must get very worse before the advent of the
Antichrist.[191] And certainly it will become terrible and grim then
far and wide in the world. Zealously understand also that the
Devil has led this nation astray too much now for too many years
and that there has been too little loyalty among the people—
though they speak well! And too many injustices have ruled in the
land, and there have not always been many people who have
thought about the remedy as eagerly as they should, but daily one
evil has been increased after another and unrighteousness has
been exalted and many laws broken all too widely throughout this
nation. And therefore we have also endured many disasters and
disgraces. And if we would experience any remedy, we then must
earn this better from God than we have done earlier. For we have
earned these miseries that now weigh us down by our greatly
deserving them, and with great merits we then must obtain reme-
dies from God—if things from now on would get better. Listen,
we know full well that too great an offense needs a great remedy
and too great a fire not a small amount of water, if that fire must
at all be quenched. And it is very necessary for everyone henceforth to obey God's law with zeal and honestly pay God's dues.[192]
In pagan countries one dares not hold back either or much of

what is prescribed by law for the worship of false gods. And everywhere we withhold God's dues all too frequently! And in pagan countries one dares not diminish either within or without any of the things that are brought to the idols and dedicated to their sacrifices. And we have completely robbed the house of God both inside and out! And nearly everywhere God's servants are deprived of honor, respect, and security![193] And one dares not injure the servants of the idols in any way among the pagan nations as it is now far and wide done to God's servants, where Christians ought to keep God's law and protect God's servants.

But what I say is true: there is need for a remedy, because what is due to God has faded away too long within this nation in every region. And the laws[194] of the people have worsened all too much, and sanctuaries have been violated far and wide, and the houses of God have been too cleanly robbed of their old rights and stripped within of all their ornaments.[195] And widows have been wrongfully forced to take a man, and too many have been much impoverished and humiliated. And the poor have been sorely betrayed and cruelly deceived, and they have been sold out of this land far and wide, completely innocent people into the hands of strangers. And infants have been enslaved through savage legal abuses far and wide throughout this nation for petty theft. And the rights of freemen have been taken away, and the rights of serfs have been restricted, and the rights of alms have diminished, and, to say it quickly, God's law is hated and his teaching scorned. And for this we often are disgraced, all through God's anger. Let the one who can, understand this! And this disaster will be shared by the whole nation, although one might not think so, unless God spares us!

Therefore it is very clear and evident among us that before this time we have more often transgressed than atoned, and because of this much has assailed this people! Nor has much helped either within or without for a long time, but there has been pillage and hunger, fire and bloodshed in almost every region all too often. And theft and murder, strife and pestilence, cattle-plague and disease, malice and hate, and the depredations of robbers have sorely hurt us and high taxes afflicted us. And bad weather very often has given us crop failure, because there was in this country, as it seems, now for many years many injustices and unstable loyalties everywhere among the people. Now very often a kinsman does not spare his kin any more than strangers nor a father his child nor sometimes even a child his own father or one brother the other![196]

Nor has any of us arranged his life as he should—neither religious according to rule nor layman according to law. But our own desires have been too often fashioned into a law for us.[197] And we have not held either the teaching or law of God or man as we should. Nor has anyone had true intentions toward another as rightly as he should, but almost everyone has deceived and hurt others in word and deed. And indeed almost everyone stabs the other in the back with shameful attacks and would do more if he could. Therefore there are here in this land great treacheries before God and before the world, and there are also in the country many who are treasonous in various ways. And the greatest treason in this world is when one betrays his lord's soul. And also a very great treason is in the world when one kills his lord treacherously or drives him out of the land. And both have happened in this country. Edward[198] was betrayed and afterward killed and after that burned. And too many godparents and godchildren have been destroyed far and wide throughout this nation in addition to all the many other innocent people who have been destroyed far and wide. And all too many holy places have been desecrated because someone had first installed some people there as he never should have done if one wanted to show respect for God's sanctuaries. And Christ's people have too often been sold out of this country now for a long time. And all this is hateful to God! Let him who wants to, believe this!

And it is shameful to speak about what has happened far and wide, and it is terrible to realize what many often do, who perpetrate this crime: that they go in together and buy for a shared purchase a common woman and practice filth on her, one after another and each after the other, like dogs who are not concerned about the filth. And afterward for a price they sell God's creatures out of the land into the hands of enemies—and she is his own purchase that he dearly bought.

Also we eagerly know where this crime happens—that a father sold a child for money and a child his mother, and one brother sold the other into the hands of enemies. And all these are great and terrible deeds! Understand this who wants to! And still there is more and manifold sins that hurt this nation! Many are forsworn and greatly perjured, and pledges are broken frequently and often. And it is clear that in this nation the wrath of God fiercely oppresses us. Understand this who can!

And lo, how can more shame happen through the wrath of God than frequently does because of our own deserts? Although some serfs escape from their lord and turn away from Christendom to the Vikings and after this it happens that the clash of swords becomes common to thane and serf, if the serf utterly kills the thane, he lies unpaid by all of the serf's kin. And if the thane utterly kills the serf whom he earlier owned, he pays the price for a thane! This very base law and shameful forced payment is common among us through the wrath of God. Understand this who can!

And many mishaps happen to this nation frequently and often. Now it has not helped either in or out, but devastation and hate has been in almost every region frequently and often. And the English now for long have been defeated and too greatly humiliated though the wrath of God. And the Vikings are so strong through the permission of God that often in battle one drives away ten,[199] sometimes less, sometimes more—all because of our sins! And often ten or twelve, each after the other, disgracefully shame the thane's woman and sometimes his daughter or kinswoman while he looks on, he who considers himself proud and powerful and good enough before that happened. And often a serf ties up the thane who earlier was his lord and makes him his own serf through the wrath of God. Alas for the crime and alas for the public disgrace that the English now have—all through the wrath of God!

Often two Vikings or sometimes three drive out the troop of Christians from sea to sea throughout this nation huddled together, for the disgrace of us all, if we earnestly understand aright any shame! But we repay with worship all this disgrace that we often endure to those who shame us. We pay them continuously,[200] and they daily humiliate us. They raid and they burn, rob and plunder and lead us to their ships! And lo, what else are all these events but the wrath of God over this nation, clear and evident?

It is also no wonder if things go wrong for us, because we know full well that now for many years people have often not been concerned about what they have done in word or deed, but this nation, as it seems, has become very corrupted through manifold sins and through many misdeeds—through murders and through evil deeds, through greedy deeds and through avarice, through stealing and through robberies, through selling into slavery and through heathen vices, through treasons and through fraud, through lawbreakings and through deceptions, through attacks on kinsmen and through manslaughters, through injuries to church-men and through adulteries, through incest and through various fornications. And far and wide through oathbreakings and through pledge breakings and through various falsehoods, things are, as we said before, ruined and perjured more than they should be, and neglect of the church's feasts and fasts are committed far and wide frequently and often.

And also in this country there are all too many lapsed apostates and hostile church-haters and savage people-haters and far and wide despisers of just divine laws and of Christ's servants, and derisive fools everywhere in the nation, who hasten into those things that God's commandments have forbidden and for the most part into those things that always belong by right to God's law. And with this far and wide it has come to the fullness of evil habits, that one is now more ashamed of good deeds than evil deeds, because too often good deeds are derided with scorn and the one who fears God reviled all too much. And all too often those who love righteousness and have in any measure the fear of God are reproached and attacked with contempt. And because it so happens that that which ought to be praised is completely derided and what ought to be loved is too much loathed, there-fore all too much is brought into evil thought and into evil deed so that people are by no means ashamed, though they sin much and they commit wrongs with all this against God himself. But they are ashamed of an empty insult so that they atone for their misdeeds just as the books teach,[201] like the foolish ones who for their pride will not seek a remedy for an injury before it is too late, though they are all willing.

Here, as it seems, too many in the country have been sorely blemished by the stains of sin. Here there are manslaughters and kin-slaughters and priest-slayers and monk-haters. And here there are perjurers and murderers. And here there are harlots and child-killers and many foul adulterous fornicators. And here there are witches and sorceresses, and here there are robbers and thieves and despoilers—and, to say it briefly, a countless number of crimes and misdeeds. And we are by no means ashamed of this, but we are greatly ashamed to begin atonement as the book teaches. And this is evident in this poor, corrupt nation. Alas, many may yet easily call much to mind besides this, which one person could not quickly relate, how wretchedly things have come about now all the while far and wide throughout this nation. And indeed, let everyone seriously consider himself and not delay about this any longer. But lo, in God's name, let us do what is necessary to protect ourselves as we most eagerly can, lest we all perish together.

There was a scholar in British times named Gildas.[202] He wrote about their misdeeds, how they provoked God so excessively with their sins that he allowed at last an army of English to conquer their country and with all destroy the noble host of the Britons. And it happened as he said through violent theft and through greed for ill-gotten gains, through the lawlessness of the nation and through the wicked laziness of God's officers who kept silent about the truth for too long and mumbled with their jaws where they should have shouted. Through the foul lust of the people and through gluttony and various of their sins they also forfeited their country and lost themselves.

But let us now do what is necessary, guard ourselves against such things. And what I say is the truth: we have known worse deeds among the English than we heard of anywhere among the Britons. And thus it is greatly necessary for us that we think about ourselves

146

and eagerly deal with God. And let us do what is necessary for us and submit to righteousness and forsake unrighteousness somewhat and eagerly atone for what we earlier broke. And let us love God and follow God's laws and do very eagerly what we have promised when we received baptism or when our sponsors were at baptism for us. And let us put word and deed rightly together and eagerly cleanse our conscience and carefully keep our oath and pledge and have a truth between us without deceit. And let us often understand the great judgment at which we all must appear and protect ourselves eagerly against the raging fire of the torments of hell and earn for ourselves those glories and joys that God has prepared for those who do his will in the world. May God help us. Amen.

BODLEY 343

The Temptation of Christ

Beloved people, we want to tell you about this holy time[203] that has now arrived, in which we have an especially greater fast and abstinence than in any other common time, when we do this for the help and cleansing of our souls and also because Christ himself established an example of this fast for us. It is written that the Savior went immediately after his baptism to a certain desert and fasted there for forty days and forty nights[204] together before he everywhere openly taught humankind. He did not fast because he ever committed a sin[205] and had need to atone for it with that fast. But he fasted so that he might heal and redeem the sins of humankind and set an example for us so we might know that everyone who thinks that he might obtain the joy of heaven now must by fasting and by alms and by frequent prayers and by bodily abstinence earn it here in the world and by no means by gluttony or by drunkenness or by bodily lusts. Moreover, Christ was suffering in the desert when the accursed Devil found him, as we are about to tell you.

St. Matthew the Evangelist[206] wrote this present gospel according to its order, saying thus: *"Ductus est Ihesus in desertum a Spiritu ut temptaretur a diabolo."*[207] He said, "The Savior was led by the Spirit into the desert so that he might be tempted by the Devil." Many people question by which spirit Christ was led into the desert. Now it says very clearly in the lesson of this gospel that the cursed Devil began to tempt him there openly. It is without doubt to be believed and eagerly understood that the Holy Spirit led him willingly into that desert and that he went there of his own will so that he would allow the Devil the presumption to begin to tempt him—by no means because the Devil had any access to our Savior or his power was such that he might come anywhere near him if he had not allowed it because of his love for us. But he did this as an example for our lives that he wanted us to know how easily he could overcome the Devil, not by his divine power alone but also through human righteousness. So likewise each person can overcome the Devil if he lives his life in righteousness and in good works.

As soon as the Savior arrived in the desert, he fasted forty days and nights together. And after this he said he was hungry.[208] Indeed, in this it was made manifest that he had a true body that might make him hunger. It is written in the Old Testament that two people fasted here before this fast. Moses fasted for forty days and nights together when he was on Mount Sinai at the Lord's command,[209] and the Lord gave him the old law, which he wrote with his own finger on two stone tablets and gave to the people and commanded that they all thereafter live by it. Elijah[210] the prophet also fasted for the same forty days and nights together, after which he ate the food that the angel brought to him and he was strengthened by that food so much that he fasted that fast. And after that fast he became filled with the wisdom of the Holy Spirit and he revealed coming events and made them clear so that he might know them as well as if he could see them in the present.

Now in this last time, the Savior once again humbled himself to fast this same fast for forty days and nights together. Why did the Devil not wish to tempt Moses and Elijah as he tempted our Savior, except that he perceived that they were men in the flesh and bound by Adam's sin and also that they had sinned in some things? For there never was a person in this middle earth so holy that he did not sin in something—except Christ alone, who is true God and true man. Never did sin attach to him!

But when the Devil came to him, he saw that he had a true body and that he was unlike all other people he had ever encountered in middle earth and that in him there was never a blemish of sin. The Devil feared that this one was—just as he was—the Son of the living God and thought then that he might find out through this tempting how this might be. He brought to him that same temptation with which he tempted and deceived the first people, Adam and Eve, and worked his will upon them. This was through gluttony, greed, and idle speech. Thus Christ wanted to overcome the accursed Devil in these same three temptations with which earlier the Devil had deceived the first people.

Then the Devil came near to the Savior and said to him: "If you are the Son of God, command that these stones turn to bread."[211] It was no difficulty for Christ to turn the stones to bread with his word, for if he had said it, it soon would have happened. And then the Devil knew very well that he was the same Lord who was at the beginning when he created and wrought all creatures and said, "Let there be light,"[212] and then immediately there was light. And so he created and made all creatures; when he desired them to be, they immediately were. Christ did not yet desire the stones to become bread then, but he desired that his divine power yet be hidden from the Devil, even though later it was strongly revealed to him.

And then he spoke to him patiently and said thus: "It is written that human life not be in bread alone but in every word that proceeds from the mouth of God."[213] Listen, we know that the human body must live by food as long as it is in this life. Thus also must the soul live by the word of God. That is, it must eagerly listen to God's teaching and ever hold it if it will obtain eternal life.

Then the Devil took the Savior into the holy city and set him up on top of the Temple[214] where the seat of the teacher was. It appears to many people marvelous to hear and also difficult to believe how the Devil ever had the presumption to dare to touch Christ's body or even come near him. Alas, if we would consider his other deeds that are much greater and more humble, then we may the more easily believe this one. Christ is the head of all holy people, and all sinful people are his limbs.[215] Truly then, the Jews were all the limbs of the Devil when they judged our Lord to death. Pilate was also the Devil's limb, when he commanded our Lord to hang bodily. What wonder was it when Christ nevertheless allowed by the presumption of the Devil to touch his body when he wanted through the Devil's limb, that is, through the hands of sinful people, to suffer death bodily? Alas, listen, it was much greater and more humble when the Devil touched him—and he suffered this for man's salvation!

Then the Devil said to Christ: "If you are God's Son, throw yourself down from this height, because it is written about God's Son that he commanded his angels about you, that they will hold you in their hands so that your foot need not strike a stone."[216] In this one gospel we read that the Devil began to recite the holy book, but then immediately lied in his first utterance, as each lie and each falsehood belongs to him. It was never elsewhere said about Christ that angels had to come to his rescue, but this was sung and written about holy people and about holy souls, because angels come to their help here in the world. And then they pass out of this life, and immediately they come where the angels give them help and protection and shield them against the hard stone that is the Devil so that they never strike it, but the angels hold them against his malice and against the fierceness of his envy.

Then Christ answered the accursed spirit and said to him, "It is written that one should not tempt his Lord God too arrogantly."[217] Listen, with one word Christ could have easily sent the Devil into eternal destruction—if he wanted to reveal his divine power; but he spoke to him patiently and overcame him with human righteousness, not with the power of his divinity. But he set an example for us that we should endure the hate of evil people and their envy and always eagerly follow the teaching of God's book.

Again the Devil took the Savior and led him onto a very high mountain and showed him all the kingdoms of middle earth and their joy.[218] Indeed Christ had no need of the kingdoms of middle earth or the transitory glory of this world, hidden or stolen, but he knows all kingdoms, either heavenly or earthly, and has all creation in his power and rules and directs them all according to his will. But nevertheless the Devil had with his falsehood and through his magic presented all middle earth's mirth together with all its worldly beauty as an illusion. Though it then be altogether a deception to one who might speak with him there, he might nevertheless see all worldly beauty together through the Devil's deceit, because the Devil may conjure up many things before people's eyes when they believe in him. Sometimes he shows himself in the likeness of an angel and yet will be once more the accursed spirit he once was.

Then the Devil spoke to Christ: "I will hand over all these things to you and give you them if you will fall at my feet and worship me."[219] Alas, listen, everyone falls painfully who now humbles himself before the Devil! No one who ever eagerly obeys the Devil will get better honor from him in return. But as much as he now eagerly obeys him, so much more terribly will it ever be so that in the end he will bring him into eternal torment.

Then Christ said to the Devil, "Get behind me, you cursed demon! Truly it is written that one must pray only to God and serve him alone."[220] Then the Devil's powers were beaten back and Christ's teaching was ever afterward growing throughout this middle earth—first through himself and later through his apostles and through the holy teachers who came afterward. Christ said that one must pray only to God almighty and serve him alone. Truly we should pray neither to angels nor to other holy people except our Lord alone, who is true God. But we nevertheless must pray to each of God's saints for help and intercession, and yet to no one else except to the one who alone is true God.

Then the Devil left the Savior and went away, and immediately angels approached him and served him.[221] In this we may openly perceive our Savior's nature, that he is both true God and true man. Certainly the Devil did not need to tempt him if he did not know full well that he was true man. Nor would angels serve him if he had not been true God. Often it has happened and still does happen that angels are sent here into middle earth to aid and help people. The apostle said about this[222] that angels are subservient spirits, and they are sent here into middle earth to serve all the people who now desire to earn with good works the ability to come to the blessedness that is eternal. Great is the honor that Almighty God has given us if we may be called his children and be like his angels if we want to keep his commandments. Let us remember how the apostle admonished, instructed, and taught us, saying thus: "Now is the acceptable time, and now is the day of salvation"[223] that every person may earn for himself eternal life with our Lord if he desires to lead his life righteously according to the doctors' teaching. We must not offend anyone lest our prayer be rejected. But in all things let us prepare ourselves as God's servants, that is, first in great patience and in tribulation and in holy vigils and in fasts and in purity and in humility and in pure thoughts and in true love of God and man. May this virtue lead man's soul into the kingdom of heaven that he possesses within!

Truly it was commanded and enjoined in the old law that every year everyone should give to God the tenth portion of worldly possessions.[224] And it is now also just and right to do this in the new law according to the teaching of the scriptures. If then it appears to someone in his spirit too hard and too difficult, let him strive to fast before God for the tenth part of his days. Listen, we know that in a year there are 365 days and six hours. And this fast is just forty-two days! And if we then subtract six Sundays on which we may take food, then there are six and thirty days of this fast. And this is the tenth part of the year. Whatever person wishes to live ascetically and abstemiously in this time will be perfect. If then it seems to some people too difficult, let them indeed strive to fast this fast best, both in psalm singing for those who know how or in the almsgiving or in holy prayers and vigils and in every good that he may do before God, so that we all in this holy time may live the more happily both before God and before the world, God being our help in this, he who lives and reigns forever in eternity. Amen.

BODLEY 343

The Transfiguration of Christ

Beloved people, St. Matthew the Evangelist,[225] who wrote this gospel, said that the Savior spoke to his disciples about Judgment Day and commanded them all to make it known to the people that he himself would seek us again at the End of the World here in middle earth in his glorious might with the angelic host and then he would judge all people, rich or poor, and give them reward according to their own deeds. And later he said that some of those who were there would not experience death before they would see himself coming into his kingdom.[226] Then, about six nights after Christ spoke this word to them, he took three of his disciples with him—Peter, James, and John—and led them up an especially high mountain.[227]

Then suddenly Christ's face became marvelously fair before the three of them, so that his countenance shone like the sun and his clothes became as white as snow. Then quickly Moses the saint who earlier had passed away from the world and Elijah the prophet appeared there with him and they spoke there with the Savior. As soon as the holy retainers had seen this great marvel, Peter said to Christ: "Lord, it is good that we are here. If you wish, we will set up three tabernacles—one for you, one for Moses, and one for Elijah."[228] And when he had said this, there suddenly came a very bright cloud, and it overshadowed them all. And a voice arose in the mist, saying thus: "This is my beloved Son with whom I am well pleased. Obey him!"[229] Then as soon as Christ's retainers had seen this great marvel and suddenly heard the voice, they became so very afraid that they could not bear it and fell to the ground full of dread.

Then the Savior approached them and touched them and raised them up and said to them: "Arise and be not afraid."[230] Then they lifted up their eyes and rose but saw neither Moses nor Elijah nor anyone except Christ alone. When they came once more down from the mountain, Christ commanded the three of them who had seen this marvelous sight not to tell anyone before he had suffered for the salvation of humankind and had arisen from death.

Beloved people, with his own words through his holy evangelist our Lord admonishes and teaches us to guard ourselves against sin and evil deeds and forsake the vices of this wicked middle earth and ever eagerly consider in this time how transitory and how ephemeral the things of this world are and how it is unknown to every person, either rich or poor, how long he might enjoy this transitory life.

Listen, we have now heard quite a wonder! He appeared to his disciples in this spiritual vision because through it he wanted to strengthen their faith and also that of all people who hear it recounted. Though the evangelist wrote this holy account with few words, nevertheless the joy and bliss that they saw there in the space of a day was greater than any human person may say or even think. The evangelist said that Christ wanted to show his own face here in the world to his disciples as brightly and as gloriously as all the saints in the kingdom of heaven would see him. And he wanted to teach us by this so we might know that everyone who thinks to obtain that heavenly kingdom must, while here in the world, be set apart from all sinful desire and from this earthly greed. We must remember that Christ said that the way is very high and very steep that leads us to heaven;[231] those people travel that way who put their hope in heaven and consider how fleeting this earthly life is and how very much it is all mixed up with sorrow. Let us remember what the apostle said: "Our mirth and our glory and our bliss is in heaven."[232] We must arrive at that mirth and at that bliss through God.

It is well said that Christ let his holy retainers up onto an especially high mountain.[233] This signifies that the faithful are set far apart from the evil neighborhood of people in the present world. Then is fulfilled what the prophet said in the psalm: "Lord, you hide your saints in the glory of your countenance, and you cover them in the kingdom of heaven and protect them from all evil things."

The evangelist said that after six days Christ fulfilled what he promised his retainers, that they should see his countenance very marvelously.[234] In this is signified that after this world all the saints will arrive at the bliss of heaven that the Lord who never lied promised them, and it has been prepared for them before middle earth was created. We read in books that the time of this world stands in the sixth age. Now, five are passed, and the sixth is now present. Now again, when this is fulfilled and ended, then all the saints will hear and see our Lord, and then they will rejoice forever in eternity.

Why did the evangelist say that the Savior's face was shining and made very glorious and shone like the sun?[235] Because the Savior wanted to establish and strengthen the faith of those who saw it, and yet again of all those who heard about it so that we all might understand that just as his face was transformed into brightness, so will all his saints be changed in appearance and glory on the Day of Judgment, just as he himself said. Faithful people shine as brightly as the sun in their Father's kingdom.

Beloved people, before the first people Adam and Eve sinned and made God angry in paradise, the stars, sun, and moon had much greater brightness than they now have. But after they sinned through disobedience and God threw them out of that great joy into this mortal life here in middle earth, then the stars had to suffer this punishment because they had to take on human nature, and because of this they then were deprived of a great part of their brightness. Nevertheless, it will happen at the End of the World on Judgment Day that God will give them back their full brightness. Then the moon will receive the brightness of the sun, and the sun will be seven times brighter than it now is. They then will also be allowed to rest from the course and the strife they now endure. This will happen when the time comes that God's children, who will all be holy people, will also receive rest from their great struggles and sorrows that they now endure and suffer. But the appearance and fairness of the stars or the saints will be like Christ's brightness, because his appearance and brightness will outshine all other light.

St. Paul the apostle speaks about the saints of Christ:[236] "Even as a star outshines another in brightness so that it is brighter than another," so will the person who will be first on Judgment Day shine there so much more gloriously and brightly than another. Because to the extent a person does good here in the world more than another and to the extent he is better in his deeds than another, so much more reward and recompense will he receive from our Lord on Judgment Day.

Listen, we truly know that the appearance and the beauty of the lordly countenance far surpasses the brightness of the sun, as it rightly is. But why did the evangelist compare the lordly countenance to the brightness of the sun, except that he could not find anything brighter or more beautiful? But nevertheless, as I just said, the beauty and fairness of Christ's countenance will surpass all the brightness of the sun. A sinful person cannot see this beauty and this glory of the lordly countenance, but this distinction is wondrously made through the great might of almighty God's Son. We all, good and evil, must look on our Lord on the Day of Judgment, but then there will be no person of the Devil who will see any part of this glory and this beauty. But sinful people will then have to see the wounds and sores on our Lord and the marks of the nails with which he was nailed onto the cross, and no part of the bliss about which I spoke earlier, because now here in the world they were more unthankful for his great humility than they should have been. Then Christ's saints will not be able to see any portion of the sores or the wounds on the lordly body, but there they will see on him the bliss and the beauty and the fairness, because here in the world they were thankful for his suffering and his humility with words and deeds.

Then on Judgment Day all faithful and sinful people will be divided in two.[237] Then after this the sinful people will be sent into eternal punishment, and the faithful people will be led into the kingdom of heaven, where they will be able to see Christ's shining countenance forever, and they will ever live there and shine in brightness. The apostle spoke about this: "The Lord will then transform the humility of our body and give it beauty and brightness according to his own likeness. What should we say that his clothes, which the evangelist spoke about and which became as white as snow, signified except the holy congregation that is the multitude and gathering of all the saints? Truly this congregation will be made white through the bath of baptism, and it will shine white and bright before God's eyes through many holy deeds. We know well that there is no one who can guard himself against all sins as long as he is here in the world so that he does not sin in some things, either in word or in deed or in thought. But nevertheless, at the end of this world on Judgment Day it will happen that the Lord will cleanse his holy church and all the saints and redeem them from every blemish, and then he will lead them, so beautiful and so unblemished, into his kingdom.

The evangelist[238] said that Moses and Elijah appeared there and spoke there with the Lord. Beloved people, what did they show him or what did they say to him? The evangelist Luke says it yet more clearly.[239] He said that Moses and Elijah appeared in glory and in wonder, and they spoke to Christ about the suffering that he later would fulfill in Jerusalem. What else do Moses and Elijah signify, who spoke up on that mountain with the Lord about his suffering, than the lordly Law and the holy prophets who were strengthened with God's Spirit and who earlier spoke many things openly before Christ's sufferings? And God revealed to them all those things that would happen, first about Christ's advent here in middle earth and then about his suffering and his resurrection and about his ascension by which he went up into heaven, and all the things that holy books now yet tell us are about to come—about Judgment Day and about the Lord's second coming into middle earth and about the resurrection of all humanity and about the future life. Without doubt all this will happen. Also indeed Moses by this signified to the people how he received human death and passed away and was buried. Rightly those people may be symbolized by Moses, who now on Judgment Day will arise from death and who earlier had passed away. Elijah never yet has suffered death, but he is yet living in a body in the place where God has put him.[240] And he will await his martyrdom there safely, until the Lord will send him again here into middle earth before the End of the World so that he will then preach and make God's teaching known and suffer his martyrdom for Christ's love in the days of Antichrist.[241] Rightly those people are symbolized by Elijah who now before Judgment Day will be found living. All people, either those who have passed away or those then living in the body, will be taken up over this airy sky in the twinkling of an eye,[242] coming toward our Lord for judgment. And after this, the great Judgment will be quickly ended, and all God's saints will then be led into eternal life.

Beloved people, ever with a thankful spirit must we understand and consider what the heavenly King suffered for us. And we should thank him for this ever with word, with deeds, and with our whole hearts. For each person, as he has more love for the almighty God, so he has a greater desire for love—and always as he feels much more greatly the sweetness of heavenly life in his spirit, so much more do all these earthly things become bitter and sour. Thus St. Peter, when he saw Christ's countenance so bright and so beautiful and the glory of the two people Moses and Elijah, then he immediately forgot all the earthly concerns he earlier had and considered them feeble on account of the joy he had then seen. Then because of this he said, "Lord, it is good for us that we are here. If you will, we will make three tabernacles here—one for you, one for Moses, and one for Elijah."[243] St. Peter was so very much overcome by the glory he had seen there, he did not consider what he said, that he intended to build an earthly house in this heavenly bliss. There is no need there in the exalted blessedness for separate houses, about which St. John the Evangelist spoke, so that the Lord showed him again for a second time a spiritual vision. When he saw and looked at the heavenly blessedness, then he said many things about the fairness he saw. He said, "I saw no temple there, no individual dwelling, but the Lord himself is that city and the temple of the noble."[244] But though St. Peter listened to that word, nevertheless he was overcome with wonder when he said, "Lord, it is good for us that we are here so that we may earn of God by a good deed and be with him and eternally see his holy countenance forever without end." When St. Peter saw Christ's countenance so bright and so beautiful and the glory of the two people who were with him, then it seemed to him, as I said before, that there was no bliss and joy except for that.

Beloved people, what should we say? What blessedness do those people receive who now with a good deed earn that they might eternally see the glory and the wonder of our Lord's blessedness? What kind of person is it who may say with a word or think in spirit how great and manifold are the joy and the fairness of faithful people when the heavenly King leads them into his kingdom where they may see forever his divine glory? And it is not only that they see there the glory of the two men just as Peter and his companions did upon that mountain, but also the unnumbered host of God's angels and all his saints. And they also might eternally look on Christ's countenance with all joy and all bliss. There each has unspeakable love toward the other, and each rejoices in the other's good and the other's joy just as in his own.

Then St. Peter said this word to Christ when suddenly a very bright cloud came there and wrapped about the outside of them all and there was a voice calling to them out of the bright cloud, saying thus: "This is my beloved Son who well pleases me. Obey him."[245] Thus they knew and understood that just as he is true man through his human nature, he is likewise true God through his divine nature and of one joy and of one might, because all faithful people stand fulfilled in him. For with great mercy Christ showed his disciples this divine vision, for he well knew that the time was nearing when he would suffer for the salvation of the people. He wanted therefore to strengthen their faith more firmly here in the world with the heavenly joy that they saw there, how beautiful his holy body would be after his resurrection.

Because of their human frailty the saints could not bear that glory, and they fell to the earth.[246] Then Christ did as a merciful teacher would do, both raised them up with his hands and also comforted them with his word and said to them, "Arise and be not afraid." When they lifted up their eyes, they saw no one except Christ alone, and the spiritual vision that they had earlier seen had all gone away. When they came down from the mountain named Tabor, Christ commanded them not to tell anyone[247] about that shining vision which they had seen there before he had suffered for the salvation of the people and had arisen again from death. Why did Christ forbid his retainers from saying and making known to anyone this shining vision, except for two reasons?

First is that he knew if it were told to the people, all the people would then be hostile to the governors and would not then permit the injury that afterward they did against Christ. But then Christ did not wish that the holy faith which would come about through his blood and through his suffering stand diminished for a while, but it must needs go according to his own will as he earlier had established it. Then it was for another reason that they could not speak about the vision. Because if it then were made known to some people, then many people would have been immediately converted through it to his faith right at the beginning. But he knew that it afterward would seem to many weak spirits very terrible when they saw his hard suffering and all the reproach and difficulty that he suffered for the salvation of the people. Thus he wanted them to await the time when it would be most profitable to tell about it and make it known to the people. He wished that his holy suffering first be fulfilled so that later his holy apostles, after they were strengthened by the Holy Spirit, would then tell about it and make it known openly to all people—his holy suffering, his resurrection, and his ascension into heaven, and also the shining vision that they will see there with their eyes and the fatherly voice that makes known his eternal blessedness which they will hear.

Now, beloved people, we have told you some things about this holy word of the gospel. Let us now turn with all our heart and all our might to the Lord and earn with a good deed that we might ascend to this height. And if we desire to love, so that we might see out Lord's countenance so marvelous and so beautiful, then let us now forsake unrighteous deeds and bodily desires and strive ever to be pure. And let us live before our Savior and guard our mouths against profitless speech and our hearts against evil thoughts. And let us earn with good deeds that we might arrive at the eternal joy when all humankind arises and receive that eternal blessedness from our Savior and see his countenance eternally and obey it and then enjoy that bliss with the heavenly King, who lives and reigns forever and ever. Amen.

BODLEY 343

The Transience of Earthly Delights

Beloved people, I ask you that as often as you go by the sepulchers of rich people you look at them and consider where their wealth has ended up together with their goods and their retinues and their worldly pride and their vanity.[248] Why do you need all this that passes and slips away like the moon's shadow with its worldly glory once so rich and now faded and dwindled and useless and defiled? But look then on those sepulchers and say to yourself, "Listen, a person once lived joyously in the world whom I once knew." Then the shattered bones would teach us and the dead dust would speak to us from the sepulcher[249] about this if they could speak: "Why, you wretched one, do you labor in greed in this world? Or why do you raise yourself up in pride, in vainglory, and in vice and follow the sun too much? Look at me, and abhor your evil thoughts and know yourself. Look at my bones here in the earth and think about yourself. I once was as you now are, and you will yet become what I now am. Look at my bones and my dust, and forsake your evil desires."

Then, beloved people, though dead bones cannot speak from a sepulcher, nevertheless we may teach ourselves something through them, because we should always remember our passing away and that we will never again go about here in the world. And thus we may do some good. But then the reward and the work once done will be scrutinized.

We should also always consider the end of this world, that is, Judgment Day, when the Lord with the heavenly host of angels will seek this middle earth for the woe and misery of sinful people and also to bring his help to holy people. Then out of the old sepulchers will arise all the bodies and the bones that have lain asleep many years in death and were held fast in the deepness of sins.[250] And then all humankind will arise together, and they will see this world sizzling, crackling with fire, and burning and the heavens in red flames. And all this middle earth will go up in fire. Then the faithful Judge will come from the clouds of heaven,[251] and he will be surrounded by the heavenly host. And then all the faithful and all the sinful will be gathered before the judgment seat of the strict Judge, and the Lord will divide them into two halves.[252] And he will place the faithful on the right side and the sinful on the left side, and he will then say to the faithful: "Come, you blessed, into the heavenly homeland and always dwell there and be in joy and bliss even like the angels, and there you will be led with merry songs of praise, and you will dwell with me there in the joy of the heavenly kingdom in the face of your Lord. There no hostility will injure you, but in the safety of the bright light you will love there in joy, because you willingly kept my law and my teaching and all the things I commanded you to keep. I saw them all carried out in your good works as I said before."

Then after this the Lord will look at the sinful people and say to them, "Depart, you cursed, from me into the great fire and into the eternal burning and into the bitter smoke of hellfire, where the flame fiercely burns and the dragons there tear the sinful with their teeth. And there the guilty will burn and the worms will devour them with foaming mouths and their faces will overflow with tears, and there will be a fearsome grinding of teeth. And the black night will never end together with the dim darkness. Nor will a beam of light ever appear, because you scorned my teaching in your hearts and you recklessly would not keep my commandments."

Then after this the wicked will be shoved weeping into the eternal fire where they will dwell in pain and eternal torment. They will see[253] the joy of the faithful and the angels and the white host of blessed people praising our Lord. And they will come there who did evil here and would not obey God's teaching. They will sink into the hot flame, where they will suffer in eternal sorrow. Then the holy and faithful people will travel into life with melody, and they will journey together with the host of angels to the upper kingdom, where they will happily dwell forever in blessedness. And they will never be separated from that eternal joy.

Thus, beloved people, we have great need to keep God's commandments zealously and earn that we might enjoy life with the citizens of heaven and not be thrown into the deepest abyss of hell. Thus we see this transitory life filled with peril and great difficulty, and every day this life wanes and worsens, and by no means do the living endure in this world, nor will anyone be left alive. All people alike are begotten in this world; nevertheless their lives are afterward not alike, and they all depart in the end. Nor can one live here in the world so long that death will not take him. And the grief of death will grip the proud and the vainglorious. And because they would not give their souls help from God's love here, they will quickly lose themselves and succeed in other things, which they would not forsake for Christ as long as they lived. But when death comes, then they will have to forsake their possessions unwillingly, and they will then have nothing.[254] Each day this present life that we love wanes, but the pain will not wane for the people who now labor according to it.

Then, beloved people, let us keep all these things in mind and consider that the human body is like a blossoming plant that dries up and shrivels on account of the sun's heat. When old age descends on it with sickness, all the fairness of youth will go away and be destroyed. But Christ's countenance is to be loved above all other things much more than the youth of the body. But set your heart on this earthly struggle and earn for yourself the heavenly kingdom, where there is eternal blessedness. There age does not groan nor does child scream. There is neither thirst there nor hunger nor weeping nor grinding of teeth nor murder nor evil. Nor does one die there, because no one is born there. There is neither sorrow there nor trouble, no longing or the strife of lust. But the kingdom of the highest King is there, and all those who have kept God's commandments dwell there in eternal joy.

And daily they see the joyous heavenly King,[255] and they live with him and with his saints and reign forever and ever.

Listen, we can understand and know about this that the almighty Lord does not wish one to be ungrateful for his gifts. There is no need for us to doubt that he does not wish us to remember the loan he granted us here in the world. As he ever gives to us more generously, so ought we give him more thanks, and the more glorious the honor, the more should the humility be. The one to whom the Lord gives much, the more he requests of in return, and the one whom he forgives much here in the world, the more he requires of him. Each high honor here in the world is enveloped in danger, and the greater the honor, the greater the danger.

We wish to give you an example of this: the tree that grows in the woods in its glory up over all other trees must then withstand the sudden strong wind. Then it is more strongly buffeted and troubled than the other trees. Also, the high rocks and cliffs that stand high above all other parts of the earth receive the greater ruin if they suddenly fall to earth. Likewise the high mountains and hills that stand high and tower over all middle earth nevertheless have the torment of sovereignty so that they are rebuked and tormented with heavenly fire and shattered with lightning. Likewise also the high powers here in the world will fall and perish and be lost. And the wealth of this world will turn to sorrow.

Nevertheless we adorn ourselves with the reddest gold and the whitest silver, and we are hung all about with the fairest jewels, yet one will abide the eternal end, and the mighty people and the richest order beds made for them out of marble and golden ornaments and command that that bed be all covered with jewels and with silver tapestries and all hung about with the most costly embroideries—even though bitter death will come and disburse it all. Then the riches and the ornaments will be destroyed and their glory broken up and their jewels disbursed and their gold shattered and their body decayed and turned to dust.

Thus the beauty of this world is nothing. Nor is the fairness of this middle earth. But it is transitory and fleeting and decaying and deteriorating and perishing and rotting and corruptible. Just so is the rich one here in the world. What has become[256] of the rich emperor and the kings whom we knew before? What has become of the aldermen who set the laws? What has become of the judgment seats of the judges? What has become of their pride except that it is covered with dirt and driven into torment? Woe to the earthly confessors unless they advise and teach with righteousness! So also is it with the laymen unless they desire and obey their penance and keep the holy teachings. What has become of the treasure of middle earth? What has become of the wealth of the world? What has become of the fairness of the people? What has become of the people who have most eagerly striven for possessions and have often left an inheritance to others? Likewise is the excessive love of earthly treasures. They are even as smoke or showers of rain when they fall hard from the sky and quickly pass away and then the fair weather comes with the bright sun.

As weak and as unstable as are earthly joys, so are the possessions among the people weak. So will the body and soul be parted when the soul departs from the body. And it is afterward completely unknown what the Judge should wish for the soul. Then nothing will be better for us or more efficacious than that we love our Lord with all our spirit and with all our strength and with all our thoughts. As it is written about this: the one who loves and sends his prayers to the Lord will ever be heard by him and receive his mercy.[257] As Christ himself said:[258] "To those who turn to me from their faults and confess their sins in my name and do penance with fasts and with the shedding of tears and with pure prayers and with alms, I will grant them my mercy and give them forgiveness and grant them my kingdom and teach them the way to heaven, where are all goodness and continual bliss and great reward. For their earthly labor I will give heavenly rest and for this transitory riches heavenly grace and for this wretched life the blessed and endless kingdom."

Lo, happy are those who love that kingdom and miserable are those who deny it. What does that person accomplish, though he treasure up all middle earth as his own possession, if the Devil reclaims his soul?[259] Or what, though he live a thousand years here in this life? It will all be unnecessary to him if after his death he is led to hell and there dwells in pain forever.

THE TRANSIENCE OF EARTHLY DELIGHTS

Let us now turn to what is better and turn to our Lord and eagerly obey him and keep his commandments. And let us visit our churches in purity and there eagerly listen to the holy teaching and speak no speech therein except to sing our prayers with quietness and earn for ourselves the upper kingdom. The King's glory is visible there, and the fair host of angels is there, together with the song of the apostles and God's praise and the worship of the highest King. There the faithful people shine as the sun and reign as angels in the heavenly kingdom. We are bidden and invited to this holy home and to the kingly sanctuary where the almighty Lord lives and reigns with all his saints forever and ever. Amen.

Cædmon's Hymn[260]

Now must we honor heaven's guardian,
the Measurer's might and his spirit's thought,
the work of the wonder-Father, the eternal Lord,
how he set a start of every marvel.
He first fashioned heaven as a roof[261]
for the children of earth, the holy Creator.
Then mankind's Guardian afterward made
middle earth, the eternal Lord,
the land for men, the almighty Leader.

Genesis A (Selection)

"Abraham and Isaac"

Then the powerful King began to prove
that soldier,[262] eagerly seek to know
what kind of courage that prince had
and spoke to him in a voice with stern words:
"Abraham, get up quickly and go,
lay down tracks and depart
with your own son. You must yourself offer
Isaac, your son, to me as a sacrifice
after you ascend the high hill,
at the boundary of the high land to which I will lead you,
up with your own feet. There you must make
a pyre for your son and yourself sacrifice
your son with the sword's edge and then with the dark fire
burn up the life's body and make me an offering."[263]
He did not delay for a while but immediately began
to prepare for the pilgrimage. The Lord of angels was
for him wondrous in words and his ruler beloved.
Then the blessed Abraham abandoned
his night's rest. By no means did he resist
his Savior's behest, but the holy man
girded himself with his gray sword, confessed that the fear
of the guardian of spirits lived in his breast. Then he began to beat
     his donkey,

the aged giver of gold[264] commanded two young
thanes to journey with him. His own kin was the third
and himself the fourth. When he was finished he left
his own home leading Isaac,
an ungrown child,[265] as God commanded him.
He hurried then much and hastened
forth on the earthway as the Lord led him
along paths in the desert until the third day,[266]
when wondrously bright over deep water
the dawn arose. Then the blessed one
saw towering a tall mountain,
as the Ruler of the sky said to him earlier.
Then Abraham said to his servants,
"My men, rest yourselves
here in this place. We will come again
after the two of us have delivered
our message to the Measurer of spirits."[267]
Then the noble one and his only son went
to the march-land where the Measurer had led him,
traveling over the woodland. The son bore the wood,
the father the fire and sword. Then with words
the man young in years began to question Abraham:
"We have, my father, fire and sword here.
Where is the offering you intend to bring
to the bright God for the burnt sacrifice?"[268]
Abraham spoke. He had considered one thing,
that he accomplish this just as the Lord commanded him.
"The true King himself, humankind's Guardian,
will find it, just as he thinks fitting."[269]
Then resolute he ascended the steep mountain
up with his offspring just as the eternal one commanded him.
So he stood at the summit of the high land
in the place where the promise-keeper, the strong one,
the Measurer, had mapped out with words.
Then he began to build the pyre, kindle fire,
and fetter the feet and hands
of his own son and then place on the pyre

young Isaac. And then quickly he clasped
the sword by its hilt, wanted to slay his son
with his own hands, feed the fire
with the blood of his boy. Then the Measurer's thane
from above, an angel, cried, "Abraham!"
with a loud voice. He stood in silence
for the messenger's word and answered the angel.
Then up out of the sky in all haste
the wondrous Spirit of God spoke in words:
"Beloved Abraham, do not slay your own son
but pull the boy alive from the pyre,
your own son! The God of glory gives him back!
Man of the Hebrews, you must receive
reward from the hand of the Holy One,
the high King of heaven, true victory spoils,
abundant gifts. The Guardian of spirits wants
to requite you with favors because his friendship
and loyalty was loved by you more than your own child."[270]
The pyre stood kindled. The Measurer of mankind
had lightened the heart of Lot's kin,
Abraham, because he had offered him back his son
Isaac alive. Then the blessed one looked,
the soldier over his shoulder, and saw a ram
standing alone and unafraid over there,
the brother of Haran, fast in the brambles.
Then Abraham took it and put it on the pyre
with great haste instead of his only son.
Then he struck it with the sword, the adorned burnt offering,
the altar reeking with the ram's blood,
sacrificed that offering to God, said thanks for that gift
and also for all those gifts given
him by the Lord forever and always.

Genesis B
(First Fragment)

"Satan in Hell"

The Ruler of all had established ten
orders of angels[271] whom he trusted well,
the holy Lord, through his hand's might
so that they would pursue his service,
work his will. Therefore he gave them wits
and with his hands created them, the holy Lord.
He had set them very blessedly. One[272] he had made so strong,
so mighty in his mind that he let him wield great might,
highest next to him in heaven's kingdom. He had made him very
      bright.
So lovely were his looks in the heavens! They came to him from the
      Lord of hosts.
He was like the lighted stars.[273] He should have given his Lord
      praise,
honored his joys in the heavens and thanked his Lord
for the gift he gave him in the light, when he let him rule for long.
      But he turned it for the worse for himself, began to raise
      trouble
for the highest Ruler of heaven, he who sits on the holy throne.
He was beloved by the Lord. It could not be hidden from him
that his angel began to be overproud,

172

lifted himself up against his Lord, sought hostile words,
proud speech in rebellion. He would not serve God,
said that his body was bright and shining,
white and light of hue. Nor could he find in his mind
that in discipleship to God he could grant
service to the Lord. He thought that he
himself had more might and strength
than the holy God could have
in allies of war. He spoke many words,
this angel overproud, thought how through his own strength
he might fashion himself a stronger seat,
a higher throne in heaven, said that his mind enticed him
to begin to build, west and north,[274]
construct castles, said it seemed doubtful
that he would follow the Lord loyally.

    "For what shall I toil?" he said. "It isn't at all important
to have a master. I may with my own hands
work many wonders. I have power great enough
to set up a goodly seat,
higher in heaven. Why must I run after his favor,
bow down to him in such slavery? I may be God, just as he!
Strong companions stand by who will not fail me in a fight,
hard, spirited heroes! They have chosen me master,
those brave fellows. Among such one may find counsel,
with such capture comrades. They are my chosen friends,
loyal in their hearts. I may be their master,
rule in this kingdom. It doesn't seem right to
me that I must at all needs flatter
God for my goods. I will no longer be his man!"

    Then the one who wields all heard all this,
that his angel began in great overpride
to rise up against his Ruler and speak such haughty words
so rashly against his Lord. Then he had to give recompense for this,
apportion work for that battle and be punished
with greatest of griefs. So must everyone
who starts a struggle against his Ruler,

with wickedness against his wondrous Lord. Then the mighty one
    was angry,
highest Ruler of heaven, threw him off the high seat.
He had gained hate from his master. He had lost his grace.
The Good One became angry at him in spirit. Thus he had to seek
    the abyss,
hard torment in hell. For this he strove against heaven's Ruler.
He banished him from his grace and hurled him into hell,
into those deep valleys where he became the Devil,
the fiend with all his fellows. Then out of heaven above
thus fell for a long while, three days and three nights
angels out of heaven into hell, and the Lord changed
them all to devils. Because they would not defer to
his word and deed, he sunk them defeated,
the Almighty God, underneath the earth
into the dim light of darkest hell.
There in the evening for unmeasured lengths
all of these fiends suffer fire renowned
when an eastern[275] wind drives at dawn,
a wicked, cold frost: always fire or spear,
some hard torment must they have!
A punishment has been prepared for them; their world
has changed. For the first time he has filled hell
with apostates. From now on only angels
would hold the height of heaven, those who had been loyal to God.
    Those other fiends lay in that fire who earlier had so much
battle against their Lord. Their torment lasts long
in the hot battle surge in the midst of hell—
fire and broad flames and bitter fumes,
smoke and darkness—because they disregarded
their loyalty to God. Their lust betrayed them,
the pride of angels. They wouldn't praise
the Almighty with their lips. But they got a large punishment:
they fell in fire to the bottom
into the heat of hell through their pride
and through their folly. They found another land
that was bereft of light and full of flames,

great peril of fire. The fiends perceived
that they received as recompense countless torments
through their great presumption and through God's power
and most of all through their own pride.
    Then the proud king spoke, he who was once most splendid of
        angels,
the whitest one in heaven and beloved of his Lord,
loyal to his Leader till they turned to folly,
so that God himself, mighty in heart,
became angry at this evil, threw him into that torment,
downward into that bed of death and then gave him a name.
The High One said he henceforth must be
called Satan,[276] commanded he take care
of the blackest hell, the abyss, and no more do battle with God.
    Satan spoke, grieved, and said—
he who henceforth had to govern hell,
watch over the abyss, who once was God's angel,
the white one in heaven, until his heart
ambushed him and his pride greatest of all—
said that he would no more honor the word
of the Lord of hosts. Inside him leapt up
his thoughts about his heart; outside him was hot,
wasting torment. Then he spoke a word:
    "This little place is very unlike
the other one we knew earlier,
high in heaven's kingdom, which the Lord granted me as mine.
Nevertheless we could not own him as almighty,
rule our kingdom. But he has not done right
and has made us fall to the bottom in fire,
to hell the hot, deprived of heaven's kingdom.
He has marked it out for mankind,
to settle it with people. This is my greatest pain,
that Adam, who was made of earth,
must hold my mighty throne,
live in delights while we endure this pain,
affliction in this hell! Alas, if I had the power of my hands
and could get out of here for one hour,

one short winter's hour, then with this host I....'[277]
But iron bands lie about me,
a chain collar crushes me. I have lost power,
the bonds of hell have so hard and fast
gripped me! Great fire is here,
above and below: never have I beheld
a more fearsome landscape. Flame never stops,
hot over all hell. Linked rings,
a cruel collar, has constricted my movement,
robbed me of motion. My feet are not free;
my hands are chained. The way out of these hell-doors
is blocked, so by no means might I
get out of these bonds. About me lie
hard irons hotly forged,
great bars. God has chained me
with these things by the neck. Thus I knew he knew
my heart. The Lord of hosts also knew
that Adam would agree with us about evil,
about the kingdom of heaven, if I had the power of my hand!
But we now endure affliction in hell. It is darkness and heat,
grim, without bottom. God himself has driven us
away into these black mists. Though he cannot accuse us of any
        sins,
that we did him harm in that land, he has deprived us of the light,[278]
cast us out into the cruelest of torments. We cannot avenge this,
pay him back with any pain. For this he had deprived us of the light!
He has now marked out middle earth, where he has made men
after his image;[279] with them will he people once more
the kingdom of heaven with pure souls. We must eagerly plot
if ever we may avenge this malice
on Adam and his offspring in like manner,
requite him for his desires if by any means we can devise it!
I do not expect further of that light which he expects long to enjoy,
prosperity with the strength of angels. Nor can we ever bring it
        about
to soften mighty God's mind. Let us take it away from the sons of
        men,

the kingdom of heaven that we may now not have, make them lose
      his favor,
so that they reject that which he commanded with his word: then he
      will be wrathful at them in spirit,
expel them from his favor. Then they must needs find hell
and these loathsome chasms. Then we can have them for lackeys,
the children of men in these fast chains! Begin now to consider this
      campaign!
If I once gave lordly gifts
to any companion while we sat contentedly
in that good kingdom and had control of our thrones,
then by no means can he repay with rewards
my gift at a greater time,
if now any of my thanes would agree
to come out from here, up through
these prison walls and have power in him
to fly with feathered wings,
wind his way through the clouds where
Adam and Eve stand, fashioned in an earthly kingdom,
wound up in wealth, with us thrown down here
into this deep dale! Now they are dearer
to their Wielder and may own the wealth
that we ought to have in the kingdom of heaven,
might with right! This role is set
for mankind! This makes my spirit sore.
It grieves me in my heart that heaven
is theirs forever! If any of you may
bring it about in any way that they forsake God's word
and his commandments, they will immediately become hateful to
      him.
If they break his rules he will be wrathful toward them.
Then their wealth will be changed and woe be fated for them,
some hard torment. Hear this, all of you,
how you may seduce them! Then softly may I lay
myself to rest in these chains, if that realm be lost to them!
He who does this will have a ready reward

afterward forever of what benefits
we may win here in this fire forever.
I will let him sit with me, whoever comes to say
in this hot hell that they have shamelessly
broken heaven's King's commands in word and deed!"[280]

Judith

[She did not] doubt[281]
his gifts in this wide world. She found there ready
help from the famous Lord when she found herself in most need,
grace from the greatest Judge, that he should guard
her from the worst terror, the Wielder of creation. The Father in
       heaven
gave her a shining gift,[282] since she ever had firm faith
in the Almighty: I have heard how Holofernes
eagerly sent out an invitation to wine and served up a banquet,
glorious in all wonders. The lord of warriors commanded
all his senior thanes to come to it. With great quickness they
did this, the shield-men, came journeying to that mighty lord,
the leader of the folk. It was on the fourth day
that Judith first found him,
that lady elfin in beauty, bright of mind.[283]

X

They went then and sat in the assembly,
proudly at the banquet, all his companions in crime,
boldly, warriors in their byrnies. There were the steep bowls
borne often along the benches, beakers also and cups
full for the feasters. They drank from them doomed,

the proud shield-warriors, though the prince did not
expect it, the terrible lord of earls. Then Holofernes,
the warriors' gold-friend, became glad in his cups,[284]
laughed and bellowed, roared and rang out
so that the children of men might hear him from afar.
How the stern one stormed and yelled,
proud and flushed with mead, often admonished
the bench-sitters to bear themselves well!
Thus the whole day long the devious one
drenched his warriors with wine,
the stern treasure-giver, until they lay in stupor;
he over-watered all his company as if they had been cut down dead,
drained of all good. Thus the master of men commanded
the feasters be filled until the sons of men
neared black night. Then the one infected with hate
commanded the blessed maid be fetched quickly
to his bed loaded with bracelets,
regaled with rings.[285] They quickly did this,
the attendants, just as their ruler ordered them,
the chief of chain-mailed men. They stepped through the noise
to the guest hall where they got
prudent Judith, and then promptly
the stout warriors started to lead
that bright beauty to the high pavilion
where the mighty one always rested
at night, noxious to the Savior,
that Holofernes! A curtain[286] was all covered
with gold there, glittering, covering
the general's bed so that the baleful one
could look through it, the lord of warriors,
on all who came inside,
the sons of heroes, yet no human
could peer in at him unless the proud one
commanded someone of his evil comrades draw
near to him, warriors enter secretly. Then they brought to his bed
the wise lady in haste. The stout warriors then went
to tell their lord that the holy lady had been

brought into his pavilion. Then the famous prince became
blithe in spirit, the ruler of cities, thought to soil
the shining lady with dirt and with shame. Wonder's Judge
would not consent, the guardian of glory, but he fixed it,
the Lord, the Wielder of hosts. Then the devilish one departed,
the lustful one, with a host of men,[287]
the baleful one, to seek his bed, where he must lose his glory,
his life within one night. For he had arranged his own end
unpleasantly on this earth, such a one as he had fashioned himself,
the stern lord of men, while he lived in this world
under the roof of clouds. Then, so clouded with wine, the mighty
      one
fell flat on the midst of his bed as if he had no sense
in his head. Heroes stepped
out of the inner room with great haste,
wine-soaked warriors, who had led
the traitor, the hated tyrant, to bed
for one last time. Then the Savior's servant,
full of glory, was fiercely mindful
of how she might with most ease deprive
the terrible one of life before the impious,
unclean one awoke. Then the wavy-locked one,
the Creator's handmaid, took a sharp, war-hardened
blade, brought it out of its sheath
with her strong, right hand. Then she named the name
of the sky's owner, the Savior of all
the world's dwellers, and said this word:[288]
"God of creation and comforting Spirit,
Son of the Almighty, I want to ask you
for your mercy in this need of mine,
O Trinity of glory! Grieved is now
my heart, heated and sad in spirit,
very oppressed with grief. Give me victory and true belief,
prince of the sky, so that with this sword I might
hew this giver of murder! Grant me my success,
stern Lord of men! Never have I had more need
of your mercy! Avenge now, mighty Lord,

wondrous Giver of glory, what makes me angry in spirit,
hot in my heart!" Then the highest Judge
inspired her instantly with courage as he does for all
who dwell here who seek help from him
with reason and right belief. Then her spirit grew great;
hope was renewed for the holy one. Then she took the heathen man
hard by his hair, drew him with her hands toward
her scornfully and skillfully laid
the wicked one down, the hated man,
as she well might wield the wicked one
most easily. Then the one with the wound locks struck
the harmful enemy with an ornamented sword,
the hostile-minded one, so that she slit half
his throat through and he lay in a swoon,
drunken and deadly wounded.[289] He was not yet dead,
all lifeless. Then earnestly she struck him,
the bold lady, with another blow,
this heathen hound, so that his head
fell onto the floor. The foul basket lay
empty fore and aft: his spirit went elsewhere
under the looming cliffs and was lowered down there,
tied up in torment forever after,
wound up with worms, bound in punishments,
chained hard in hellfire
after its journey hence. Nor need he hope,
drowned in darkness, that he may depart
from the room full of worms, but remain there
forever and ever without end
in the darkest home, bereft of hope's joy.

XI

Then Judith had fought for famous glory
in the fight, just as God had granted her,
the Lord of the skies, who loaned her victory.
Then the clever maid quickly brought

the bloody head of the war-hunter
in the sack that her servant,
a bright-cheeked lady of virtuous life,
had brought there for food for them both,
and she gave it all gory into her hand,
her heart full of thoughts, to bear it home,
Judith to her attendant. Then immediately they went out
from there,²⁹⁰ both of those damsels, with daring,
until they came in courage,
the triumphant maidens, out of that army,
and they could see clearly
the walls of the wondrous city gleam,
Bethulia. Then, bearing rings, they
hurried forth along the foot path
until, glad in heart, they had gotten
to the gate in the wall. Warriors sat,
men watching, holding ward
in the fortress, as earlier to the folk
Judith had admonished, sad in mind,
the clever maid, when she went on her quest,
the courageous lady. Then the beloved one
came once more to her people, and then the clever woman
quickly commanded one of her men
to come to her from that wide-walled fortress
and quickly let her come in
through the gate in the wall. And she said a word
to the triumphant people: "I can now tell you
a noteworthy thing, that you need no longer
sorrow in spirit. God is gracious toward you,
the King of glory! This has become known
far and wide throughout the world, that splendid
glory is about to come to you and renown be given to you
for the shameful deeds you long have endured!"
The fortress-dwellers were filled with joy
after they heard how the holy one spoke
beyond the high wall. The people hurried;
the host was in haste toward the fort's gate,

man and women together, a multitude and crowd,
a troop and a torrent, thronged and ran
about the Lord's handmaiden, many hundreds,
old and young. The spirit of each one
was made glad in that city of mead
after they understood that it was Judith
who had come back home! And then in haste
they let her in with humility.
Then the clever one adorned with gold commanded
her mindful handmaiden
to uncover the head of the war-hunter
and to proffer it bloody as proof
to the city's people, how she succeeded in battle.
Then the princely maid spoke to all the people:
"Here you can clearly see, leaders of the nation,
victorious heroes, the head
of the hateful one, the heathens' general
Holofernes, how lifeless he is,
he who most of men taxed us with murders,
sore sorrows, and wanted still
to add even more. But God did not
give him longer life to molest us
with griefs. Through God's help
I drew life from his body. Now I desire
to ask every one of you city people,
you shield-fighters, to fit yourselves
quickly for a fight when the God of creation,
the merciful King, calls out of the east
the shining light. Bear forth your shields,
and your boards before your breasts and your coats of mail,
your shining helmets into the host of enemies!
Fell the leaders of that folk with decorated swords,
the lead-spears fated to die! Your foes are
doomed to death, and you will gain glory,
fame in the fight, just as the Lord,
the Mighty One, has shown you through this hand of mine!"[291]
Then the keen host was quickly outfitted,

the bold ones for the battle. The kingly ones marched,
comrades and companions bearing victory banners,
went to the fight, forward in righteousness,
heroes under helmets, out of the holy city
at the very break of day. Shields made a din,
roared loudly. The lean one rejoiced in this,
the wolf in the woods with the pale raven,
the slaughter-greedy bird. Both knew
that the warriors wanted to give them
their fill among those fated to die. But right behind them
flew the eagle eager to eat, the one with dewy feathers,
the dark-coated one, sang a battle song,
the one with a horny beak.[292] The battle warriors marched,
fighters to the battle covered with their boards,
hollow linden-shields, those who earlier
had suffered the abuse of the aliens,
the contempt of the heathens. Harshly was it
all paid them back in the shield-play,
those Assyrians, after the Hebrews
had arrived under their battle-banners
at their campsite. Then they quickly
let fly showers of shafts,
battle-snakes from their horned bows,
steel-hard arrows. Loudly stormed
the grim warriors, spewed spears into
the press of the ones hardened in battle. Heroes
were angry, they who owned the land, with that hated race,
marched with stern mood, stouthearted,
awoke none too gently the ancient enemies
heavy with mead, drew with their hands
swords from sheaths, shining with ornament, those warriors,
proven edges, earnestly slew
the Assyrian battle sergeants,
plotters of evil, spared not a one
of that battle-people, neither peasant nor lord,
of those once alive whom they could overcome.

XII

So in the morning those young men
chased the aliens all the while,
until they understood, those who were angry,
the champions of that people, the chief guardians,
that the Hebrew men had surely shown
them the swinging of their swords.
They went to announce this to the oldest
of their elder retainers, roused up the warriors,
and preached them in fright a fearful gospel,
a morning's slaughter to the mead-weary,
a horrible play of swords. Then immediately, as I heard,
doomed warriors woke from sleep
and surged in a press toward the pavilion
of the wicked one, those weary-hearted men,
toward the tent of Holofernes. They thought at once
to recount the battle to their ruler
before the horror, the might of the Hebrews,
fell on him from above. They all figured
that the prince of men and the bright maid
were together in that beautiful tent,
Judith the noble and that nasty lecher,
awful and fierce. But none of the earls
dared wake that warrior or find out
what that banner-bearing hero
had done to the holy damsel,
the Measurer's maiden. The host approached,
the Hebrew folk, fought sorely
with hard weapons of war, paid with sword hilts
the ancient argument, with fated swords
the old grudge. The glory of the Assyrians
was greatly diminished on that day,
their pride laid low. Warriors stood
about their lord's tent, sorely excited,
with moody minds. Then altogether
they began to cough, cry loudly

and gnash their teeth,[293] knowing no good,
suffering sorrow with their teeth. Then their glory came to an end,
their happiness and deeds of courage. The warriors thought to
      waken
their dear lord. It did them no good!
Then late, too late, one of the battle warriors
got bold enough, one brave in battle, to peep
into that pavilion as need pushed him.
Then he spied the pale one sprawling on the bed,
the giver of his gold, emptied of spirit,
cut off from life. Quickly he fell
in terror to the earth, began to tear his hair
and also his clothing, his courage shattered,
and said this word to the warriors
who were outside, all dejected:
"Here is made manifest our own destruction,
revealed to be coming, that the time has closely
pressed upon us with tribulation so that we now must perish,
together fall in battle. Here lies our leader
hewn with a sword, beheaded." Then sad at heart they
threw their weapons down,[294] left weary-hearted,
hurried away in flight. On their tracks fought
a big, powerful people until the greatest part
of that host lay, fallen in the fight
on the victory-field, fractured by swords,
as comfort for wolves and also consolation
for slaughter-greedy fowls. Then they fled, those who yet
lived, from the hated shield-men. Hard behind
them came the troop of Hebrews, honored by victory,
exalted by fame. The Lord God had given them
fair aid, the almighty Master.
Then quickly with swords cunningly adorned
the hearty heroes made a war path
through the hated crowd. They hewed shields,
sheered through the shield wall. The shooters were
made bold by the battle, those Hebrew men.
On this occasion the thanes sorely sought

the spear-fight. There on the ground fell
the greater half of the head-count
of the Assyrians, the host of earls
of that hateful kin. Few came back
alive to their home country. Bold as kings,
the warriors turned to the way back among that carnage,
reeking of raw bodies. Those who lived there
had a chance to grab gory plunder
among the most hated of their ancient enemies,
now dead—shining adornments,
boards and broadswords, bright helmets,
worthy treasures. The wardens of the homeland
had overcome their enemies gloriously
on that battlefield, sent with their swords
their old enemies to sleep. They rested on the road,
those who were most loathsome alive
of the countries of the living. Then all that kin,
the most famous of the people, proud, wavy-haired,
for the length of a month lugged and carried
to their bright city of Bethulia
helmets and hip-swords, gray byrnies,
war gear of warriors adorned with gold,
treasures more famous than any man
among the sages might tell,
all the things the warriors won in glory,
bold under their banners and in battle,
through Judith's clever counsel,
the brave girl. As a gift those heroic earls
brought her from that outing Holofernes's own
sword and bloody helmet and also his broad byrnie
bedecked with red gold and all the ruler of warriors
owned of treasure, that insolent one, or his inheritance,
bracelets and bright treasure. They gave them to that bright lady,
the ready-witted one. For all this Judith
gave glory to the Lord of hosts, he who had given her honor,
fame in this world's kingdom and also wealth in heaven,
victory's gift in the glory of the sky, because she had true faith

in the Almighty always. Indeed in the end she did not doubt
the reward for which she long yearned. For this may the beloved
    Lord
be given glory forever, who created the wind and the air,
the skies and the broad earth and also the bold streams
and the joys of heaven—all through his own mercy![295]

CYNEWULF

The Fates of the Apostles

Listen![296] I set this song, tired of travel,
sick in spirit, gathered it far and wide:
How those nobles made known their courage,
bright and wondrous.[297] There were twelve,
wonderful in their works, chosen by the Lord,
beloved in life. Their praise sprung far and wide,
their might and fame, throughout middle earth,
thanes of the Lord, no little glory.
Led by lot[298] was the holy group
where they should decree the Lord's law,
preach it before the people.[299] Some in Rome—
bold, brave—gave up their lives
through Nero's narrow snares—
Peter and Paul.[300] The Apostolate is
honored far and wide among all folk.

    Likewise Andrew[301] in Achaia
laid his life at risk before Aegius.
He did not consider the might of kings
anywhere on earth, but chose for himself
eternal, everlasting life, unending light,
when battlehard amidst the noise of the multitude,
he tasted the gallows after the tumult of battle.

Listen! We have also heard learned people
narrate the nobility of John.[302]
As I have heard, he was of all
most beloved by Christ because of his kindred
among the male sex, after glory's king,
the creator of angels, sought the earth
through a woman's womb, the Father of all.
In Ephesus all the time he
gave the people lessons. From there life's way
he sought, a journey, shining joys,
bright wealth. His brother was not lax
with his own journey, but through the swinging of the sword
among the Jews, James[303] had to
lose his life before Herod,
his life from his flesh. Philip[304] was
among the Asians. From there he sought
rich eternal life by death on the rood,
when in Hieropolis he was hung
on the gallows by a band of battlers.
        Indeed, his fate became known far and wide:
that he laid his life at risk in India,
the battle-mighty hero, Bartholomew.[305]
Then in Albania Astrages,
a heathen blind in spirit, commanded his head
be severed because he would not submit to paganism,
worship an idol. To him was glory's gladness,
the wealth of life, more loved than the goods that fade.
        Likewise Thomas[306] valiantly ventured
in other parts of India
where the minds of many were enlightened,
their spirits strengthened through his sacred word.
Afterward through wondrous power he awakened
the bold one, the king's brother, before
the multitude through the Lord's might, so he rose from death,
young and battle grim. His name was Gad.
And so, he laid down his life for the people,
his own in war. A wave of swords took him

through the hands of heathens. The holy one fell there,
wounded before the hosts. From there as reward for victory
his soul sought glory's light.

Listen! We have heard through holy books
that among the Ethiopians truth went up,
the lordly decree of God. The dawn of day awoke,
the light of faith. The land was cleansed
through Matthew's[307] famous message.
Then Irtacus, angry in mind,
the savage king, commanded that weapons kill him.

We have heard that James[308] in Jerusalem
was done to death before the priests.
Through the stroke of a staff he fell
brave, blessed before the envious ones. Now he has
eternal life with glory's king, reward for war.

Nor were those two careless in the conflict,
in the sword play. The land of Persia
sought Simon[309] and Thadeus,[310] ready to travel,
men bold in battle. Both
lived their last day together. The princes
had to do this work in the heat of weapons,
look for victory's reward and lasting joy,
delight after death, when life was
cut from body. All of them had contempt
for transitory treasures, idle hoards.

Thus those princes, twelve proud ones,
met their ends.[311] Unending glory
they bore in their hearts, honor's thanes.

Now then I ask the one who loves
the whole of this song to ask help
from the sacred troop for me in my sorrow,
peace and protection. Lo, I have need of friends,
gentle ones on the journey, when I must seek
my long home alone, the unknown dwelling,
leave in my tracks my body, my bit of earth,
my slaughter-remains, to await as solace for worms.

Here the one mighty of mind
may find, he who likes lays,
who it was who set this song.[312] **Wealth** stands at the end;
earls enjoy it on earth. Nor may they ever stay together,
dwelling in the world. **Joy** must diminish,
Ours on earth. Afterward the transitory
adornments of the body will decay, even as **Water** spills.
When the **Torch** and **Horn** seek strength
in the narrow night, then **Need** lies on them,
the service of the king. Now you may know
who has been made manifest to men in these words.
    Be mindful of this, the man who loves
the whole of this song, that he help me
to find comfort. I must go far from here,
seek elsewhere alone a dwelling,
set out on a journey, out of this earth,
I know not where. Unknown are the dwellings,
house and homeland, just as it is for everyone,
unless he possess a sacred spirit.
    But let us be keen to call out to God,
send our prayers into that bright place,
that we may have that hall,
a home on high where there is the greatest of hopes,
where the King of angels pays to the clean
an eternal reward. Now may his praise remain
great and glorious and his might endure,
eternal and rejuvenated over all creation. Finit.

Guthlac A

It is the greatest of joys when angel encounters
blessed soul at the beginning.[313] They relinquish the joys of earth,
forsake the fleeting delights, and are separated from the body.
Then says the angel—he is of an elder order—
one spirit greeting another, announces to him God's message:
"Now you must depart and go to where you have desired
long and often. I will lead you there.
The ways are winsome for you, and glory's light
is brightly revealed. You now are a traveler through time
to the holy home." Sorrow never comes there,
robbery or reproach, but the joy of angels is there,
peace and prosperity and soul's rest.
And there always and ever must be joy,
gladness with God when he gives
his judgments here on earth. He grants eternal
reward in heaven, when the highest
King of all kings rules the city.
Those are the buildings that never become run down.
Nor does life diminish in the face of miseries
for those who live in them, but for them the longer there the better.
They partake of youth and God's compassion.
There must the steadfast souls
come after death, those who teach and keep

Christ's law here and raise up his laud.
They have overcome the cursed spirits, received glory's rest,
whither the spirit of men must ascend
earlier or later, when he cares for his own
spirit here, so that it may come
good, clean of blemishes, into the kingdom.
There are many orders[314] throughout middle earth
under the heavens, which ascend in ever
holier ranks. We may by right
belong to any one of them
if we desire to keep the holy commandment.
A wise person may now enjoy the prosperity
of good times and wish a way
forth for his spirit. The world is disturbed;
the love of Christ grows cold. Many tribulations
have arisen throughout middle earth,
just as years ago God's evangelists
said with words and announced to all
through prophesy as it now has proven true.[315]
The splendor of earth grows old for each noble thing,
and each species of blossom turns from its beauty.
The end time of each seed
is measured in might. Therefore one need not
hope for improvement for this earth,
that it ever furnish us with fair joy
over the afflictions we now endure
before the end of all creatures
that he set alive in six days,[316]
who now bring forth their species under the skies,
great and small. This globe
is separated into parts. The Lord sees
where they dwell who keep his commandments.
Every day he sees the sentences
that he appointed through his own word
wane and change from the world's law.
He finds many, but few are chosen.[317]
Some wish to hear about ways of life,

weigh in words and then not do the work.
The wealth of earth is the highest hope
for them over eternal life. It must
become estranged from every earth-dweller.
Therefore they now scorn the spirit of the saints,
those who set their hearts in heaven.
They know that the homeland abides eternally
for all the multitude who throughout middle earth
serve the Lord and desire to deserve
that dear home. Thus this worldly wealth
will be exchanged into the greater good
when they over whose heads hover
the Lord's fear feel desire for it. They will be
rebuked by that great glory, spend this life
according to the commandments and wish
and expect the better life. They buy glory,
give alms, aid the poor,
are openhanded with their own treasures,
love with their gifts those who have less,
daily serve the Lord. He sees their deeds.
Some then dwell in deserts,[318]
seek out and set up of their own will
homes in the darkness. They await heavenly
houses. Often he who will not allow
them life leads them to hateful terror,
grants them fear, sometimes idle glory.
The crafty killer has power over both;
he harries hermits. Before them angels stand,
ready with spiritual armor,[319] are mindful of their aid,
hold the lines of the holy, know their hope is in the Lord.
These are the proven soldiers who serve the king
who never misplaces payment for those who persevere in his love.

We can now narrate what lately
was made known by a holy man,
how Guthlac[320] governed his spirit
in God's will, withstood all evil,

earthly nobility, turned thoughts upward
to his home in heaven. He had hope in that,
after he who readies life's road
for spirits had enlightened him and given him the grace
of the race of angels to begin alone
and submit to a mountain[321] home and give to God
in poverty all his pomp
which in youth he had to hand over
to worldly joys. From heaven a holy
guard beheld him, he who eagerly urged
that bright spirit into spiritual goodness.
Listen, we have often heard that the holy man
loved in his earliest age
many dangerous things.[322] There was a time, however,
in God's ordaining, when an angel
gave to Guthlac in his understanding
the wish to subside from the lusts of sins.
The time was at hand. About him two
wardens watched, made battle,
the angel of the Lord and the ugly spirit.
Many times they taught him
different things in the thoughts of his mind.
One said all of the earth
under the heavens was perishing and praised
the lasting goods in heaven where in the glory of their victory
the souls of the saints await
God's joys. He eagerly gives
reward for their deeds to those who want to receive
his gift with gratitude and forsake
this world utterly for the life eternal.
The other urged him to seek by night
a group of thugs and through boldness
strive after the world as outlaws do
who do not mourn for the life of the man
who brings booty into their hands,
if they can profit from the plunder.[323]
So they urged him on either side

197

until the God of hosts granted an end
to the argument and decided for the angel.
The fiend was put to flight. Later the Spirit of comfort
stayed to give aid to Guthlac,
loved him and taught him ever more eagerly
to love the joys of the land,
the mansion on the mountain. Often danger came there,
terrible and unknown, malice of the old enemies,
big in deceit. They displayed to him
their own appearance, and there earlier
set up many seats. They started a journey from there,
a wide wandering, cut off from glory,
sporting in the air. That spot of land was
concealed from men until the Measurer revealed
a barrow in the woods, when the builder came
who raised up there a holy home,
not because he covetously cared
for the fleeting wealth of this life but that he might free
that land fairly for God after he overcame the enemy,
Christ's champion. He was accosted
in the time that men yet remember
who still honor him for his spiritual
wonders and hold up his wisdom's
fame—that the saintly servant
came with his courage and sat alone
in the hidden place. There he raised up and recounted
the praise of the Lord. Often with words he proclaimed
God's gospel to those who loved
the manners of the martyrs when the Spirit revealed
to him the prudence of life, so that he prevented
the joys of his body and worldly bliss,
soft seats and banquet days,
also idle joys of the eyes,
proud apparel. God's fear was
too much in his mind for him to partake
of human glory, giving thanks.
Guthlac was good. He bore in his spirit

heavenly hope. He reached the health
of eternal life. An angel was near him,
a trusty protector of the peace who, one of a few,
stayed in that marchland.[324] For many there
in Britain he became an example when,
a blessed fighter, he ascended the barrow,
hard in battle. He boldly girded himself
with spiritual arms.[325] He blessed that area,
first raised up Christ's rood
for himself as a help. There the warrior
overcame many dangers. Many of God's martyrs
became great there. Guthlac's
precious portion we ascribe to the Lord.
He gave him victory and great wisdom,
mighty protection when a multitude
of enemies came with sudden attacks to raise a feud.[326]
They could not with envy abandon him
but granted many temptations to Guthlac's
spirit. Aid was near him. An angel
trimmed him with boldness when they angrily bullied him
with wicked waves of fire. They stood about him
like footmen, said that he had to feel fire in the barrow
and let the burning gulp down his body
so his sufferings would suit well
his spirit-weary kin if he himself would
no longer seek the joys of men
away from that battle and observe
willingly his rights of kin among the race
of men and let the fight alone.
Thus he who spoke for all the crowd of enemies
angered him. Guthlac's spirit was afraid
by no means, but God gave him
courage against the terror so that the guilty gang
of the old enemies suffered shame.
The makers of reproach were full of rage,
said that Guthlac alone with God himself
made the most difficulties for them

after he broke the barrows in pride
in the desert where they dwelled,
wretched adversaries.[327] Earlier they could
enjoy the time after their torments there,
when, weary from their wanderings, they came
to rest for a secret stretch of time. They united
in the quiet that was allowed them for a little while.
The secret place stood in the Lord's mind
idle and empty, far from his homeland.
It awaited the visit of a better warden.
The old enemies have a grudge against this;
thus they always endure sorrow.
They cannot enjoy a home upon the earth,
nor does the air lull them for the rest of their limbs,
but they endure homes without any shelter.
They cry out in care, wish for death,
desire that the Lord through the stroke of death
put an end to their pain.
They were not able to injure Guthlac's spirit,
nor separate his soul from his body
by a sore stroke, but they raised up
harmful words through their lies. They lay aside laughter,
suffered in sorrow when the stronger
guardian overcame them in that place. The outlaws
had to give up grieving the green barrows.
Nevertheless they yet said sore words,
God's enemies, made many promises
that he had to suffer the separation of death
if he longer awaited a more hateful meeting,
when they would come with a greater group
of those who sorrowed little for his life.
Guthlac gave answer against them, said that they could not boast
in their deeds against the Lord's might. "Though you promise me
      death,
he who directs your distress will save me from these injuries.
God alone is almighty. He may easily protect me.
He will save my life. I will say many

truths to you. I can without trouble
and alone protect this place from you.
I am not so bereft, as I stand before you,
of a troop of men, but a mightier part
of godly spiritual secrets dwell
and well up in me, which will keep me angry.
Alone I will easily build me here
a house and a shelter. In the heavens
are lessons belonging to me. Little doubt have I
that an angel will lead me to all
profitable prosperity in words and deeds.
Go away now, wretched ones, weary in spirit,
from this spot on which you here stand,
flee onto the far paths! I wish
to gain peace from God. Nor shall my spirit
endure deception from you, but the Lord's hand
will protect me with power. Here shall be my
earthly home, no longer any of yours!"
Then a cry arose. The outlaws
stood about the barrow in groups. A noise broke out,
a cry of the woeful. Many called,
spokesmen of the enemies, boasted in their iniquities:
"Often have we surveyed between the seas
the customs of the peoples, the fury of the proud ones,
who led their lives aimlessly.
We have not met in all middle earth
more pride of any man.
You have declared that you desire to go
home among us, you who are God's miserable wretch.
How shall you live, even if you own that land?
No one will feed you there with food.[328]
Hunger and thirst will be hard enemies against you
if you go alone from your own land
like a wild beast. That is no beginning!
Go from this place! One can give you
no better advice than that of all this troop.
We will be gracious to you if you give us obedience,

or again we will seek you out when you least expect it
with a bigger troop so that none need
harm you with their hands. Nor will your body fall
from the wounds of weapons. We can
fell that dwelling with our feet. The folk
will trample you with troops and hosts of horses.
Then they will be angry, those who will overwhelm you,
trample and tear you and wreak vengeance on you,
bear you away with bloody tracks. If you despise our request,
we will accost you with injuries. Start desiring deliverance!
Go where you look for friends, if you want to live!"
Guthlac was ready. God gave him
an answer and made him mighty in courage.
He did not change with their words but said sorrow
to his enemies. He knew enough the truth:
"This wilderness is wide, with many a refuge,
unhealthy homes for wretched spirits.
They are liars who live in these places.
Although you call them all out
and also work up a wider conflict,
you will encounter here in your envy
a fruitless effort. I will not consider
drawing a sword against you with a daring hand,
a weapon of this world, nor will this place
be bought for God by bloodshed,
but I think I will comply with my Christ
by a dearer gift. Now that I have gone up
into this place, you have proclaimed with idle words
many homes for me. My heart is not
afraid or fated to die, but he who governs
the deeds of every one among the race of men
will protect me in peace.[329] There is nothing you
can give one in this life, nor are you allowed to do
me any injury. I am the Lord's servant.
He often comforts me through an angel.
Therefore longings little bother me,
give me grief. Now the spiritual

herdsman keeps me. My hope is in God.
Nor is worldly wealth anything to me[330]
or makes me yearn for much in my heart,
but God gives me my needs
every day through human hands."
Thus he exulted, he who stood against many,
wonder's warrior worthily upheld
by the strength of angels. All the host of enemies
departed from that land. Nor was the time long
that they thought to yield to Guthlac.
He abided in the barrow, lived in courage
and humility. He had pleasure in the house,
forsook the longings for fleeting joy.
By no means did he cut himself off from mercy toward men,
but prayed for the prosperity of every soul
when in that loneliness he lay
his head on the earth. His heart
was afire with a happy spirit from heaven.
Often with an angel near him he considered
how he need enjoy the niceties
of this land least with his body.
By no means did he doubt his faith
through fear of the wretched spirits, nor did he forsake
the time when he had to toil for the Lord,
lest the slumber of sleep or slack heart
take away his courage when he woke up.
A warrior must thus campaign for Christ
ever in his soul and hold his spirit
ever in fear of the one who will follow
every soul where he may set his seal on it.
They always found Guthlac in God's
will firm when wild in flight
they came to him through the clouds of night,
those who kept the unhealthy homeland,
seeking whether his joy in that land had lessened.
They wanted sorrow to seek him out
in his heart for human love so he would journey back

again to his homeland. That was not his intent
when an angel greeted him eagerly
in his solitude and gave him grace
that no desire might deprive him
of the Measurer's will. But he remained
in the Teacher's true faith. Often he spoke in words:
"Indeed it is fitting for the one whom the Holy Spirit
guides in his will and strengthens his works,
invites with respectful words, to whom he promises life's rest
that he listen to his Leader's teaching,
and not let the old enemy again turn
his soul from his God. How will my spirit
gain help unless I give God
an obedient mind so that the heart's musings...?[331]
...earlier or later make an end,
so that you can awfully afflict me.
Nor can my body divide death
from this fleeting creature, but it must fall,
as must all this earth on which I stand here.
Even if you wickedly attack my flesh with waves
of fire, with greedy flame,
never will you turn me from these words while my wits last.
Even if you afflict it with sorrows, you will not reach my soul,
but you will bring it to what is better. Therefore I will abide
what God gives me. Death for me is no sorrow.[332]
Even if my bones and blood both turn
to increase the earth, my eternal portion
will pass over into joy, where it will possess
a fairer home. The hermitage on this mountain
is not bigger or better than is fit for me,
who daily endures in suffering
the Lord's will. Nor will the Lord's servant
love more material wealth
in his heart than is appropriate for him alone
so he may have the necessary nourishment for his body."
Then again as earlier the enmity and wrath
of the old enemies was aroused. Another unlittle

sound was unloosed when the cry of the care-spirits
arose in the air.[333] Ever Christ's praise
grew and lived in Guthlac's
good spirit, and the God of hosts
protected him on the earth as he holds in health
every soul when its higher spirit
thrives in virtues. He was one of them.
He did not run after the world, but he raised into glory
the joy of his heart. Who was greater than he,
a single soldier in our times,
a warrior made manifest so that Christ before him
made known more worldly wonders!
He defended himself against the awful attacks
of wicked ones, of wretched spirits.
They were bloodthirsty in their battle rush
with greedy claws. God did not desire
his soul to suffer sorely for this
in his body-home. He let the harmers
grab him with their grasping hands
yet established a safe refuge against them.
They then heaved him up into the high air,
gave him might beyond all mankind
so that before his eyes appeared all
doings of men in monasteries
under the control of holy herdsmen
who lead their lives in lust
with idle possessions, excessive riches,
and showy clothing, as is the custom of the young,
where the fear of God does not grieve them.
By no means could the enemies exult,
but quickly they were crushed in the success
that had been loaned them for a little while,
and they could no longer break his body
with miseries.[334] He was by no means harmed
from what they had put him through for punishment.
They led him through the air to the dearest dwelling
on earth so that again he ascended

to the barrow in the woods. The killers wailed,
grieved, and mourned that a son of man
could overcome them with miseries and come alone
in such poverty for their punishment
and they could not pay him with greater pains
in a settlement of vengeance. Guthlac set
his hope in the heavens, trusted in salvation.
He had saved his life from the seizure of enemies.
The fierce temptation of the wretched fiends
was overcome. The solider stayed
happily on the hill. His glory was with God.
It seemed in his spirit that he was blessed
among humankind, he who kept here
his single life safe, so that the hand of the enemy
could not harm him at the uttermost end,
when the Lord's judgment led him
to the last parting from life.
Nevertheless, mindful of their misfortunes,
the scoffers yet promised him poverty
with bitter, spiteful speech. Faithfulness was made known
when God rewarded Guthlac's
courage with mercy because he made battle alone.
The wretched spirit spoke to him with words:
"By no means did we need to torment you thus so much
if you courageously would have heard the counsel
of friends, when you first came
wretched and miserable into this warfare,
when you spoke a boast that the Holy Spirit
would shield you easily against afflictions
on account of the token that turned
the hand of humans from your noble face.
Many exist in this way given over
to guile. They do not accept God,
but they lavish their bodies for the love
of pleasant foods. Thus you give God
due worship with foolish delights.
You conceal much from the people that you keep in your mind.

Your deeds are not secret, though you do them in darkness.
We led you aloft, dragged you from the joys of the land,
wanted you to see for yourself that we told you the truth.
For all this you remain in affliction, because you could not avoid it."
Then it happened that God wanted to give
him back some thanks after his suffering,
since he hoped for martyrdom in his heart.
He bestowed on him wisdom in the thoughts of his breast,
a firm and mighty mind. He stood against
many old enemies, built up with courage,
said to them to their sorrow that they had
to give over the green field to him without victory:
"You are scattered! Guilt has settled on you!
You cannot ask God for any gift
or seek mercy with mild obedience.
Though he allowed you for a little while
to possess power over me,[335]
you would not partake of that with patience
but led me aloft in anger
so I could observe from the air
the buildings of the lands. The light of the sky
was shiningly shown to me, though I felt grief.
They put me to such shame that I easily forbore
the easy ruler and severe spirit
of young ones in God's own temples.
They wanted by this to scorn the praise of the saints.
Then they sought what was worse and by no means judged
the better according to their deeds. You will nevertheless not be
        hidden.
I will later tell you the truth.
God made youth and the joys of men.
They cannot bear old age
in their earliest prosperity, but they take pleasures
in the joys of the world until a pile of winters
overruns their youth and their spirit yearns
for the form and presence of the former way of life
that many throughout middle earth,

as is fitting, follow in their habits. Men reveal
wisdom to the people, abandon pride,
after the spirit flees the folly of youth.
You do not make this clear, but you clamor
about the sins of the guilty, by no means wish to glorify
the courage and customs of the faithful.
You rejoice in crimes, look for no comfort,
so you can win relief from these wanderings.
You often stand among those who steal. Restraint comes for that
     from heaven.
Then he sends me victory, he who became man for us,
he who determines the length of every life."
Thus the saintly warrior spoke.
The martyr had been separated from the sins
of humankind. He still had to suffer
a portion of pain, though the Lord
directed his duties. Listen! That seemed
a wonder to the people, that he would
let the miserable spirits manhandle him more
with their greedy grasps. And yet it happened!
What was more, he himself sought
middle earth and bled his blood
at the hands of killers. He had control over both
life and death when he willingly endured
the enmity of his pursuers humbly on earth.
Therefore it is now agreeable that we announce
the deeds of the devout, give the Lord praise
for all the examples by which books open up
his wisdom through his wondrous works.
Grace was given to Guthlac
in godly strength. It is important to say that
all that he endured in his courage was ordered.
The almighty Father himself established
his servant against the secret
old enemies, where his soul was
tempted and found clean. It is known far and wide
throughout middle earth that his heart was happy

in God's will. There is still much more
to say of what he himself suffered
under the close bonds of the criminal spirits.[336]
He always well scorned the sorrow of his soul
for the sake of the Protector who preserved his spirit
so that his faith did not hesitate in his breast
and discontent did not disturb his spirit,
but his steadfast heart lived in holiness
until it had outlasted its affliction.
Harsh were the throes; the thanes[337] were grim.
They all announced the end of his life.
By no means could they condemn him to death,
those shepherds of sins, but his soul waited
in his body for a better time.
Eagerly they understood that God wished
to save him from their enmity and pass severe judgment
on their distress. Thus God can guard
each of the blessed, he who alone
is almighty against every affliction.
Nevertheless the angry outcasts brought him
enraged in spirit, glory's soldier,
the holy sacrament's son, to hell's mouth,
where the doomed spirits of the wicked ones
begin after death's slaughter to seek
their first entrance into that horrible house,
the profound pits down under the cliffs.
They alarmed him, aggressively threatened him
with terror and enmity impiously,
with a fearsome journey, as is the custom of fiends,
when they want to trick trustworthy
souls with sins and deceits.
They began grimly to torment God's
hero in his heart. They made many promises
that he would go into that grim terror,
move about condemned among the inmates of hell,
and there suffer fire in fetters.
They wanted to drag, those miserable monsters,

the Measurer's champion with wicked words
into despair. It could not be done!
The care-laden creatures, hateful to Christ,
spoke to Guthlac grimly:
"This is not seemly for you, who are neither
the Lord's cleanly tempted servant nor God's soldier
well known in words and deeds,
holy in your heart. Now you must sink
deep into hell. By no means have you
the Lord's light in heaven, the high home,
a mansion in the sky, because you committed too many
sins and frauds in your fleshly body.
Now we want to pay your wage
for every little wrong where it will be most loathsome
for you in the cruelest contest of the soul."
The blessed man made them an answer,
Guthlac with God's strength in his spirit:
"Do what you wish, if the Lord Christ,
life's Light-giver, will allow you,
the Lord of hosts, and lead
his suppliant into the fearsome fire.
It is in the control of glory's King,
he who crushed you and drove you into captivity,
into close confinement, the saving Christ.
I am his humble errand boy,
a patient servant. I shall suffer
in all things everywhere his only judgment
and eagerly be under his will
in the thoughts of my spirit ever and always,
sincerely obey my Savior
in habits and thoughts and thank him
for all the gifts that God created
first for angels and then for earth-dwellers.
And I will bless with a blithe heart
life's Light-giver and sing him praise
day and night with a fitting demeanor,
honor in my heart heaven's Guardian.

Never will it be allowed from above
by the mercy of the light that you may
speak to the Lord, but you must sing
in death your welling woe with weeping,
have lamentation in hell and by no means
the holy praise of heaven's King.
I will honor the high Judge
in my days with words and deeds,
love him in my life. Thus teaching and honor
is brought to blossoming speech
in the one who does his will in his words.
You are oathbreakers. Thus in exile
have you long lived, sunk in fire,
dismally deceived, bereft of the sky,
deprived of joy, fallen into death,
clasped by crimes, despairing of life,
so that you sought safety in your blindness.
In days of old you eagerly despised
the splendid creation, the spiritual joy in God,
when you laughed the holy Lord to scorn.
You could not always experience joyful days,
but were shoved in shame for your sins
on account of your pride into eternal fire,
where you must endure death and darkness,
lamentation forever and ever. Never will you feel relief for that!
And I believe in the one who began life,
the eternal Ruler of all creation,
that for his mercy and might he never
will forsake me, the Savior of souls,
because of the bold deed by which in my body
and in my soul I soldiered
for the Lord for a long while
through the mystery of his manifold powers.
Therefore I believe in the brightest
glory of the Trinity who holds in his hands
heaven and earth in his high counsel,
so that you may never drag me in your dire rage

with trouble into torments,
my murderous and evil enemies,
black and bereft of victory. Truly I am
beautifully filled with faith in the light
and love of the Lord in my heart,
my breast on fire for a better home,
my limbs illumined for the best eternal house where the homeland
is fair and joyful in the Father's glory.
there never will rays of light or life's
hope be given you in God's
kingdom before humankind's Savior
because of your pride, which surged in your spirits
through idle boasts all too much.
You expected and hoped in your hostility
that you would be in glory like God
your Creator. Then a worse thing came upon you
when the Ruler in his wrath sank you
down into that dark misery where ever afterward
a pyre was kindled mixed with poison,
joy cut off from you by a calamitous judgment,
the company of angels. So now ever it must
be and always that you own the weariness
of burning waves, by no means blessings.
Nor can you suppose, separated from glory,
that you can shove me under the shadow of shame
sinfully with your crafty snares,
nor bind me under in a blaze of fire
in the house of hell, where a home has been made for you,
a black eternal night, war without end,
savage slaying of the spirit. There mourning you
must endure death while I will own
the joy of delights with the angels in the upper
kingdom in the skies, where the true King lives,
help and health of the race of heroes,
together with his retainers and their company." Then came
the Lord's messenger,[338] holy from heaven, who in laughter
commanded the wretched spirits in divine dread,

bade them quickly bear the innocent one
out of that exile, glory's soldier,
all whole in limbs, so that the loved
spirit could go into joy all prepared
in God's protection. Then the gang of fiends
became dismayed because of that dread. The illustrious one
spoke, the Lord's dear thane; he shone with daylight.
He had Guthlac's spirit, the brave guardian,
in his keeping, prosperous in power.
He bound the thanes of darkness in distress,
settled need on them and commanded them constantly:
"Let him have neither broken bone nor bloody wound,
bruise of the body nor any hurt
from that damage that you may do to him,
but set him sound where you seized him.
He shall govern the plain. You cannot grab from him his hermitage.
I am the judge. God gave me the command
to tell you in haste that you must heal
all his hurts with your own hand and then
be obedient to his own authority.
Nor shall I keep my countenance
from your gang. I am God's thane.
I am one of the Twelve, the most trusted,
whom he loved in his heart in human form.
He sent me hither from heaven,
saw that you troubled with torments
his suppliant on earth on account of your enmity.
He is my brother. His suffering has caused me sorrow.
I will cause it where my comrade dwells
in his hermitage (for I wish to hold
peace with him now that I can help him)
that you will often view my visage.
Now I will continuously come to see him.
I will lead to the Lord in testimony
his words and works. He will know his deeds."
Then Guthlac's soul was gladdened
after Bartholomew had brought forth

God's message. Those slaves stood
ready, obedient. Little of the Lord's
word did they miss. Then God's warrior,
blessed in judgment, left on the beloved journey
to that agreeable portion of earth.
They carried him and kept him from injury,
held him in their hands and protected him from a fall.
Their going under the fear of God
was smooth and soft. Triumphant came
the builder to the barrow. Many species
blessed him with bold words.
The offspring of the trees' birds gave tokens
of the blessed one's return. Often had he offered
them food when they flew hungry about his hand,
greedily ravenous. They rejoiced in his help.
Thus that merciful spirit moved away
from the gladness of humankind, served God,
took his joy in the wild beasts after he scorned this world.
Peaceful was the victory-plain and the new hermitage,
fair the songs of the birds, blossoming in the earth.
Cuckoos announced the spring. Blessed and one
in heart, Guthlac could enjoy his home.
The green field stood in God's keeping.
The herdsman who came from heaven
had frightened the fiends. What fairer
pleasure could happen in the life of the people
of which our elders remind us
or we ourselves have afterward known?
Listen! We are witnesses of these wonders!
All this has occurred in our time
and age.[339] Therefore none of the race of our elders
upon the earth need doubt this.
But God does things like this to give
strength to the life of spirits lest the frailer heart
must needs turn from the testimony
when they could touch the truth in front of them.
Thus the almighty one loves all creation

under the heavens in their bodily homes,
the tribes of men throughout middle earth.
The Wielder wishes that we always cleverly
pursue wisdom, so that, in payment
for his gifts, his truth that he gives
and sends us as an apostle and for our understanding
might become our path. He makes broad for our souls
the gentle paths of life, made straight in light.
Indeed, that is not the least that Love makes known
when it builds in the human heart
spiritual grace. Thus through his glory
he raised up Guthlac's days and deeds.
This prince was firm in opposition to the fiends,
secure against sins. Afterward he struggled
little there in his loyalty. In humility
he often sent his words up to God,
let his prayer go into the land of light,
thanked the Ruler that he had to remain
in grievous pains until through God's will
a greater life would be given him.
Thus was Guthlac's soul sent
into the upper heavens in the embrace of angels.
They led him lovingly before the face[340]
of the eternal Ruler. Reward was given him,
a seat in the sky where he could
ever and always be assured of a home,
to live there gladly. God's son
is a merciful guardian, the mighty Lord,
the holy herdsman, heaven-kingdom's keeper.
Thus the souls of the steadfast may
ascend up into the eternal dwelling,
the fatherland of the skies, those who follow here
in words and works the Glory-king's
enduring doctrine and at their life's end
earn on earth eternal life,
homes on high. They are the people of the eucharist,
chosen champions, beloved to Christ.

ANGLO-SAXON SPIRITUALITY

They bear bright faith in their breasts,
holy hope with a clean heart.
They honor the Wielder, have wise thoughts,
are eager to go forth to the Father's land.
They prepare a place for the spirit and with intelligence
overcome the enemy and forbear
sinful lusts in their hearts. They eagerly honor
brotherly love. They labor themselves
in God's will, give their souls ornaments
of holy thoughts, follow heaven's king's
commandments in the land. They love fasting,
protect themselves from evil and seek prayer,
travail against sins, keep what is true and right.
They do not do penance for that after their passing,
when they pass into the heavenly palace,
go quickly on their journey to Jerusalem,
where they may eagerly gaze on God's face
forever and always in joy,
in peace, and in his sight. Pure truth lives there,
fair, fast in glories, forever and ever
in joy among the living of that land.

Advent Lyrics

...to the King[341]
You are the wall-stone that the workers once
rejected from their work.[342] It well befits you
that you are the head of this famous hall
and gather together the wide walls
and with a firm joint the unbroken flint
so that throughout all cities of earth all the sight of eyes
will forever wonder at the Wielder of glory.
Now make clear through your cleverness your own work,
loyal, victory-bright, and immediately leave
wall against wall. Now it is necessary for this work
that the Craftsman come, the King himself,
and then restore, since it is now ruined,
the house under the roof. He rose up that body,
limbs from the earth. Now life's Lord will
rescue that miserable heap from the hostile ones,
the wretched ones from dread, as he often did.
O you Ruler and you righteous King,[343]
who holds the lock, opens life,
the blessed way upward denied to others,
the beautiful, wished-for journey, if their works do not last.
Now, we speak these words in need
and pray to the one who created the people

that he not elect to announce
a pitiful thing, that in prison
we sit sorrowing, await the sun,
until life's Lord reveal to us the light,
become the herdsman of our hearts,
and wind our feeble wits about with glory.
Do for us, whom he has granted glory, this great thing,
when we had to move about in misery,
in this narrow land, lacking a home.
Therefore he who tells the truth may say
that he ransomed the human race
when it had wandered far away. The Virgin[344] was young,
a maiden without fault, whom he chose as his mother.
This marvel happened without the love of man
so that the bride was pregnant for the child's birth.
Nothing before or after was equal to this
in the world, to the woman's yearning.
It was a mystery, the Maker's secret.
All spiritual grace spread throughout the surface of the earth.
There many wise ones were enlightened
in enduring doctrines by life's Creator,
which before had lain shrouded under shadows,
the songs of the seers, when the Wielder came,
he who makes wondrous every word
of those who often want to exalt
the name of the Creator in a quick-witted way.

O sight of peace,[345] saintly Jerusalem,
choicest seat of kings, Christ's city,
homeland of angels, in you alone
the souls of the faithful find rest,
boasting in glories. Never will a mark of blemish
be seen in that safe dwelling,
but each crime, curse, and conflict
withdraws far from you. You are full of wonder,
hope of the holy, just as you are named.
Now cast your gaze throughout this grand creation

and also on the roof of the sky, widely scan
in every corner how the King of heaven
seeks you everywhere and, oh, comes himself
and finds a dwelling in you just as in former days
wise prophets said in words,
proclaimed Christ's birth, spoke comfort to you,
choicest of cities. Now that child has come,
awakened for the reversal of the works of the Hebrews.
He brings you bliss, loosens your bonds
forced on you by your sins. He knows narrow need,
how the miserable ones must await mercy.
O joy of women[346] throughout the glory of wonder,
most magnificent maiden on the earth's surface,
of whom sea-folk[347] ever have heard spoken,
say something of that secret that came upon you from heaven,
how you ever experienced pregnancy
on account of that child's coming and knew
no bedding with a man according the human habit.
Truly we have never heard that such a thing
ever happened in earlier days,
that you by special gift grasped this,
nor need we expect such an event
in the time to come. Indeed, in you truth has lived
worshipfully now that you have borne in your bosom
the glory of wonders, and the great virginity
by no means was corrupted. As all the children of men
sow in sorrows, so will they reap once more,
bear children in pain. The blessed Virgin,
St. Mary, always full of victory, said,
"What is this marvel at which you are amazed
and mourn, moaning with grief,
son and also daughter of Salem?
Ask in curiosity how I kept my bridal
gift, my maidenhood, and also became the mother
of the glorious God's son. Therefore that is not a mystery
made known to men, but Christ revealed
in David's dear relative

that Eve's guilt is all removed,
the curse cast away, and the lesser gender
made glorious. Hope has been grasped,
so that blessing may now be shared by both
man and women forever and always
in the upper joy of angels
always abiding with the faithful Father."

O rising sun,[348] brightest of angels,
sent to men all over middle earth,
and loyal light of the sun
bright beyond the stars, you always
send light of yourself in every season!
As you, God from God eagerly begotten,
Son of the faithful Father, ever were
without beginning in heaven's high glory,
so now in need your own creatures
beseech you boldly that you yourself
send us the bright sun and come
to shed light on those who long
have dwelt here in darkness, covered
in clouds of continual night, enveloped in sins,
and have had to suffer dark death's shadow.
Now we hopefully believe in the health
granted to the multitude by the word of God,
which in the beginning was equally eternal with God,
the Father almighty, and now afterward became
flesh, free from sins, whom the Virgin bore
for the aid of the afflicted. God was with us,
seen to be without sins. He dwelt with us,
the mighty Measurer's child and the Son of Man
peaceful among the people. He can give thanks
to the victory Lord always for his actions,
because he wished to send us his own self.

O God of spirits,[349] how skillfully
are you named with the right name,

Emmanuel, just as the angel uttered it
first in Hebrew! It was afterward explained
amply according to its hidden meaning: "Now the Keeper of the
     heavens,
God himself, is with us."[350] Thus in days gone by
people spoke truly of the King of all kings
and also the pure priest who was to come.
So once the famous one, Melchizedek,[351]
discerning in spirit, revealed the divine glory
of the eternal All-ruler. He was the lawgiver,
the bringer of lore to those who long
hoped for his coming here as was promised them,
that the Wielder's Son himself wanted
to cleanse the kin of the earth,
likewise also seek out even the abyss
by the power of the spirit. Now softly they
abided in bonds till the Son of God
should come to those in care. Therefore they spoke
thus, disabled by distress: "Now come,
heaven's high King, yourself, and bring us a life
of health, weary ones, slaves of pain, worn down
by weeping, by bitter, burning tears. The remedy
belongs only to you for those who bear overmuch pain.
Seek here with eager spirit us captives.
Do not leave thus behind you a big crowd
when you turn away from here, but have mercy on us,
according to your kind, Christ the Savior,
glory's prince. Let not the wretched have power
over us. Give us eternal gladness
in your wondrous glory, so that we may worship you,
marvelous King of hosts, whom you once made
with your own hands. You have a home
in the heights forever with the ruling Father."

"O my Joseph,[352] Jacob's son,
kin of David the famous king,
now you must firmly separate from friendship,

221

take leave of my love!" "I am suddenly
deeply distressed, bereft of my reputation,
because I have heard many rumors about you,
wide sorrows and sore words
of harm. And they speak spite to me,
many insulting words. I must shed
mourning tears. God easily may
heal the heaviness of mind in my heart,
comfort the miserable one. Alas, young maiden,
Virgin Mary!" "Why do you mourn,
cry out in cares? I never have
found any fault in you or suspicion of
works of evil, and still you speak words
as if you yourself were filled
with every sin and crime." "I have had
too many pains from this pregnancy!
How can I avoid this evil speech
or find any answer
against these wicked people? It is widely known
that I freely took from the bright temple
of the Lord a pure lady,
free of crimes. And now she is corrupted
by I know not whom. It doesn't avail me
either to say something or be silent. If I speak the truth,
then must David's daughter die,
destroyed by stones. Still harder for me
is to 'heal a murder': a man who lies
afterward lives hated in every land,
reviled among the folk." Then the Virgin revealed
the right secrets and said thus:
"Truly I tell you by the Measurer's Son,
the Helper of spirits, that still have I no knowledge
of any man anywhere on the earth
by living with him, but it was allowed
me, young in years, that Gabriel,
heaven's high angel, should give me salutation.
He truly said that the Spirit of the skies

would illumine me with light should I bear
life's glory, the bright Son, the great God's child,
the radiant Ruler of wonder. Now I am his temple,
formed without fault. In me the Spirit
of comfort has dwelled. Now drop all this
sore care of sorrow! Give eternal thanks
to the famous Son of the Measurer, that I have become his mother
yet remain a virgin, with you reputed to be
his earthly father. Indeed, prophesy
will find fulfillment in himself."

O you true and you tranquil
King of all kings,[353] Christ almighty,
how you were once begotten a child
in all worldly glories with your wondrous
Father through his skill and strength!
There is now no earl under the air,
a man so wise, one so very intelligent,
who can say to the sea-folk,
recount rightly, how the guardian of the skies
at the beginning took him as his freeborn child.
That was the first of those things among the folk
that the people of the Gentiles had heard proclaimed
to have happened under the clouds, that the wise God,
life's fountainhead, separated light
and dark in a princely way. And in him was the power
of judgment. And the Leader of hosts commanded it like this:
"Now let there be forever and always
light, a glittering joy to each living creature
that will be begotten according to its kind."[354]
And then it immediately occurred, when it had to:
light illuminated the tribes of the nations,
bright with stars according to the circuit of the seasons.
He himself set it that you his Son be
a co-dweller with you, the one and only Lord,
before any of this ever happened.
You are the wise one who worked all

this wide creation with your Wielder.
Therefore there is no one so quick-witted or so intelligent
who can clearly affirm your origin
among the children of men. Come now, Maker of victory,
Measurer of humankind, and kindly show
your mercy here! There is need for us all
to learn your mother's lineage,
through the right mysteries, now that we may not
relate from afar anything of your Father's.
Bless this middle earth mildly
through your coming here, Savior Christ,
and, high Lord of heaven, command
those golden gates that in bygone ages
so long ago stood locked be opened,[355]
and then seek us in your own advent,
humble on the earth. We have need of your help!
The damned wolf, the dark shadow
of death, has dispersed your flock, Lord,
scattered it all about. That which, Wielder,
you earlier bought with your blood the baleful one
now sorely crushes and takes into captivity
despite our desire and needs. Therefore, Savior, we
earnestly ask you in our hearts' thoughts
that you grant us help in all haste,
sorrowful exiles, that the torment's slayer
might tumble in poverty into the pit of hell
and your handiwork, Creator of heroes,
might arise and come in righteousness
into the upper kingdom of the princely people,
from where the dark spirit once in his sinful lust
deceived and seduced us, so that we, dispossessed of glory,
would have to endure torment ever without end,
unless you the more quickly, eternal Lord,
living God, guardian of all creatures,
wish to free us from the foe of the nations.

O you illustrious one on middle earth,[356]
the purest woman in all the world
of those who ever were and will be fashioned,
how rightly all who can recount it,
people on the earth, proclaim your name
with a blithe heart and say that you are the bride
of the best ring-giver of heaven's roof.
Likewise also, the highest in the heavens,
Christ's thanes, sing and say
that you are by holy might marvelous Lady
of the hosts of wonder of all worldly
orders under the heavens and also of hell's dwellers,
because you alone of all people
gloriously considered, courageous in mind,
that you would bring your maidenhood to the Measurer,
offer it without sins. None such
ever came, any other over all the people,
a bride adorned with bracelets, who later sent
the bright gift to the heavenly home
with a clean spirit. Therefore the Creator of victories
commanded his high angel to fly here
out of his famous order and quickly announce
to you the abundance of might[357]—that you would bear
the Son of God by a sinless birth
as mercy for the people and, Mary,
ever after keep you always spotless.
We have also heard what long ago
was truly said about you by some prophet
in the old days named Isaiah[358]—
that he was led so that he looked at
all life's habitations in the eternal home.
Thus then the wise prophet peered throughout this country
until he stared at the place where a noble
entranceway was established. All that
huge door was decorated with costly treasure,
wound about with wondrous bands. He very much
expected that no one of the people could ever

at all in eternity raise up
bars so firmly bolted
or unlock the clasp of this castle's gate
before God's angel with a glad thought
revealed the way and spoke this word:
"I can tell you that truly it happened
that the Wielder himself wishes yet
at some time to pass through these golden gates
by the strength of the Spirit, the Father almighty,
and look for the earth through those fast latches.
And they will then stand eternally after him
always and ever so closed up
that no one else except God the Savior
will evermore again unlock them."
Now is it fulfilled what the wise one then
gazed at there with his own eyes.
You are the wall's door through whom the Wielder Lord
alone journeyed out into this earth
and so encountered you adorned with virtues,
clean and chosen, Christ almighty.
So the Lord of angels locked you
after him once more immaculate in every
way, life's Ring-giver, with a great key.
Show us now the mercy that the messenger,
God's angel Gabriel, brought.
Indeed, we the people of this city pray
that you will speak comfort to the congregation:
your own Son. Then will we be able,
one in spirit, all to hope,
now that we behold that Child before your breast.
Intercede now for us with daring words
that he leave us no while longer
in this dale of death obeying heresy,
but that he carry us into the Father's kingdom
where we henceforth will live lacking sorrow
in glory with the God of hosts.

O you holy Lord of the heavens,[359]
you were from ancient times coexistent
with your heavenly Father in the noble home.
Not one of the angels had yet been made,
nor any of the great, glorious host
who care for the kingdom up in the skies,
the glory-seat of God and his thanes,
when first you were yourself setting in order
this wide creation with the eternal King,
the broad, abundant land. To both of you belong
the high Spirit firm in help. Savior Christ,
we all ask you in our humility
to hear the cry of the captives,
your suppliants, O saving God—
how we are distressed by our own desires.
Accursed spirits, hostile hell-foes
have hard beset the exiles,
bound them with baleful ropes. Remedy belongs
all to you alone, eternal Lord.
Help those in trouble, so that your coming here
may comfort the miserable, even though we have made
a feud against you through our lust for iniquities.
Have mercy on your servants and consider our miseries,
how we totter with a tired spirit,
move wretchedly about. Come now, King of heroes.
Do not delay too long. We have need of mercies,
that you free us and faithfully give us
the healthful gift, that ever after we
may always thrive in the thing
that prospers among the people—your will.

O the heavenly Trinity, full of honors,[360]
beautiful, high, and holy,
blessed far and wide throughout the broad plains,
those bearing speech, poor inhabitants of earth
must in right with all their might
praise you highly now that the honorable

Savior God has given notice that we can know him.
Therefore they, with energy, enlarged in good opinion,
the steadfast race of seraphim,
always exulting up with the angels,
sing in unwearied strength,
very high with a loud voice,
fairly far and near. They have the choicest
of service with the King. Christ granted
that they enjoy with their eyes his presence
always and ever, brightly adorned,
worship the Wielder far and wide.
And with their feathers they guard the face
of God almighty, the eternal Lord
and eagerly throng about his throne,
seeing which of them can in the courts
of peace play in flight closest to our Lord.
They laud the Beloved and in light
say these words and give glory
to the kingly Fashioner of all creatures:
"Holy you are, holy, prince of high angels,
true King of victory, Lord of lords,
always you are holy! Ever will your judgment
dwell on earth among the rulers in every age,
be worshiped far and wide. You are the God of hosts,
because, Protector of heroes, you have filled heaven
and earth with your glory, Guardian
of all creatures. Eternal salutation
be to you in the highest and on earth honor,
bright among the people. Beloved,
blessed among the nobles be the one who comes in the name
of the Lord for help to the wretched. To you in the highest
be eternal praise ever without end!"

O listen![361] It is a marvelous change in the life of man
that mankind's merciful Creator
got from a Virgin flesh without guilt.
And she knew nothing of a man's embraces!

228

Nor did the Maker of victory come through man's
seed in the world. But it was a greater wonder
than all those living on the earth could understand
in its mystery, how he, the marvel of the skies,
the high Lord of heaven, could give help
to mankind through his mother's womb.
And the Savior of the nations deals out every day
his pardon as help to the people,
going forth like this, the God of hosts.
Therefore we should loyally laud him
with words and works. That is good advice
to everyone who has intelligence,
that he always and most often and most heartily
and most eagerly give God worship.
He will repay him with rewards for that love,
the holy Savior himself,
even in the country to which he has never before come,
in the joy of the land of the living,
where he may have a home in happiness ever after,
dwell forever and ever, all without end. Amen.

The Lord's Prayer I[362]

Holy Father, you who dwell in heaven,
honored be the joy of your glory. May your name be hallowed
in your works by the sons of the people. You are the savior of men.
May your spacious kingdom come and your will firm in counsel
be raised under the roof of heaven and also on the wide earth.
Give us for this day just dignity,
our continued loaf, comforter
of men, steadfast Savior.
Do not let us be tossed too much in temptation,
but, Ruler of the people, give us good deliverance
from every evil forever and ever.

Psalm 121[363]

I raise my eyes to the high hill
where I found help, faithfully at need.
My help is also lovely from the Lord,
he who made heaven, also the earth.
He will not place your foot in the power of the enemy
nor consider sleep, he who keeps you safe.
Indeed, he never sleeps nor slumbers much
who now must hold in his mind
the folk of Israel from foes without.
The holy Lord holds you
and your powerful Protector will
hover at your right hand, always at need.
The sun shall not singe you by day
nor the moon in my night,
but the holy Lord will hold you eagerly
against every evil everywhere
and likewise preserve your soul.
The eternal Lord will always hold
your going out and coming in, the true King of souls,
from this time forth forever and ever.

Soul and Body II

Indeed, it behooves every hero
to ponder his own soul's pilgrimage,
how deep it is when death comes,
sunders the siblings who were once together,
body and soul. It will be a long time
before the spirit takes from God himself
either torment or glory according to how that earthen
vessel earlier worked it here in the world.[364]
The spirit must come, clamoring with cares,
every seventh night, the soul to find
the body with which it was burdened
long ago, for three hundred years unless[365]
the eternal Lord earlier arranges it,
the almighty God, and ends the world.
Then, so care-laden, it will call in a cold voice,
the spirit speak grimly to that dust:[366]
"What have you endured, dreary one? How have you oppressed
        me?
The earth's filth will fall away
like the loam! Little have you thought
what you later would become in your soul's journey,
after it was led away out of its own body!
Wretch, what torment for me! Listen, you little thought

to be worm's food. How far is this from here!
And out of heaven the almighty Measurer
sent you a soul through an angel,
through his own hand in his princely power,
and then bought you with holy blood!
Yet you bound me with hard hunger
and held me prisoner in the torments of hell!
I lived inside of you. Enfolded in flesh,
I could by no means come out of you, and your
sinful lusts sank me down. It often seemed to me
that it would be thirty thousand winters
till your death day. Listen, I awaited our
divorce with difficulty. The end is not very good!
You were proud of your food and full of your wine.
You thundered in glory, and I was often thirsty
for God's body, the sustenance of the spirit.
You thought then that though you were strongly stirred
by the flesh and by foul lusts
here in this life, you were made stable by me
while I had to live in the world,
and that I was a spirit sent by God into you.
Never did you have need to honor me
through the lust of your desires by such hard pains in hell.
Now you must nevertheless endure the shame of my
          embarrassment
on that awful day when the Only Begotten
assembles all the race of humans.[367]
You are now no dearer to any living person
as a mate—neither to mother nor to father
nor to any sibling—than the swarthy raven
after I journeyed alone out of you
by the self-same hand by whom I once was sent.
They may not receive from you those red trappings—
gold or silver or any of your goods—
but here you must abide, bereft of your bones,
torn from your sinews. And I your soul must
often seek you out against my will

to abuse you with words as you once did me.
You are deaf and dumb. Your joys are nothing.
I must needs by night still seek you out,
sorrowed by sins and soon go from you
again at cock-crow, when holy people
who sing their songs of praise to the living God
seek the dwellings that you ordained for me
and those horrid homesteads.
And many earthworms must gnaw you,
slit your sinews, swarthy creatures,
gluttonous and greedy. Your follies are nothing—
those which you paraded before the people here on earth.
Therefore it had been better, much better
than if all the successes of earth were yours—
unless you give them back to God himself—
that at the beginning you had become a bird or fish in the sea
or toiled for food like an animal on the earth,
an ox footing about a field without understanding
or the grimmest of beasts, where God willed,
wild in the wasteland, yes, even if
you had become the worst of the race of worms
than you had ever lived as a man on the earth
or ever had to submit to the sacrament of baptism.
When for us both you must make answer
on that great day when to all the dwellers here
in the world those wounds will be revealed
that criminals once caused,
then will the Lord himself listen to every deed,
in the words of each and every mouth
for requital from those wounds. But what will you
say there to the Savior on Judgment Day?
Then joint will be too little grown on a limb;
for each of them especially will you not
pay the penalty when the Lord
becomes dreadful in judgment? But what will we both do
when he has brought us both back to life again?
Shall we then once more enjoy together

such miseries as you once made for us?"
Thus the soul berates the body. Then it must go away,
seek out hell's abyss, by no means heaven's joys,
driven by its deeds. The dust just lies where it was.
It cannot give anything in answer
or offer any refuge
to the sad spirit, help or comfort.
Its head is split, hands splayed apart,
jaws gaping, gums torn.
Sinews are sucked out, neck gnawed.
Worms savagely rob the ribs,
drink the corpse like crooks thirsty for blood.
The tongue is pulled out into ten pieces
for the benefit of the hungry. Therefore it cannot briskly
exchange words with the wretched spirit.
The worm is named Glutton, whose jaws will be
needle-sharp. He first draws near
to the earth-grave before all others.
He tears out the tongue and drives through the teeth
and for a feast opens them up for others.
And he eats the eyes upon the head—
nourishment for worms when the weary
body lies cold that long before
was covered with clothes. Then it will be morsels
for worms, food in the earth. Every wise one
among the people may bring this to mind.

Judgment Day I

It must happen that the sea will surge,
a flood over the land. Life will have an end
for each and all.[368] Often may the one who wishes
hold this truth in his own heart.
Our Lord has set himself an advent here
on that proud day, highest of powerful kings.
Then the King of humankind will kindle
the land with fire. That will not be a little
gathering to convene! Flame will be fueled
once fire has grabbed the ends of the earth,
the burning flame the bright creation.
All this wide world will be filled with embers,
cruel coals, since now grim-minded
men rule, boastfully rebel
against their Lord, do business with laughter,
until the guardians of sin[369] seduce them
so they seek hell with a heap of the damned,
fly away with the fiends. Fire will find them
in troublesome torture. Day never shines there[370]
lightly in the sky, but it always stands locked
once terror has taken hold of the soul.
It is narrow above, and it is hot inside.
It is not a grand house, but the greatest of horrors is there,

not a hopeful home, but the abyss of hell is there,
a terrible trip for the one who often
mars the peace with his mouth. Nor does he know that murky
creation: how eternally it stands without end
for the one who is thrown there, a sacrifice for his sins,
and there endures his fate forever.

      Who then is smart enough for this or knows so much
that he can ever explain heaven's height,
the heritage of God, so eagerly as he stands, heart
clean and ready, to the one who wishes to fear
this speech so deeply? The day will come
when we will bear forth each fault,
our customs and thoughts. That will be a cruel court,
a harsh jury. Heat will grow cold.
Then there will be nothing in this world but water's sound.
The fish's homeland will flow over the earth.
There will be neither blood nor bone, but every child
with body and soul will seek payment
for all we earlier did on earth,
good or evil.[371] No greater horror
will ever happen in this world, and this is widely known.
Stars will not sparkle here, but splendor will fade,
the glory of the world. Thus I always want
to teach the people to praise God's
glory on high in hopes of heaven,
to live in belief and always work for
the Lord's love in this world before that lofty day
preaches with a fanfare the fiery flame,
the grim superpower. Nor will any earl's glory
last long in this life after light's guardian
sends fire over all the face of the earth.
The powers of the air kindle. Flame quickens,
a burning darkness. Bloodshed will be
proclaimed to many, the menace of the mighty King.
All the bright creation will tremble; brands will leap.
On that deep day highest heaven will resound.

Then men and women will let go of the world,
misery of the earth. Then they will see their work in eternity.
Then will be made known who lived life
in purity. For them will be a ready reward.
There has ever been hope in the heavens since our Savior,
middle-earth's Measurer, was bound fast
on that black beam through the construction of a mast[372]
with sad clamps. Christ knows all
good deeds. By no means should a sinful soul
boast of this, that he is bound toward heaven
when he too often derides holy doctrine,
scorns it as a scandal. Nor does he know of that dread
a part, a perception of evil, before it falls on him.
When the calamity will come then will he discover it.
Throughout middle earth it will be made known to many
that he will be led to the crowd on the left,[373]
worse than if he might wander toward the right hand,
released from sins. He thinks it little,
he who enjoys his wants, glad for wine,
who sits drunk at the feast, who does not despair of his journey,
what might happen for him after this world.
     Then the Lord of spirits, glory's Leader,
will grant his desires after this doom
to the one who now sorely considers his sins,
who endures great dread of mind.
Then life's Wielder will reward him,
the Shepherd of heaven, after his journey hence,
with his good deeds, since he grieved so much,
sorry for his sins. Nor must he be too slow
nor too late for these lessons, he who wishes to live with God,
enjoy that building which the bright Father
will ready for us,[374] Ruler of spirits.
It is the victory Lord who will adorn the dwelling,
who will build it brightly. The pure will
go to it without sins, just as the Wielder says,
King of all kings. Thus all of the living,

those who understand this well, will obey the Wielder,
those who wish to climb the heights of the heavens.
　　　Yet it will happen, though it be heaped with earth,
the body with loam, that it will take life,
spirit after the grave. The people will be summoned,
all Adam's offspring to the meeting.
Then spirit and skeleton will be united[375]
together for that journey. That will reveal the truth,
when on that great day we gather,
a crowd at the cross. Then many judgments will be made,
all that has happened under heaven—hot or cold,
good or evil. Eagerly will he listen,
the highest of heaven's kings, to the deeds of heroes.
Never has horn been sounded so strongly
nor trumpet blown[376] that the bright voice
will not be heard the louder by men all over middle earth,
the world of the Wielder. The plains will tremble
at the message that he has in mind for all of us.
　　　Now echo this word: it will be known
that I cannot deny this doom under the heavens,
but it must come to pass like this for each of the peoples,
burning flame over all the bright dwellings.
Later, after that fire, life will be laid down firmly.
He who considers this well will have wealth in heaven.

The Phoenix

I have heard that far from here
in the eastern parts is the princeliest of lands,
renowned among the people. That region of the earth
is not accessible to many of the chieftains
of middle earth, but is removed
through the might of the Measurer from all evildoers.
Beautiful is all that meadow, blessed with joys,
with the sweetest scents on the earth.
That island is unique, its Creator noble,
courageous, prosperous in might. He created that land.
There heaven's door is often open
to all the blessed, the sweetness of song revealed.
It is a winsome field, green forests
ranging wide under the skies. Neither rain nor snow
nor breath of frost nor blast of fire
nor downpour of hail nor fall of hoarfrost
nor heat of the sun nor constant cold
nor hot weather nor winter's shower
harms anyone.[377] But blessed abides
the field and whole. Flowering with blooms
is that noble land. There neither hills nor mountains
stand steeply nor cliffs of stone
tower high as here among us.[378]
Neither does glen or dale or dim cave

or barrow or slope. Nothing unsmooth
ever lies there, but the princely plain
blossoms under the clouds, blowing with delights.
That bright field is twelve fathoms higher,
as wise sages in their wisdom
let us learn in their books,
than any of the hills that tower on high
brightly here among us under the heavens' stars.
That victory-field is serene. The sun-grove gleams.
Winsome are those woods. Fruits do not decay there,
bright blossoms, but the trees ever stand
green, just as God commands them.
In winter and summer alike those woods are
hung with flowers. Leaves never fade
there under the sky. Nor does fire ever scorch
them forever and ever before that ending
which will come upon the world. When long ago the sea's flood,[379]
the power of water, covered all the world,
the circle of earth, then the princely plain
stood firm against the wave's surge,
entirely safe against the rough surf,
blessed, unblemished through God's grace.
Thus will it abide in bloom until the fire's coming,
God's Judgment, when the graves,
the dark chambers of champions, will be opened.
There in that land is no loathsome foe,
neither weeping nor revenge, no sign of woe,
neither age nor illness nor narrow death,
neither loss of life nor the coming of what is hateful,
neither sin nor strife nor sorrowful suffering,
neither the struggle of poverty nor the loss of possessions,
neither sorrow nor sleep nor heavy sickness
neither winter's storm nor weather's uncertainty,
rough under the heavens. Nor does hard frost
or cold icicles afflict anyone.
There neither hail nor hoarfrost fall to the earth.
Nor does a windy cloud or water fall there,

stirred up by the air. But there streams of water,
wondrously beautiful, spring up from wells
and water the earth in fair fountains,
winsome water out of the midst of the woods
when each month it breaks brim-cold
out of the earth's sod and goes out through all the grove,
courageously at its due season. It is the Lord's command
that twelve times the water's surge
should gloriously flow through that glade.
Those forests are hung with fruit,
beautiful blossoms.[380] There by no means ever
do those forest ornaments fade, holy under the heavens.
Nor do the yellow flowers fall there onto the ground,
the beauty of the wood-beams. But marvelously are
the boughs always brimming among the trees,
fruit made fresh in every season.
On that grassy field they stand green,
adorned delightfully by the Holy One's might,
the brightest of groves. By no means broken
is that forest in hue, where the holy fragrance
lasts throughout that joyous land. It is never changed
forever and ever before the wise ancient Worker
finishes it, he who fashioned it in the beginning.
Guarding that wood is a wondrously fair
bird strong in feathers; it is named Phoenix.
There the recluse rules its realm,
behaves boldly. Never will death harm him
in that pleasant plain while the world lasts.
He gazes at the sun's going
and toward the coming of God's candle,
the gracious gem, studiously staring
when the noblest of stars stands up
lighting the east over the wavy water,
the Father's ancient work shining with adornments,
the bright beacon of God. The stars are hidden,
gone under the waves in the western regions,
concealed in the dawn. And the dark night

departs in dreariness. Then the one strong in the hunt,
the bird glorious in feathers, gazes eagerly
at the ocean's current under the air over the sea
when it comes up, gliding from the east,
the light of the sky over the wide sea.
Thus the noble bird inhabits in lasting beauty
the well-streams at the water fountain,
where the glorious one bathes before the beacon's arising,
the coming of sky's candle, in that brook
twelve times. And always as often
he partakes of that pleasant spring
brim-cold at every bath.
Later in high spirits he lifts himself,
after the bath's play, onto a high branch
from which he can regard the sun's rise
toward the east,[381] when the sky's taper
quickly kindles over the restless sea,
the light's luminary. The land is adorned,
the world made wonderful when glory's gem
illuminates the abyss over the ocean's expanse
throughout middle earth, most famous of stars.
As soon as the sun looms high over
the salt streams, the gray bird
leaves its branch, bright from the grove,
travels quick in feathers in flight in the air,
sings and sounds a harmony together to the sky.
Then so fair is the bird's bearing,
so stirred his breast, boastful with bliss,
that he mixes in songcraft a more wondrously
bright speech than ever the sons of men
heard under the heavens after the high King,
glory's Worker, established the world,
heaven and earth. The sound of that harmony
is sweeter and more beautiful than every song
and more winsome than every melody.
Neither trumpet nor horn nor sound of the harp
nor voice of anyone on earth

nor the organ nor the sound of song
nor the swan's plectrum nor any of those pleasantries
that the Measurer created as delight for men
throughout this sad world may rival that revelry.
He sings like this and sounds a harmony blessed with joys
until the sun in the southern sky
sinks down. Then he keeps silence
and starts to hear. He stirs his head,
courageous, quick of thought, and shakes three times
his feathers quick in flight: the bird is silent.
He always marks the hours twelve times
day and night. It is thus decreed
for that grove's inhabitant that he may enjoy
the plain with pleasure and possess its wealth,
life and favor, the adornments of the land,
until he abides, the wood-grove's guardian,
a thousand winters of this life.
Then old, full of years, the gray-feathered one
becomes heavy. The birds' joy
abandons the green earth, the blooming land.
And then he seeks a spacious kingdom
of middle earth where no men live,
a place to live and a homeland. There he receives
an earldom, most mighty over the race of birds,
prominent among the people. And for a time among them
he guards the wilderness. Then the one formidable in flight
wings westward, beset by years,
flying with quick feathers. Birds throng
all about the noble one. Each one wants
to be thane and follower of the famous lord
until they seek the land of the Syrians
in a great band. There the pure bird
will suddenly depart, until it guards in the desert
some ground in the shadows in a wood-grove,
covered and hidden from crowds of heroes.
He will live there and rule a fast-rooted tree
under heaven's mantle, whom men call

THE PHOENIX

Phoenix on the earth from this fowl's name.
The king glorious in might has, I've heard,
the Measurer of mankind, granted to that tree
to be alone of all trees
growing upon the earthway,
the brightest of blooms. Nor may anything bitter
harm it grievously, but, always guarded,
it dwells uninjured while the earth lasts.
Then the wind rests and the weather is fair.
heaven's gem shines pure and holy.
Clouds are gone; the glory of the waters
stands still. Every storm is
silenced under the sky. From the south appears
the warm weather-candle; it lights the multitudes.
Then he begins to build in the branches,
prepare a nest. He has great need
in the urging of his intelligence
to exchange old age for life,
to succeed to a young spirit. Then far and near
he gathers and collects the most gracious
of winsome roots and wood blossoms
for its resting place, each one nobly scented
from among the winsome roots that wonder's King,
the Father of every creature, created
over the earth for the lordly race of our ancestors,
the sweetest under the sky. Then he himself bears
into the innards of that tree bright treasures.
There the wild bird builds a house
in that desert on the tall tree,
beautiful and lovely, and lives there
himself in that solar and surrounds up there
his body and feathers with the shade of the foliage
on each side with healthful scents
and the best blossoms of the earth.
He sits ready for his sojourn. When the gem of the sky,
the sun most hot in the summer,
shines over the shadows and fulfills its role,

lighting up the land, then his house
is heated by the bright heavens.
The roots warm up; the winsome dwelling steams
with sweet smells; then in the glow
the bird burns in the fire's grip with his nest.
The funeral pyre is kindled. Then the fire swallows up
the house of the sorrowful one. It hastens wildly;
the yellow flame burns and eats the Phoenix,
wise from former years. Then the fire tastes
the loaned body. Life leaves on a journey,
the fated soul's hoard, when flesh and bone
light the funeral pyre. Nevertheless new life
comes again for him after a while,
when the embers begin again
after the conflagration to close together,
shrunken to a ball. Then the brightest nest
is clean, consumed by the pyre,
the hall of the hero. The corpse has cooled,
the bone-vessel broken, and the burning abates.
Then out of the pyre in the ashes
the form of an apple may be found.
Out of it grows a worm, wondrously fair,
as if he were drawn out of eggs,
shining from a shell. Then he grows in the shade,
so that at first he is like an eagle's fledgling,
a fair young bird. Then further still
he grows in joys until he is like the form
of an old eagle, and afterward
clothed with feathers as he was at his creation,
brightly blossoming. Then he becomes big,
all renewed, begotten once again,
sundered from sins, as men
bring the fruits of the earth for food
back home in the harvest,
pleasant provisions, before winter's advent
at reaping time, lest a rain shower
spoil them under the heavens. There they find help,

joy in their food, when frost and snow
in great might thatch the meadows
with winter's garment. The wealth of earls
must again come forth from these fruits,
through the nature of the grain that was sown a seed
previously in purity. Then the sun's gleam
is loaned, life's token;
it awakens worldly treasure, so that the fruits
are once again begotten of their own nature,
adornments of the earth. Thus the bird becomes
young again, once grown old in years,
enfolded in flesh. He partakes of no food,
a meal upon the earth, unless to enjoy a portion
of the dew of honey that often drops down
in the silence of the night. By this the spirited one
sustains its life until again it seeks
its ancient throne, its own homeland.
When the bird, bold in feathers, is grown
among the herbs and its life is new,
young, full of gifts, then from the ground
he gathers his body, great of limb, which earlier
the flame took away, the leavings of the fire,
cleverly collects his crumbled bones
after the fire's force and then brings bone
and ember, the pyre's leavings, again together
and then covers the slaughter-spoils with plants,
fairly adorned. Then he is driven
to seek again his own homeland.
Then with his feet he grasps the fire's leavings,
clasps them with his claws and seeks in joy
again his country, his sun-bright seat,
his happy homeland. All is made new,
body and feathers, as it was in the beginning
when God first placed him in that noble plain,
firm in victories. He brings his own bones
there, those that earlier the fire's surge,
the flame, overwhelmed on the funeral mound,

together with the ashes. Then all together
the battle-crafty one buries bone and ember
on that island. The sun's sign
is renewed for him when the sky's ray,
most gleaming of gems, comes up over the sea,
the joy of noble stars, and illuminates the east.
The bird is ever bright of hue,
framed with colors about the breast in front.
Behind his head is bright green,
marvelously mixed, blended with purple.
Then his fantail is fairly divided—
some brown, some red, some cleverly
specked with shining spots.
The wings are white behind, and the neck green
below and above, and the beak lights up
like glass or gems. His jaws gleam
inside and out. His eyes by nature
are stark and in form like stones,
bright gems when smart smiths
set them in golden goblets.
Round his neck like a ring of sun
is the brightest of bracelets embroidered with feathers.
Beautiful is the belly beneath, wondrous fair,
bright and shining. His shield above,
over the bird's back, is linked with ornaments.
His shanks are grown over with scales,
his feet yellow. Every way unique,
the bird in color is like a peacock
joyfully tall, as the books tell.
He is not slow, not sluggish,
heavy or sad, as some birds,
who limp on their feathers late through the air,
but he is swift and quick and quite light,
pretty and pleasant, with markings of glory.
Eternal is the Lord who bestows on him that bliss!
Then he departs to seek out the plains,
his former dwelling out of this fatherland.

THE PHOENIX

As the bird flies, he appears to the folk,
many people throughout middle earth.
Then they assemble from the south and the north,
the east and the west, all in troops,
travel from far and near in a host of folk
where they contemplate the Creator's gift
fair in that bird as in the beginning
the true King of victory bestowed on it a better nature,
fairer in adornments than is found in the race of birds.
Then men all over the earth marvel
at its beauty and form and make it known in their books,
mark it with their hands in marble
when the day and the hour reveal to the retainers
the adornments of the one swift of flight. Then the race of birds
throngs in heaps on each half,
approach from distant parts, praise in song,
make famous the spirited one with mighty speech,
and thus they hem in the holy one in a ring,
in flight through the air. The Phoenix is in their midst,
thronged by hosts. The people behold,
admire the marvels, how the willing band,
host after host, honor the wild one,
confess it in strength and proclaim him king,
lead the loved ruler with joys,
the kingly one to his country, until the solitary one,
quick of wing, soars away so that the singing host
may not follow him. Then he finds a homeland,
the retainers' joy, out of this region of the earth.
Thus the blessed one again visits
his old home after the hour of death,
the fair earth. Birds turn back
sad-hearted from the battle hero
again toward their dwellings. Then the noble one
is now young in its home. God alone knows,
the almighty King, its own nature,
whether female or male. None of mankind
knows this except the Measurer alone,

how his ways are wondrous,
a fair, ancient law, about the bird's birth.
The blessed one may use this dwelling,
the welling springs in the woody grove,
dwell in this plain until there pass
a thousand seasons.[382] Then life ceases
for him. Through the funeral fire
he is consumed, yet he comes again,
marvelously awakened, wondrously to life.
Therefore he does not sorrow droopingly for death,
the awful agony of departing, for he always
knows new life after the flame's rush,
fresh life after the fall, when boldly
through the bird's form it becomes restored
again from the ashes, becomes young again
under the heavens' dome. In himself he is both
son and his own father[383] and ever also
heir again of his old possessions.
The Mighty One, mankind's Creator,
gave him the gift to be so marvelously
again the same as he once was,
enfolded in feathers, though fire take him.

Thus each of the blessed chooses eternal
life for himself after the long tribulation
through dark death, so that he may
enjoy the Lord's gift after his life
in lasting joy and later always dwell in glory as gift for good deeds.
This bird's nature is very like
that of the chosen ones, Christ's thanes.
It is a beacon in the city showing how they might hold bright joy
under heaven through the Father's help
in this time of trouble and steer themselves
to high glory in the upward homeland.
We have understood that the Almighty
made man and woman[384] through his wondrous
power and placed them there in the best

part of the earth, which the people's offspring
name paradise, where there was no
lack of blessedness while they wanted to keep
the word of eternity, the Holy One's speech,
in the new delight. There enmity damaged them,
the ancient enemy's envy, who offered them
the fruit of the tree,[385] so that they both tried it,
the ill-advised apple, over the command of God,
tasted the forbidden fruit. It became bitter
for them there, misery after the meal—and for their children also,
a sorrowful banquet for their sons and daughters.
Their greedy teeth were grievously
punished after the guilt. They bore God's anger,
bitter, baleful sorrow. For that their children
afterward paid the penalty, those who partook
of that morsel against the eternal decree. Therefore they must,
sad at heart, give up the joy of home
through the adder's enmity, who secretly deceived
our ancestors in the old days
by a sneaking spirit, so that they sought
a living far from there in death's den,
a baleful place. A better life was
hidden from them in darkness, and the holy plain
was fast enclosed by the enemy's deceit
for many winters until the wondrous King
opened it again by his advent
for all the holy ones, the joy of humans,
the comfort of the weary and our only hope.
Like this, as the learned ones tell us
in their words and make known in their writings,
is the bird's life, when old he leaves
home and dwelling and descends into age.
He departs weary in spirit, beset by winters,
to where he finds the high refuge of the forest
in which with twigs and weeds he winds
the noblest new dwelling place,
a nest in the woods. He has great need,

again young in body, to receive once more
life after death past the flame's fury,
be young again and visit once more
his old territory, his sun-bright seat
after the fire's bath. So our forefathers,
our ancestors, abandoned
the pleasant plain and the wood's homestead
lovely in their tracks, went on a long journey
into the hand of harms where their enemies,
the wretched monsters, often marred them.[386]
Nevertheless there were many who well obeyed
the Measurer under the heavens, holy servants,
with famous deeds, so the high King of heaven,
God, became gracious in spirit to them.
That is the high tree in which now the holy ones
keep a dwelling place, where no poison
of the old enemies may harm them in any way,
a token of hate in this troubled time.
There he works a nest for himself against every harm
with famous deeds, the Lord's fighter,
when he provides alms for the poor,
for those at a loss for wealth, and calls on the Lord,
the Father, for help. He hurries forth
from this transitory life, snuffs out sins,
murky deeds of guilt, keeps the Measurer's law
boldly in his breast, seeks out
prayer with a pure heart and bends his knee
nobly to the earth, flees every evil,
grim guilts, because of the fear of God.
Glad in spirit he desires to do the most
good deeds. God is his shield
on every occasion, the Wielder of victories,
the host's gracious giver. These are the herbs,
fruits of the flower, that the wild bird
harvests under the heavens from far and wide
for its dwelling place, where he places a nest
marvelously safe from every injury.

THE PHOENIX

Thus now in their dwelling place the Savior's soldiers
work his will in spirit and strength,
aim at famous deeds. The Almighty, Eternal One
will blessedly pay them back a reward for that.
From those plants a dwelling place will be fixed for them
in the city of glory, reward for their work,
because they held the holy teaching
hot in their hearts, welling up in their minds.
Day and night they loved the Lord,
chose in the light to believe in the beloved
over worldly wealth. Nor has he hope in joy
to own for long his short life.
Thus a blessed earl earns with courage
a heavenly home with the high King,
eternal joy until the end comes
of his numbered days when death takes him,
the slaughter-hungry warrior, mighty in weapons,
the age of everyone and in the depths of the earth
swiftly send the captured soul,
the short-lived body, where they will be for long
until the advent of fire, enfolded in earth.
Then many of the kin of men
will be led to Judgment.[387] The Father of angels,
the true King of victory, will call a synod,
the Lord of retainers, to judge with righteousness.
Then all people on earth will
rise up as the almighty King will
command, the captain of angels, with the sound
of trumpets over the wide abyss, the Savior of souls.
Dark death through the Lord's might
will end for all the blessed. The noble will throng,
move in multitudes, when this world
that has done badly will burn up in shame,
ignited in a pyre. Everyone will be
frightened in his soul when fire will burst
the transitory riches in the land. The flame will taste
the treasures of the earth, gluttonously grip

253

the apple-red gold, greedily gulp down
the adornments of the land. Then into the light
will come the pretty and pleasant sign
of this bird in the open time of this age
when all power will be proclaimed
from the burial mounds. Bones will be gathered,[388]
limbs and body together and the life's spirit
before Christ's knee. Gloriously the King
will shine with the saints from his high seat,
the beautiful jewel of wonder. Well to those who
will please God in that grim time!
There the bodies will gladly go,
made clean from sin, spirits move
into their vessels of bone when the burning ascends
high to heaven. The terrible pyre
will be hot for many when everyone,
steadfast or sinning, will seek the Measurer's judgment,
soul and body from its grave in the ground,
frightened, afraid. Fire will be in an army,
will kindle crimes. Then the blessed there will be
embraced by their deeds after the time of trial,
their own works. Thus the noble ones are
the winsome plants with whom the wild bird
set out a new nest for himself
so that suddenly it surges with fire,
is swallowed up under the sun with himself in it,
and then after the flame again accepts
life, renewal. So everyone in the race of man
enfolded in flesh shall be
unique and young again, he who here
works his own will so glory's King,
mighty at the judgment, will be mild to him.
Then the holy spirits will speak out,
the steadfast souls raise a song
clean and chosen, praise the King's glory,
voice after voice, ascend to glory,
spiced in beauty with their best deeds.

Then the souls of the people will be purified,
brightly polished through the burning of fire.
No one of the human race should reckon
that I sing a song with lying words,
write with eloquence only. Hear the wisdom
of Job's[389] songs. By the spirit's breath,
inspired in his breast, he spoke boldly,
worshiped glory and spoke this word:
"I do not scorn it with my inward thoughts,
that I choose a burial bed in my nest,
depart a wretch from here, while though weary in body,
on the long journey, covered with clay,
grieving for past deeds into the bosom of this ground
and then after death through God's gift
know new life like the bird,
the risen Phoenix after the resurrection,
joys with the Lord where the beloved choir
praises the dear one. I may never be able
to await the end of life,
of light and love. Though my body
must become moldy in the grave
for the worms' will, nevertheless the God of hosts
will save my soul after the time of death
and wake it up in wonder. Never does that hope
break for me in my breast, for I hold fast
the coming joy in the King of angels."
Thus in days of old the wise one
sang with glad spirit, God's herald,
about his arising into eternal life,
so that we might more eagerly see
the glorious token that the bright bird
signifies through the fire. He finds
the bones that are left, ashes and embers,
after the fiery burning. Later the bird
brings them in his feet to the Prince's palace,
toward the sun. There they afterward sit
for many winters made new in form,

all young again, where no one
in that land may threaten them with malice.
So now after death through divine might
souls with bodies will travel together,
beautifully adorned, most like the bird,
in blessed prosperity with the fragrance of princes,
where the steadfast sun lights up
beautiful over the hosts in the city of heaven.
Then for the steadfast souls Christ
the Savior will shine[390] high over its roofs.
Fair birds will follow him,
brightly reborn, exulting in bliss
into the cheerful home, the chosen spirits
forever and ever. There the enemy may not
harm them maliciously, the hostile, shameless one,
but they will ever live there guarded by light,
as the Phoenix bird beautiful in glory,
in God's peace. The good deeds of them all
will brightly shine in the happy home
before the face of the eternal Lord,
ever in peace, even as the sun.
There the bright crown, wondrously woven
of ark-stones, will be lifted over the heads
of each of the blessed. Their heads will beam,
gloriously covered. The King's crown
will wondrously adorn each of the steadfast
with light in that life, where the long joy
eternal and young again will never dwindle
but they will live in beauty, loaded with glory
in fair adornments with the Father of angels.
Nothing of sorrow will they have in those homes,
no disputes, no poverty, no days of trouble,
no hot hunger, no hard thirst,
no misery, no old age. The noble King
will give them every good thing. There the host of spirits
will praise the Savior and make known the might
of heaven's King, sing praise to the Prince.

THE PHOENIX

The peaceful host sings a melody with the loudest of sounds
clearly about the holy high seat of God,[391]
blissfully bless the best of rulers,
the blessed with the angels sounding in unison thus:
"Peace be to you, true God, and the power of wisdom,
and to you be thanks who sit on the glory throne
for the young gifts, every good thing.
Great, unmeasured, is the might of your strength,
high and holy! The heavens are
fairly filled, Father almighty,
with your glory of glories, your wonder,
up with the angels and together on the earth.
Grant us peace, founder of beginnings. You are Father,
almighty in the heights, Ruler of the heavens!"
Thus declare the doers of righteousness,
saved from sin, in the great city.
They confess his kingly glory. The steadfast host
sings in the sky the praise of the Emperor
to whom alone is eternal worship
for this time forth without end. Never, ever had he
beginning, origin of his blessedness. Though he was begotten
here on earth in the identity of a child
in middle earth, nevertheless the abundance of his might
dwelled holy, high over the heavens,
judgment unbreakable. Though he had to endure
the torment of death on the rood tree,
dreadful pain, on the third day
he received life again after his body's ruin
through the Father's help. Thus the Phoenix,
young in the dwellings, signifies the might of God's Son
when he awakened again from the ashes
in his life of life, full grown in his limbs.
Thus the Savior sends us help
through his body's loss, life without end,
as the bird fills his two feathered
wings with winsome sweet herbs,
fair fruits of the earth, when he must depart.

These are the words, as the writings tell us,
the song of the holy ones whose hearts
hasten to heaven, to the merciful God
in joy of joys, where they bring to the Measurer
the winsome fragrance of words and deeds
as a gift in that great creation,
in that life in light. May praise always
be given him forever and ever, and splendor of glory,
honor and authority in the upper
Kingdom of heaven. He is King in righteousness
of middle earth and the glory of his might
wound around with wonder in the beautiful city.
The author of light has allowed us[392]
to earn here on earth,
win with our good deeds gaudia in heaven,
where we may with the King maxima
seek and sit in the high seat,
live in love, light, and peace,
possess the mansions of magnanimous joy,
enjoy blessed days without end,
and sing him praise of perennial laud,
blessed with the angels. Alleluia.

The Dream of the Rood

Listen,[393] I'll tell the loveliest of dreams,
what I dreamt in the dark of night
after reason-bearers lay at rest.
It seemed I saw a wondrous tree
led aloft, wound in light,
the brightest of beams. That beacon was
all covered with gold. Gems stood
fair at the ground's surface; likewise there were five
up at the crossbeam. All beheld there the Angel of the Lord,[394]
fair through eternal decree. There was no felon's gallows there,
but holy spirits beheld him,
people of earth and all this glorious creation.

      Rare was this victory-beam, and I stained in sins,
mauled by misdeeds. I saw glory's tree,
graced with garments, shine with joy,
girded with gold. Gems had
worthily covered the tree of the wild.
Yet through that gold I could glimpse
the old war of wretched ones, for it first began
to bleed on its right side. I was all driven with sorrows;
afraid I was of the fair vision. I saw that eager beacon
change clothes and colors. Sometimes it was soaked with liquid,

drenched with a flow of blood. Sometimes it was adorned with
   treasures.
     Lying a long while I nevertheless
beheld sorrowing the Savior's tree
until I heard it utter words,
begin to speak, the best of woods:
     "It was long ago, it yet lives in my mind,
that I was felled in a forest's end,
removed from my root. Rough enemies there seized me,
made me there into a marvel, ordered me to raise up their felons.
Bullies bore me there on their shoulders until they set me on a
   hill.[395]
Enough enemies fastened me there. I saw then mankind's Master
hurry with great eagerness to climb on me.
I dare not there and then bend or burst
against the Lord's word. Then I saw the earth's
surface tremble.[396] I could have felled all those fiends, but I stood
   fast.
"Then the young hero ungirded himself, he who was God
   Almighty,
strong and stern. He ascended the wretched gallows,
mighty in the sight of many, when he wanted to redeem mankind.[397]
I trembled when the hero hugged me. I nevertheless dared not bow
   to earth,
fall to the ground's surface, but I had to stand fast.
I was raised up a cross; I raised up a powerful King,
the Lord of the heavens. I dared not lower myself.
They pierced me with dark nails; then my wounds opened wide,
gaping gashes.[398] I dared not injure any of them.
They mocked us both together. I was all dripping with blood,
smeared from that man's side when he gave up his spirit.
I have suffered much on that hill,
evil events: I saw the God of hosts
sorely stretch out. Darkness covered up[399]
with clouds the Creator's corpse,
the shining brightness. A shadow went forth,

wan under the clouds. All creation wept,
spoke the king's fall: Christ was on the cross.
    "But eager ones came there from afar
to that Prince. I perceived it all.
Sorely was I driven with sorrows, yet I bowed down into the war-
      riors' hands,[400]
humble, with great zeal. They took there the almighty God,
raised him out of that heavy torment. Then the troops forsook me,
standing soaked in blood: I was all wounded with arrows.
They laid down the limb-weary one, stood about at his body's head.
They beheld there heaven's Lord, and he rested himself awhile,
weary after the great war. Then they began to work him a grave,
the warriors in the slayer's sight. They carved it from bright stone;
they set in it the works of victories. Then they began to sing a woe-
      ful song,
wretched in the eventide. Then they wished to journey again,
weary ones, away from the famous Lord; he rested then in a very
      small band.
Yet we stood steady a good while,
weeping there until a voice went up
of warriors. The corpse went cold,
the fair life-house. Then someone began to fell us
all to earth: that was a fearsome fate!
He covered us in a deep pit, but the Lord's companions,
his friends, found me there,
girded me with gold and silver.[401]
    "Now you may hear, beloved hero,
how I had to abide the deeds of bullies,
sorrowful cares. The time has now come
that people on this plain far and wide
and all this wondrous creation worship me,
pray to this sign. On me God's Son
suffered a time; thus glorious I now tower
under the heavens, and I may heal
all and some of those in awe of me.
Once I was turned into the hardest of torments,

261

loathsome to all, before I opened up
life's way to them, to those wielding speech.

"Hear me! Then glory's prince honored me
over all trees of the wood, heaven's Warden,
just as he did his mother, Mary herself;[402]
the almighty God gave her honor
for all people over all other women.

"Now I beseech you, my beloved hero,
that you proclaim this dream to the people,
reveal with words that it is wonder's tree
on which for mankind's many sins
and Adam's deeds of old almighty God suffered.
There he partook of death, yet with his great power
the Lord rose again to restore mankind.
Then he went up to heaven. He will come here
to this middle earth to seek mankind
on Doomsday,[403] the dear Lord himself,
almighty God, his angels with him,
and he will then judge, he who wields judgment,
all and some, according to their earnings,
which earlier they found in this fleeting life.
Nor may anyone be unafraid there
of the word that the Wielder says.
He will ask before the multitude where that man might be
who wished for the Lord's name to know
bitter death, just as he earlier did on that beam.
But they will then be afraid, and few will think
what they will start to say to Christ.
Nor is there any need for one to be afraid,
who before bore in breast the best of beams,
but through that cross each soul shall seek
a kingdom away from the world's ways,
he who wishes to dwell with the Wielder."

Then I prayed to the beam in a blithe mood,
with great zeal, there where I was all alone,
in a small company. My spirit was
pushed toward an outward path. I felt

many pangs of longing. It is now my life's hope
that I will find the victory-wood
alone more often than other men,
worship it well. My will for that
is great in my spirit, and my safety is
right in that cross. I have few friends
powerful on earth, since they have departed
from the world's joys, sought wonder's King,
and live now in heaven with the high Father,
dwell in glory. And every day
I look for that time when the Lord's cross,
which I once beheld here on earth,
will fetch me in this fleeting life
and bring me where the bliss is great,
joy in heaven, where the Lord's hosts are
seated at the banquet. Endless bliss is there.
It will set me where forever I will
dwell in wonders, taste well
happiness with the holy. May the Lord be my friend,
he who earlier suffered here on earth,
on this gallows tree for our trespasses.
He redeemed us and returned our lives,
gave us a heavenly home. Hope was renewed
among blessings with bliss for those who suffered burning there.
The Son, mighty and successful, was victorious
in that quest, when he came with many,
a host of spirits into God's glorious kingdom,
the almighty ruler, to the bliss of angels
and all the saints who earlier dwelt in glory
in heaven, when their Creator came,
almighty Lord, back to the land of his home.

Maxims II

A king shall hold a kingdom. Cities are seen from afar,
cunning craft of giants,[404] those that are on this earth,
wondrous work of masonry. Wind is swiftest aloft.
Thunder at times is loudest. The glories of Christ are large.
Fate is quickest. Winter is coldest,
Lent the frostiest; it's longest cold.
Summer is the prettiest in sunshine: the sun is hottest,
the harvest most blessed; it brings to heroes
the summer's fruits that God sends them.
Truth is clearest, treasure dearest,
gold for everyone, and the old one wisest,
experienced in past years, he who before has done much.
Woe is wondrously sticky. Clouds sail.
A young prince must prepare for war
good companions and give rings.
Courage must live in earls. The edge must
abide in battle against the helmet. The hawk must abide
wild on the glove.[405] The wolf must be in the grove,
wretched lonely one. The boar must be in the woods,
great in tooth. The good one must stay in his country
to build homes. The spear must be in the hand,
a javelin worked with gold. The gem must be in the ring,
standing steep and curved. The stream must mingle
its waves in the mere's water. The mast must be on the ship,

hanging a sail-yard. The sword must be on one's chest,
a mighty iron. The dragon must be in the barrow,
old, exulting in treasures. The fish must be in the water
bringing forth its kind.[406] The king must be in the hall,
giving bracelets. The bear must be on the heath,
old and awful. The river must flow
down in a gray flood. An army must march
together in a glorious troop. Faith must live in an earl,
wisdom in a man. In the country a wood
must bloom with blossoms. On the earth a hill
must stand green. God must be in the heavens,
the Judge of deeds. A door must be in the hall,
the wide building's mouth. A boss must be on a shield,
fast defense of fingers. A bird must sport
above in the air. In a deep pool a salmon
must dart like a shot. Showers must be in the heavens,
mixed with wind, coming into this world.
A thief must go about in dark weather. A troll must dwell in the fen,
alone within the land. With secret skill a lady must
visit her female friend—if she does not want to cause it among the
     people
that someone buys her with bracelets. The sea must flow with salt,
cloud and ocean about every land,
flowing with mighty floods. On the earth cattle
must multiply and beget offspring. A star must shine
clearly in the heavens, just as the Measurer commanded.[407]
Good must oppose evil, youth age,
life must oppose death, light darkness,
army against army, enemies against others,
foe against foe, fighting about the land,
stirring up sin. A clever person must consider
the strife of this world, condemn criminals to hang,
fairly make recompense for the faults they committed
against mankind. The Measurer alone knows
whither the soul must wander afterward,
and all those spirits who come and go before God
waiting for judgment after the day of death

into the Father's embrace. The future is
hidden and secret. Only the Lord understands it,
the Father who redeems. No one may return
here under our roofs who may relate to the people
here in truth what the Measurer's land is like,
the settlements of the victory people where they themselves dwell.

Notes to the Introduction

1. For the events leading up to Edward's death, see Peter Hunter Blair, *An Introduction to Anglo-Saxon England* (Cambridge: Cambridge University Press, 1959, 1977), pp. 104–15; for a comprehensive study of Edward's reign, see Frank Barlow, *Edward the Confessor* (Berkeley and Los Angeles: University of California Press, 1970).

2. For Halley's Comet, see Nigel Calder, *The Comet Is Coming* (New York: Viking Press, 1980), pp. 9–26; and John North, *The Norton History of Astronomy and Cosmology* (New York: Norton, 1995), pp. 394–95.

3. See David M. Wilson, *The Bayeaux Tapestry: The Complete Tapestry in Color with an Introduction, Description, and Commentary* (New York: Alfred A. Knopf, 1985). The comet is depicted in this volume on Plate 32.

4. For a thorough though controversial account of that ascendency from the Celtic point of view, see John Morris, *The Age of Arthur: A History of the British Isles from 350 to 650* (London: Orion Books, 1973). See also John Davies, *A History of Wales* (London: Penguin, 1993), pp. 44–79. For the Anglo-Saxon point of view, see Blair, *Introduction*, pp. 1–54. For the effect of the migration period on later Old English literature, see Nicholas Howe, *Migration and Mythology in Anglo-Saxon England* (New Haven, Conn.: Yale University Press, 1989).

5. See Michael Winterbottom, trans., *Gildas: The Ruin of Britain and Other Works* (Totowa, N.J.: Roman and Littlefield, 1978). For an assessment of Gildas's *oeuvre*, see W. F. Bolton, *Anglo-Latin Literature* (Princeton, N.J.: Princeton University Press, 1967), pp. 27–37.

6. Winterbottom, *Gildas*, p. 14.

7. Winterbottom, *Gildas*, p. 15.

8. Winterbottom, *Gildas*, p. 26.

9. For the demographics and geography of the Anglo-Saxon kingdoms, see David Hill, *An Atlas of Anglo-Saxon England* (Toronto: University of Toronto Press, 1981).

10. See Leo Sherley-Price, trans., *Bede: A History of the English Church and People*, revised by R. E. Latham (Harmondsworth: Penguin, 1955, 1968), pp. 99–100.

11. See Paul Meyvaert, "Diversity within Unity, a Gregorian Theme," *Heythrop Journal* 4 (1963): 143.

12. Sherley-Price, *Bede*, p. 127.

13. For a study of the Conversion, see Henry Mayr-Harting, *The Coming of Christianity to Anglo-Saxon England*, 3d ed. (University Park: Pennsylvania State University Press, 1991).

14. For Anglo-Saxon paganism, see Blair, *Introduction*, pp. 120–24; and Karen Louise Jolly, *Popular Religion in Late Saxon England* (Chapel Hill: University of North Carolina Press, 1966).

15. For Celtic paganism, see Gerhard Herms, *The Celts* (New York: St. Martin's Press, 1976), pp. 150–63; Peter Berresford Ellis, *The Druids* (Grand Rapids, Mich.: Eerdmans, 1994); Proinsias MacCana, *Celtic Mythology* (London: Hamelyn, 1970); and Anne Ross, *Pagan Celtic Britain: Studies in Iconographical Tradition* (Chicago: Academy Chicago Publishers, 1967, 1996). For the wider contact between the Western church and European paganism, see J. N. Hilgarth, ed., *Christianity and Paganism, 350–750* (Philadelphia: University of Pennsylvania Press, 1969).

16. For a debate over the authenticity of this letter, see Dom Suso Brechter, *Die Quellen zur Angel-sachsenmission Gregors des Grossen* (Munster, Westphalia: Aschendorff, 1941), pp. 13–111, who rejects Gregorian authorship; Margaret Deansley and Paul Grosjean, S.J., "The Canterbury *Editio* of the Answers of Pope Gregory I to St. Augustine," *Journal of Ecclesiastical History* 10 (1959): 1–49, who think it contains some authentically Gregorian material; and Paul Meyvaert, "Bede's Text of the *Libellus Responsionum* of Gregory the Great to Augustine of Canterbury," pp. 15–33 in Peter Clemoes and Kathleen Hughes, eds., *England Before the Conquest: Studies in Primary Sources Presented to Dorothy Whitelock* (Cambridge: Cambridge University Press, 1971), who convincingly reasserts its authenticity. See also Meyvaert, "Diversity Within Unity," 142–43; Paul Meyvaert, "Les Responsiones de S. Grégoire le Grand à S. Augustin de Cantorbéry," *Revue d'Histoire Ecclesiastique* 54 (1959): 879–94; and Margaret Deansley, "The Capitular Text of the *Responsiones* of Pope Gregory I to St. Augustine," *Journal of Ecclesiastical History* 11 (1961): 231–34.

17. Sherley-Price, *Bede*, p. 86.

18. Sherley-Price, *Bede*, Book II, Chapter 2.

19. Sherley-Price, *Bede*, Book III, Chapter 4.

20. See Peter Biller and A. J. Minnis, eds., *Handling Sin: Confession in the Middle Ages* (Rochester, N.Y.: York Medieval Press, 1998); Rosamond Pierce, "The 'Frankis' Penitentials," *Studies in Church History* 2 (1975): 31–39; Robert Cecil Mortimer, *The Origins of Private Penance in the Western Church* (Oxford: Clarendon Press, 1939); Ludwig Bieler, "The Irish Penitentials: Their Religious and Social Background," *Studia Patristica* 8 (1966): 329–39; Oscar D. Watkins, *A History of Penance*, 2 vols. (1920; reprinted New York: Burt Franklin, 1961); John T. McNeill, *A History of the Cure of Souls* (New York: Harper & Row, 1951); Thomas P. Oakley, "The Origins of Irish Penitential Discipline," *Catholic Historical Review* 19 (1933–34): 320–32; Oakley, "Celtic Penance: Its Sources, Affiliations, and Influence," *Irish Ecclesiastical Review* 52 (1938): 198–264. For the important penitentials themselves, see John J. McNeill and Helena M. Gamer, *Medieval Handbooks of Penance* (New York: Columbia University Press, 1938). For the influence of the doctrine of penance on Old English literature, see Robert C. Rice, "The Penitential Motif in Cynewulf's *Fates of the Apostles* and in His Epilogues," *Anglo-Saxon England* 6 (1977): 105–19; Allen J. Frantzen, *The Literature of Penance in Anglo-Saxon England* (New Brunswick, N.J.: Rutgers University Press, 1983); and Robert Boenig, *Saint and Hero: Andreas and Medieval Doctrine* (Lewisburg, Pa.: Bucknell University Press, 1991), pp. 30–54.

21. For a recent thorough investigation of Theodore's life and contribution to English Church history, see the various essays in the volume honoring the thirteen-hundredth anniversary of Theodore's death in 690, Michael Lapidge, ed., *Archbishop Theodore: Commemorative Studies on His Life and Influence* (Cambridge: Cambridge University Press, 1995). Of particular importance in this volume are the following essays: Lapidge, "The Career of Archbishop Theodore" (pp. 1–29); Henry Chadwick, "Theodore, the English Church and the Monothelete Controversy" (pp. 88–95); Thomas Charles-Edwards, "The Penitential of Theodore and the *Iudicia Theodori*" (pp. 222–35); and Christopher Hohler, "Theodore and the Liturgy" (pp. 222–35). For the importance of the school Theodore and his companion Hadrian established at Canterbury, see Michael Lapidge, "The School of Theodore and Hadrian," *Anglo-Saxon England* 15 (1986): 45–72; and Michael Lapidge, "The Study of Greek at the School of Canterbury in the Seventh Century," pp. 169–94 in Michael W. Herren, ed., *The Sacred Nectar of the Greeks: The Study of Greek in the West*

in the Early Middle Ages (London: King's College, University of London, 1988).

22. For Wilfred's career and troubles, see D. P. Kirby, ed., *Saint Wilfred at Hexham* (Newcastle upon Tyne: Oriel Press, 1974); see also Bolton, *Anglo-Latin*, pp. 66–68; and Trent Foley, *Images of Sanctity in Eddius Stephanus'* Life of Bishop Wilfred, *an Early English Saint's Life* (Lewiston, N.Y.: Edwin Mellen, 1992).

23. For Benedict Biscop, see Bolton, *Anglo-Latin*, pp. 62–66.

24. For a discussion of the knowledge of Greek in Anglo-Saxon England, see Mary Catherine Bodden, "The Preservation and Transmission of Greek in Early England," pp. 53–63 in Paul E. Szarmach, ed., *Sources in Anglo-Saxon Culture* (Kalamazoo, Mich.: Medieval Institute Publications, 1986); and Boenig, *Saint and Hero*, pp. 23–25.

25. For a collection of Aldhelm's works in translation and a study of them, see Michael Lapidge and Michael Herren, trans., *Aldhelm: The Prose Works* (Ipswich: D. S. Brewer, 1979). For an assessment of Aldhelm's *oeuvre*, see Bolton, *Anglo-Latin*, pp. 68–100.

26. See Lapidge and Herren, *Aldhelm*, p. 18.

27. For Bede, see Peter Hunter Blair, *The World of Bede* (Cambridge: Cambridge University Press, 1970, 1990); and Bolton, *Anglo-Latin*, pp. 101–85.

28. For Alcuin, see W. F. Bolton, *Alcuin and Beowulf* (New Brunswick, N.J.: Rutgers University Press, 1978), pp. 11–94.

29. Ep. 183.22, *Quid Hinieldus cum Christo?* For analysis of this remark, see W. F. Bolton, *Alcuin and Beowulf*, pp. 100–103; and Stanley B. Greenfield, *A Critical History of Old English Literature* (New York: New York University Press, 1965), p. 1. For a similar letter of Alcuin to Higebald that does not cite the monks' interest in heroic literature as a contributing cause to their difficulties, see Colin Chase, ed., *Two Alcuin Letter-Books* (Toronto: University of Toronto Press, 1975), pp. 50–51.

30. See Morris, *Age*, pp. 381–405.

31. For the Vikings, see John Marsden, *The Fury of the Northmen* (New York: St. Martin's Press, 1993); Blair, *Introduction*, pp. 55–115; and Alfred P. Smyth, *King Alfred the Great* (Oxford: Oxford University Press, 1995), pp. 51–148.

32. Quoted in Marsden, *Fury*, p. 139.

33. A. H. Smith, ed., *The Parker Chronicle, 832–900* (London: Metheuen, 1935), pp. 25–26; the translation is my own.

34. See Marsden, *Fury*, p. 148.

35. See Smyth, *Alfred*, pp. 3–50.

36. See Michael Swanton, *Anglo-Saxon Prose* (London: Dent, 1975), pp. 30–31.

37. See Henry Sweet, ed., *King Alfred's West Saxon Version of Gregory's Pastoral Care*, Early English Text Society 45, 50 (London: Oxford University Press, 1871, 1872; reprinted 1958).

38. See Thomas Miller, ed., *The Old English Version of Bede's Ecclesiastical History of the English People*, Early English Text Society 95, 96, 110, 111 (London: Oxford University Press, 1883; reprinted 1959).

39. See Henry Sweet, ed., *King Alfred's Orosius*, Early English Text Society 79 (London: Oxford University Press, 1883; reprinted 1959).

40. See Dom David Knowles, *The Monastic Order in England: A History of Its Development from the Times of St. Dunstan to the Fourth Lateran Council, 940–1216*, 2d ed. (Cambridge: Cambridge University Press, 1963), pp. 31–56; Blair, *Introduction*, pp. 173–78; and Cora E. Lutz, *Schoolmasters of the Tenth Century* (Hamden, Conn.: Archon Books, 1977), pp. 23–40.

41. For this linguistic feature, see Robert Boenig, "Very Sharp/Unsharp, Unpeace/Firm Peace: Morphemic Ambiguity in *Beowulf*," *Neophilologus* 76 (1992): 275–82.

42. See D. G. Scragg, ed., *The Battle of Maldon* (Manchester: Manchester University Press, 1981).

43. For Edward's life, see Barlow, *Edward the Confessor*.

44. Residual resistance continued longest in the fenlands around Ely under the leadership of a minor thane named Hereward. See Victor Head, *Hereward* (Phoenix Mill, Stroud, Gloucestershire, U.K.: Sutton Publishing, 1995).

45. For broad surveys of this literature and its artistic merits, see Greenfield, *Critical History*; C. L. Wrenn, *A Study of Old English Literature* (New York: Norton, 1967); and Kenneth Sisam, *Studies in the History of Old English Literature* (Oxford: Clarendon Press, 1962).

46. The dating of *Beowulf* has been much under debate. See Colin Chase, ed., *The Dating of Beowulf* (Toronto: University of Toronto Press, 1981); Kevin S. Kiernan, *Beowulf and the Beowulf Manuscript* (New Brunswick, N.J.: Rutgers University Press, 1984); and R. D. Fulk, *A History of Old English Meter* (Philadelphia: University of Pennsylvania Press, 1992).

47. See Thomas Pyles and John Algeo, *The Origins and Development of the English Language*, 3d ed. (New York: Harcourt, Brace, Jovanovich, 1982), p. 109.

48. See, for instance, *The Riming Poem*, contained in the Exeter Book.

49. For a convenient tabulation of Sievers's five types, see Frederic G. Cassidy and Richard N. Ringler, eds., *Bright's Old English Grammar and Reader*, 3d ed. (New York: Holt, Rinehart, and Winston, 1971), pp. 275–87.

50. See John C. Pope, *The Rhythm of Beowulf*, 2d ed. (New Haven, Conn.: Yale University Press, 1966); and Robert P. Creed, "A New Approach to the Rhythm of *Beowulf*," *Publications of the Modern Language Association* 81 (1966): 23–33.

51. See John Leyerle, "The Interlace Structure of *Beowulf*," *University of Toronto Quarterly* 37 (1967): 1–17.

52. For examples of this visual art, see Carl Nordenfalk, *Celtic and Anglo-Saxon Painting* (New York: George Brazillier, 1977).

53. For the literary implications of the appositional style, see Fred C. Robinson, *Beowulf and the Appositive Style* (Knoxville: University of Tennessee Press, 1987).

54. Margaret Schlauch, "The 'Dream of the Rood' as Prosopopoeia," pp. 23–34 in *Essays and Studies in Honor of Carelton Brown* (New York: New York University Press, 1940).

55. For runes, see R. I. Page, *Runes* (Berkeley and Los Angeles: University of California Press, 1987).

56. See G. S. Kirk, *The Songs of Homer* (Cambridge: Cambridge University Press, 1962), pp. 56–69, 280–81.

57. E. Talbot Donaldson, trans., *Beowulf: A New Prose Translation* (New York: Norton, 1966), p. 3.

58. R. K. Gordon, trans., *Anglo-Saxon Poetry* (London: Dent, 1926), p. 78.

59. For the records of Sutton Hoo, see Rupert Bruce-Mitford, *The Sutton Hoo Ship-Burial*, 3 vols. (London: British Museum, 1975–83).

60. Robert Boenig, "The Anglo-Saxon Harp," *Speculum* 71 (1996): 290–320.

61. Albert B. Lord, *The Singer of Tales* (Cambridge, Mass.: Harvard University Press, 1960).

62. See, for example, Francis P. Magoun, Jr., "The Oral-Formulaic Character of Anglo-Saxon Narrative Poetry," *Speculum* 28 (1953): 446–67.

63. See, for instance, Katherine O'Brien O'Keeffe, *Visible Song: Transitional Literacy in Old English Verse* (Cambridge: Cambridge University Press, 1990); and John Miles Foley, "Literary Art and Oral Tradition in Old English and Serbian Poetry," *Anglo-Saxon England* 12 (1983): 183–214. Compare Seth Lerer, *Literacy and Power in Anglo-Saxon Literature* (Lincoln, Nebraska: University of Nebraska Press, 1991).

64. In 1624 a divine named William Guild published Ælfric's sermon as polemic in trying to prove that the new Anglican doctrine of the eucharist was also the one held in the early English Church. See Boenig, *Saint and Hero*, pp. 61–62.

65. For discussion of the eucharistic controversies of the early Middle Ages, see Boenig, *Saint and Hero*, pp. 55–77; Charles E. Sheedy, C.S.C., *The Eucharistic Controversy of the Eleventh Century Against the Background of Pre-Scholastic Theology* (Washington, D.C.: Catholic University Press of America, 1947); and Gary Macy, *The Theologies of the Eucharist in the Early Scholastic Period* (Oxford: Clarendon Press, 1984).

66. For Aldhelm's prose style, see Bolton, *Anglo-Latin*, pp. 68–100.

67. For Ælfric's prose style, see Greenfield, *Critical History*, pp. 50–51.

68. Dorothy Whitelock, "Archbishop Wulfstan, Homilist and Statesman," *Transactions of the Royal Historical Society*, 4th Series 24 (1942): 27.

69. Dorothy Bethurum, *The Homilies of Wulfstan* (Oxford: Clarendon Press, 1957), p. 28.

70. J. P. Kinard, *A Study of Wulfstan's Homilies* (Baltimore: John Murphy, 1897), p. 19.

71. Angus McIntosh, "Wulfstan's Prose," *Proceedings of the British Academy* 35 (1949): 117–18.

72. Bernard McGinn, "The End of the World and the Beginning of Christendom," pp. 58–89 in Malcolm Bull, ed., *Apocalypse Theory and the Ends of the World* (Oxford: Blackwell, 1995), p. 58. For a discussion of eschatology in the context of Old English sermonic literature, see Milton McCormick Gatch, "Eschatology in the Anonymous Old English Homilies," *Traditio* 21 (1965): 117–65.

73. See McGinn, "Beginning of Christendom," p. 69; and Mayr-Harting, *Coming of Christianity*, p. 217.

74. See McGinn, "Beginning of Christendom," pp. 66–67.

75. For the theological implications of Christ the Victor, see Gustav Aulen, *Christus Victor* (New York: Macmillan, 1951).

76. For the sources of *The Phoenix*, see Michael J. B. Allen and Daniel G. Calder trans., *Sources and Analogues of Old English Poetry: The Major Latin Texts in Translation* (Cambridge: D. S. Brewer, 1976), pp. 113–20.

77. Allen and Calder, *Sources and Analogues*, pp. 118–19.

78. See, for instance, Greenfield, *Critical History*, p. 184; N. F. Blake, "The Form of *The Phoenix*," pp. 268–78 in Martin Stevens and Jerome

Mandel, eds., *Old English Literature: Twenty-two Analytical Essays* (Lincoln: University of Nebraska Press, 1968), p. 275; and Alvin A. Lee, *The Guest-Hall of Eden: Four Essays on the Design of Old English Poetry* (New Haven, Conn.: Yale University Press, 1972), p. 120.

    79. Allen and Calder, *Sources and Analogues*, p. 114.

    80. See Allen and Calder, *Sources and Analogues*, p. 114.

    81. See Allen and Calder, *Sources and Analogues*, pp. 118–19.

    82. Quoted in Bernard McGinn, *Antichrist: Two Thousand Years of the Human Fascination with Evil* (San Francisco: HarperSanFrancisco, 1994), p. 98.

    83. See McGinn, "Beginning of Christendom," p. 60.

    84. See McGinn, "Beginning of Christendom," pp. 62–63.

    85. See McGinn, "Beginning of Christendom," pp. 70–71.

    86. See McGinn, "Beginning of Christendom," pp. 71–72.

    87. For an account of the reception of this text, see Rodney L. Petersen, *Preaching in the Last Days: The Theme of "Two Witnesses" in the Sixteenth and Seventeenth Centuries* (New York: Oxford University Press, 1993), pp. 28–58.

    88. See Bernard McGinn, ed., *Apocalyptic Spirituality* (New York: Paulist Press, 1979), pp. 81–96. Though Wulfstan shows little interest in the mythic aspects of Antichrist in his *Sermo Lupi ad Anglos*, an Old English translation of Adso's work, which emphasizes the immanence of Antichrist's coming, was possibly prepared for him. See Richard K. Emmerson, "From Epistola to Sermo: The Old English Version of Adso's Libellus de Antichristo," *Journal of English and Germanic Philology* 82 (1983): 1–10.

    89. See Herbert W. Benario, trans., *Tacitus: Agricola, Germany, Dialogue on Orators* (New York: Bobbs-Merril, 1967), p. 47. For an analysis of the ethical injunction to die with one's lord in battle, see Rosemary Woolf, "The Ideal of Men Dying with their Lord in the *Germania* and in *The Battle of Maldon*," *Anglo-Saxon England* 5 (1976): 63–81.

    90. Scragg, *Battle of Maldon*, p. 67.

    91. See Mayr-Harting, *Coming of Christianity*, Chapter 13, "Saints and Heroes," pp. 220–39.

    92. Mayr-Harting, *Coming of Christianity*, p. 221.

    93. For a translation of Felix's Life of Guthlac, see Clinton Albertson, S.J., *Anglo-Saxon Saints and Heroes* (New York: Fordham University Press, 1967), pp. 165–222.

    94. See Robert C. Gregg, trans., *Athanasius: The Life of Antony and the Letter to Marcellinus* (New York: Paulist Press, 1980).

95. See Mayr-Harting, *Coming of Christianity*, pp. 229–39.

96. See Robert Boenig, *The Acts of Andrew in the Country of the Cannibals: Translations from the Greek, Latin, and Old English* (New York: Garland, 1991), pp. xxxiii-xxxiv.

97. André Vauchez, *The Spirituality of the Medieval West from the Eighth to the Twelfth Century*, trans. Colette Friedlander (Kalamazoo, Mich.: Cistercian Publications, 1993), p. 59.

98. Albertson, *Anglo-Saxon Saints and Heroes*, p. 20.

99. For an analysis of *Heliand* that emphasizes this idea, see G. Ronald Murphy, S.J., *The Saxon Savior: The Germanic Transformation of the Gospel in the Ninth-Century Heliand* (New York: Oxford University Press, 1989), especially pp. 11–32.

100. See Josef A. Jungmann, *Pastoral Liturgy* (London: Challoner Publications, 1962), Part I.

101. Vauchez, *Spirituality*, pp. 15–16.

102. Vauchez, *Spirituality*, p. 16.

103. See Vauchez, *Spirituality*, pp. 40–44; see also Barbara H. Rosenwein, *Rhinoceros Bound: Cluny in the Tenth Century* (Philadelphia: University of Pennsylvania Press, 1982), pp. 89–93.

104. See Knowles, *Monastic Order*, pp. 31–56.

105. For the importance of books for the Anglo-Saxon liturgy and a useful classification of them, see Helmut Gneuss, "Liturgical Books in Anglo-Saxon England and their Old English Terminology," pp. 91–142 in Michael Lapidge and Helmut Gneuss, eds., *Learning and Literature in Anglo-Saxon England: Studies Presented to Peter Clemoes on the Occasion of His Sixty-Fifth Birthday* (Cambridge: Cambridge University Press, 1985).

106. For English translations of these lives, see Albertson, *Anglo-Saxon Saints and Heroes*.

107. For the use of the Vulgate as opposed to the Old Latin version of the Bible in Anglo-Saxon England, see Richard Marsden, "Theodore's Bible: The Pentateuch"; and Patrick McGurk, "Theodore's Bible: The Gospels," pp. 236–54 and 255–60, respectively, in Lapidge, *Theodore*.

108. For the history and nature of liturgical troping, see Willi Apel, *Gregorian Chant* (Bloomington: Indiana University Press, 1958, 1990), pp. 429–42; for the Anglo-Saxon manuscripts containing tropes, termed *tropers*, see Gneuss, "Liturgical Books," pp. 104–6.

109. For the Winchester troper, compiled in Winchester sometime between A.D. 990 and 1010, see Apel, *Gregorian Chant*, p. 449n; and David Fenwick Wilson, *Music of the Middle Ages: Style and Structure* (New York: Macmillan, 1990), pp. 103–4.

110. This example, taken from Kyrie II in the *Liber Usualis*, is given as an example of troping by Richard Hoppin, *Medieval Music* (New York: Norton, 1978), p. 151.

111. For an analysis of this preface, see Suzanne C. Hagedorn, "Received Wisdom: The Reception History of Alfred's Preface to the *Pastoral Care*," pp. 86–107 in Allen Frantzen and John D. Niles, eds., *Anglo-Saxonism and the Construction of Social Identity* (Gainesville: University Press of Florida, 1997).

112. For a comprehensive case against using linguistic means to date Old English poems, see Ashley Crandell Amos, *Linguistic Means of Determining the Date of Old English Literary Texts* (Cambridge, Mass: Medieval Academy of America, 1980); for a partial rehabilitation of those means, see Fulk, *History*.

113. See John C. Pope, *The Homilies of Ælfric: A Supplementary Collection*, 2 vols. Early English Text Society 259, 260 (London: Oxford University Press, 1967, 1968).

114. The linkage of pagan gods and goddesses with humans who purportedly lived in the remote past is a theory known as *euhemerism*, named after its first proponent, Euhemeros, a Greek philosopher who flourished about the year 300 B.C.; his work *Sacred History*, extant only in fragments, contains this theory.

115. For this work see Antonette dePaolo Healey, *The Old English Vision of St. Paul* (Cambridge, Mass.: Medieval Academy of America, 1978).

116. For a summary of the various attempts at solving this vexing problem as well as this theory, see Boenig, *Saint and Hero*, pp. 74–77.

Notes to the Texts

Blickling Homily X: The End of the World

1. This list is a good indication of the oral nature of this, and by extension, other Old English sermons and homilies.

2. See Psalm 34:17: "When the righteous cry for help, the LORD hears and delivers them out of all their troubles." This and subsequent quotations from the Bible are taken from the Revised Standard translation, unless otherwise noted. Bible passages embedded in the Old English texts, however, are translated directly from the Anglo-Saxon authors' renderings.

3. The signs of the end times are troubles and afflictions for the righteous. The Apocalypse, of course, recounts such difficulty at great length. The reference here, though, is likely to Matthew 24:21–22: "For then there will be great tribulation, such as has not been from the beginning of the world until now, no, and never will be. And if those days had not been shortened, no human being would be saved...."

4. Matthew 24:7: "For nation will rise against nation and kingdom against kingdom, and there will be famines and earthquakes in various places."

5. Matthew 24:12: "And because wickedness is multiplied, most men's love will grow cold."

6. These good deeds are enumerated in Matthew 25:31–46—feeding the hungry, giving water to the thirsty, welcoming the stranger, clothing the naked, and visiting the sick and those in prison.

7. Matthew 24:14: "And this gospel...will be preached throughout the whole world...and then the end will come."

8. This is possibly a reference to either Matthew 10:34: "I have not come to bring peace, but a sword," or Revelation 1:16: "...from his [the glorified Christ] mouth issued a sharp two-edged sword...."

9. These phrases are echoes of the Nicean Creed.

10. Compare Matthew 6:19–21: "Do not lay up for yourselves treasures on earth, where moth and rust consume and where thieves break in and steal, but lay up for yourselves treasures in heaven, where neither moth nor rust consumes and where thieves do not break in and steal. For where your treasure is, there will your heart be also."

11. The address of the corpse to the passerby is an old commonplace among writers of medieval exhortations to repent. Its origins are likely in Genesis 3:19, God's curse of Adam after the Fall: "...you are dust and to dust you shall return." In the Middle English period, this commonplace developed into the ubiquitous "Earth upon Earth" poems. See Hilda M. R. Murray, ed., *Erthe upon Erthe, Printed from Twenty-four Manuscripts*, Early English Text Society 141 (London: Oxford University Press, 1911).

Blickling Homily XIV: The Birth of John the Baptist

12. The feast of St. John the Baptist is June 24, traditionally known as Midsummer's Day—a survival of pagan solstice celebrations.

13. The birth of John the Baptist is recounted in Luke 1:5–24, 57–80.

14. The custom in the church, except in the two instances the homilist mentions, was to honor saints on the anniversaries of their death.

15. Luke 7:28: "I tell you, among those born of women none is greater than John; yet he who is least in the kingdom of God is greater than he."

16. Luke 7:26.

17. Luke 1:13–17.

18. Galatians 2:20.

19. This encounter is narrated in Luke 1:39–56.

20. There is a gap in the text here; the words in brackets, of course, are supplied by the context.

21. See John 1:23: "He [John] said, 'I am the voice of one crying in the wilderness, "Make straight the way of the Lord," as the prophet Isaiah said.'" The reference is to Isaiah 40:3.

22. *Angel* originally meant "messenger" in Greek.

23. There is a gap in the text here; the missing words are supplied by context.

24. Luke 3:7. See also Matthew 3:7, 12:34, and 23:33.

25. There is a gap in the text here; the missing words are supplied by the original passage in the Bible.

26. Compare Luke 9:3: "And he said to them, 'Take nothing for your journey, no staff, nor bag, nor bread, nor money; and do not have two tunics.'"

27. Matthew 24:39.

Blickling Homily XVII: The Dedication of St. Michael's Church

28. The feast of St. Michael the Archangel, otherwise known as Michaelmas, is September 29. He is mentioned in Daniel (10:13, 12:1) as the guardian of Israel and in both Jude (verse 9) and, more important, Revelation 12:7–9, as an adversary of Satan: "Now war arose in heaven, Michael and his angels fighting against the dragon; and the dragon and his angels fought, but they were defeated and there was no longer any place for them in heaven. And the great dragon was thrown down, that ancient serpent, who is called the Devil and Satan, the deceiver of the whole world—he was thrown down to the earth, and his angels were thrown down with him." The legend of Michael's appearance on Mt. Gargano dates to the fifth century. For more information about his cult, see the entry under his name in David Hugh Farmer, *The Oxford Dictionary of Saints*, 3d ed. (Oxford: Oxford University Press, 1992).

29. The cultus of Archangel Michael was particularly associated with the dedication of churches. Not only is he associated with the church described in this piece (which was founded in the fifth century in southeast Italy), but the day of his feast was originally the day another church (this one near Rome) was dedicated to him. In England many churches were named after him, numbering 689 by the end of the Middle Ages. Perhaps the sermon was delivered at the consecration of one of them.

30. Perhaps an allegorical interpretation of Michael's protection of the bull is in order. Michael is protector of Israel, the bull in the wilderness is Israel itself as it searches for the promised land; Garganus and his men would then allegorically represent Pharaoh and his army. See Daniel 12:1: "At that time shall arise Michael, the great prince who has charge of your people."

31. The archangel Michael was associated with military exploits

279

because of his role in defeating the dragon in Revelation 12:7–9. See note 28, above.

32. This mountain storm perhaps echoes that on Mt. Sinai, where Moses ascended to receive the Law. See Exodus 19:16: "On the morning of the third day there were thunders and lightnings, and a thick cloud upon the mountain...."

33. It is not the prophet but the psalmist who utters these words from Psalm 104:4. The Vulgate misconstrues the Hebrew, a more accurate translation (RSV) being, "who makest the winds [= *spiritus*] thy messengers [=*angelos*], fire and flame thy ministers." But compare Hebrews 1:7: "Of the angels he says, 'Who makes his angels winds, and his servants flames of fire.'"

34. This is a tithe of the normal forty-day fast.

35. Perhaps this spring is reminiscent of the water issuing from the rock Moses struck in Numbers 20, or the living water promised by Christ to the woman of Samaria in John 4.

36. The reference is to Hebrews 1:14: "Are they not all ministering spirits sent forth to serve, for the sake of those who are to obtain salvation?" The Epistle to the Hebrews was normally ascribed to St. Paul in the Middle Ages.

37. The nine orders of angels were proposed by Pseudo-Dionysius in his *Celestial Hierarchy*.

38. The following description is taken from the *Visio Sancti Pauli*; see Healey, *St. Paul*, pp. 23–24.

Blickling Homily XIX: St. Andrew

39. That is, on the feast of St. Andrew, November 30.

40. This unwillingness to eat the poison is neither in the Greek nor the Latin sources for this homily.

41. The word here is Old English *Mod*, a word with a wide semantic range, including "mind," "spirit," and "courage."

42. Matthew is here rather more afraid of death than his counterpart in the *Praxeis* and Casanatensis.

43. The Old English is *wæs geworden to him*, literally, "happened for him."

44. The Old English homilist omits the passage about the tablets in each prisoner's hand.

45. Note the cannibalistic tendency of the Old English word *flæslic*.

46. The sentence is in Latin. The Old English translation follows: an intrusion of the source onto the translation.

47. Singular, not plural here: the Old English Homilist elliptically moves from the three men to Christ, who is one of them.

48. In the sources, Christ changes himself and the angels into the likeness of men; theologically astute, the Old English homilist remembers that the incarnate Christ has no need for such transformation. Note also the intrusion this sentence makes in the normal order of conversation. The homilist left out this statement earlier and must now insert it.

49. Note the hierarchical structure here.

50. Note how most of the conversation between Andrew and Christ is omitted here.

51. See Acts 1:6–11.

52. That is, Andrew.

53. Note all the verbs for perceiving and knowing and seeing: in Old English they are *onytap, witon, ongeaton*. There are metaphorical connections here with Matthew's earlier blindness and regained sight.

54. The Old English homilist repeats *he* here, a syntactical redundancy not repeated by this translation.

55. Doubtless this is singing psalms, the activity of St. Paul in prison; see Acts 16:24–26, where the prison doors are likewise opened miraculously.

56. In Old English this is, *hie wæron cyssende*—again a repeated subject. Note also the imperfect tense, probably mimetic of the excitement of reunion: literally, "Then the blessed Matthew and the holy Andrew, they were kissing each other."

57. Matthew 10:16: "Behold, I send you out as sheep in the midst of wolves; so be wise as serpents and innocent as doves."

58. This is liturgically the bishop's act of ordaining someone for the priesthood.

59. Literally this is *on lande*, perhaps a scribal error for *on blinde*, "blind."

60. That is, Matthew.

61. Peter, of course, is Andrew's more famous brother.

62. The repetition *men...men* ("people"..."people") may be intentional association of the victims and captors, a slight reminder that evil is self-destructive.

63. Literally this is, "and they said," a syntactical disorder perhaps mimetic of the leaders' confusion.

64. Note the shift in pronoun from second person plural to first person plural.

65. This is in Old English *he hine forleton*, language that echoes that of Christ on the cross in the West Saxon gospels, *Min God, min God, to hwi forlete þu me* (Mt 27:46, cf. Mk 15:34).

66. In Old English this is *hine bismriende mid myclere bismre*, literally, "mocking him with great mocks," an imitation of biblical idiom.

67. See above, note 65.

68. That is, the apostles. See Luke 21:18: "But not a hair of your head will perish"; compare Matthew 10:30 and Luke 12:7.

69. See Matthew 5:18: "For truly, I say to you, till heaven and earth pass away, not an iota, not a dot, will pass from the law until all is accomplished."

70. The syntactical disorder of this sentence is perhaps mimetic of the suddenness of the image's response to Andrew's prayer.

71. Perhaps this is an inversion of the fiery cherubim who exclude Adam and Eve from Eden; see Genesis 3:24: "He drove out the man; and at the east of the garden of Eden he placed the cherubim, and a flaming sword which turned every way, to guard the way to the tree of life."

72. In Old English this is, *þegnunge gearwode beforan his fotum*; the metaphor is drawn from the Anglo-Saxon *comitatus* relationship between lord and thane, and the biblical allusion is to Moses parting the Red Sea. See Exodus 14:21–22: "Then Moses stretched out his hand over the sea; and the LORD drove the sea back by a strong east wind all night, and made the sea dry land, and the waters were divided. And the people of Israel went into the midst of the sea on dry ground, the waters being a wall to them on their right hand and on their left."

73. This is reference perhaps to the liturgical phrase, *Kyrie eleison*, "Lord, have mercy."

74. This is an interesting inversion of Christ's Golden Rule found in Matthew 7:12: "So whatever you wish that men would do to you, do so to them; for this is the law and the prophets"; compare Christ's stricture, "...the measure you give will be the measure you get" (Mt 7:2).

75. "Convert" here and "turn" at the beginning of the sentence are both forms of the same Old English verb, *hweorfan*.

76. That is, the Mermedonians.

77. Note the interesting variant on the great *shema* prayer of ancient Israel: "Hear, O Israel: The LORD your God is one LORD!" (Dt 6:4).

Vercelli Homily II: The Day of Judgment

78. Compare Revelation 6:12–13: "...and the sun became black as sackcloth, the full moon became like blood, and the stars of the sky fell to the earth...."

79. For the apocalyptic trumpets, see Revelation 8:7—9:20, 11:15–19.

80. For the resurrection of the dead for Judgment, see Revelation 20:11–15. For a treatment of medieval attitudes toward resurrection, see Caroline Walker Bynum, *The Resurrection of the Body in Western Christianity, 200–1336* (New York: Columbia University Press, 1995).

81. This detail appears in other Old English sermons. See, for instance, Vercelli Homily XV, lines 138–40, as explained by D. G. Scragg, *The Vercelli Homilies and Related Texts*, Early English Text Society 300 (Oxford: Oxford University Press, 1992), p. 66.

82. For the torments of hell, see Revelation 20:10, "...and the devil who had deceived them was thrown into the lake of fire and sulphur where the beast and the false prophet were, and they will be tormented day and night for ever and ever"; and Revelation 21:8: "But as for the cowardly, the faithless, the polluted, as for murderers, fornicators, sorcerers, idolaters, and all liars, their lot shall be in the lake that burns with fire and sulphur, which is the second death." See also Daniel 12:2, Romans 9:22, 1 Thessalonians 1:10, and Mark 9:48. For a treatment of medieval artists' depictions of this torment, see Clifford Davidson and Thomas H. Seiler, eds., *The Iconography of Hell* (Kalamazoo, Mich.: Medieval Institute Publications, 1992).

83. For the history of Antichrist, see McGinn, *Antichrist*, especially pp. 33–113, which deal with the legend from the beginnings of Christianity through the early Middle Ages. The figure of the Antichrist, mentioned in the Bible (1 John 2:18–22, 4:3, 2 John 7), was a favorite subject of medieval theologians, prophets, and politicians. For anthologies of medieval writings about the end times and Antichrist, see Bernard McGinn, ed., *Visions of the End: Apocalyptic Traditions in the Middle Ages* (New York: Columbia University Press, 1979); and McGinn, *Apocalyptic Spirituality*). See also Richard K. Emmerson, *Antichrist in the Middle Ages* (Seattle: University of Washington Press, 1981); and Richard K. Emmerson and Bernard McGinn, eds., *The Apocalypse in the Middle Ages* (Ithaca, N.Y.: Cornell University Press, 1992).

84. That is, the Day of Judgment.

85. See Revelation 20:11. See note 80, above.

86. For the career of the apocalyptic dragon, see Revelation 12:1–17.

87. The reference is to the Lord's Prayer, Matthew 6:12.

88. Scragg suggests (*Vercelli*, p. 69), Job 22:29 for the reference here: "For God abases the proud, but he saves the lowly."

89. Compare Matthew 5:5: "Blessed are the meek, for they shall inherit the earth."

90. See Revelation 21:23: "And the city [i.e., the New Jerusalem] has no need of sun or moon to shine upon it, for the glory of God is its light, and its lamp is the Lamb."

Vercelli Homily VI: Christmas Day

91. Psalm 118:24.

92. The Emperor Augustus's sympathy for Christ's birth might be explainable by the fact that people in the Middle Ages often interpreted the poet he patronized, Virgil, as in effect a prophet who foretold Christ's birth in his Fourth Ecologue. He is also credited with a sibylline vision of the birth of an unknown Jewish divinity, one recounted in the *Laterculus Malalianus*, a Latin version of John Malalase's Greek *Chronicle* produced in the latter seventh century in Anglo-Saxon England, possibly by Archbishop Theodore. See Jane Barbara Stevenson, "Theodore and the *Laterculus Malalianus*," pp. 204–21 in Michael Lapidge, *Theodore*, p. 213.

93. This action foreshadows Christ's harrowing of hell.

94. The sermon here until almost the end follows the legendary *Euangelium pseudo-Matthae*. For the relevant passages, consult Scragg's footnotes in *Vercelli*, pp. 129–31.

95. Luke 2:14.

96. The account of Herod's murderous intentions and the flight to Egypt are found in Matthew 2:1–18.

97. A leaf is missing here, which evidently recounted the story of the child Jesus rescuing the Holy Family from the dragons, performing various miracles, and then shortening the journey to Egypt. The *Euangelium pseudo-Matthae* supplies the information.

98. For a masterful interpretation of the iconography attending the fallen idols, see Michael Camile, *The Gothic Idol: Ideology and Image-Making in Medieval Art* (Cambridge: Cambridge University Press, 1989); see especially pp. 1–26.

99. See Luke 2:52: "And Jesus increased in wisdom and in stature, and in favor with God and man."

Vercelli Homily XI: Rogation Day

100. This is the first and longer of two rogation-day sermons in the Vercelli Book. The other (Vercelli Homily XII) immediately follows it. The three rogation days immediately precede the feast of the Ascension; Vercelli Homily XIII, a fragment, also addresses the themes of rogation days. The main source of Vercelli Homily XI is Caesarius of Arles's *Sermo ccvii*.

101. According to Scragg, *Vercelli*, p. 219, Vercelli Homilies XI and XII "contain the only known references to Peter in connection with Rogationtide."

102. The reference, perhaps, is to the lanterns carried in the parable by the Wise Virgins. See Matthew 25:1–13.

103. Compare Matthew 24:13: "But he who endures to the end will be saved."

104. The ubiquitous interpretation in the early penitentials was that penance was a medicine to cure sins. See Frantzen, *Penance*, pp. 30–31.

105. Ecclesiasties 3:4.

106. John 16:33 and John 16:20, quoted by the Vercelli homilist, following Caesarius of Arles, in that order.

107. Psalm 126:5.

108. 2 Corinthians 5:6.

109. The New Jerusalem is described in Revelation 21:9–14.

110. Luke 6:25.

111. This is a reference to the Viking invasions.

112. That is, in the liturgy for the rogation days.

Ælfric: St. John the Apostle

113. The feast of St. John the Apostle is December 27. The non-biblical details are taken from the apocryphal *Acts of John*.

114. The association of St. John with the bridegroom at the Wedding at Cana (Jn 2:1–11) is legendary and extra-biblical.

115. See John 19:26–27: "When Jesus saw his mother, and the disciple whom he loved standing near, he said to his mother, 'Woman, behold your son!' Then he said to the disciple, 'Behold, your mother!' And from that hour the disciple took her to his own home."

116. See Revelation 1:9: "I John, your brother, who share with you in Jesus the tribulation and the kingdom and the patient endurance, was on the island called Patmos on account of the word of God and the testimony of Jesus." The identification of John the Evangelist with John the

Divine (who wrote the Apocalypse) was not challenged until modern times. John's exile on Patmos, legend has it, was his punishment during the Domitian persecution.

117. Matthew 21:9.

118. This apocryphal miracle is reminiscent of Christ's healing of St. Peter's mother-in-law, whom he commands to serve and prepare a meal after the miracle. See Matthew 8:14–15: "And when Jesus entered Peter's house, he saw his mother-in-law lying sick with fever; he touched her hand, and the fever left her, and she rose and served him."

119. The story is recounted in Matthew 19:16–22.

120. The following story is a long allegorical descant on the dominical words in Matthew 6:19–20: "Do not lay up for yourselves treasures on earth, where moth and rust consume and where thieves break in and steal, but lay up for yourselves treasures in heaven, where neither moth nor rust consume and where thieves do not break in and steal."

121. This is perhaps a reference to Matthew 6:28–30. See note 10, above.

122. Compare Job 1:21: "And he [Job] said, 'Naked I came from my mother's womb, and naked shall I return....'"

123. This distinction among the three gospels that share passages (Matthew, Mark, and Luke—the synoptic gospels) and John is basic to New Testament studies still today, when John's emphasis on Christ's divinity is still explicated.

124. John 1:1–3.

125. This is a possible reference to Mark 16:17–18: "And these signs will accompany those who believe: in my name they will cast out demons; they will speak in new tongues; they will pick up serpents, and if they drink any deadly thing, it will not hurt them; they will lay their hands on the sick, and they will recover." These verses are part of the section (Mark 16:9–19) that was added to complete the seemingly fragmentary Gospel of Mark. They are thus extra-biblical and represent the same outlook as that of the apocryphal Acts of the Apostles, full of improbable miracles. Compare the poisonous drink given to the apostle Matthew at the beginning of the Blickling Homily on Andrew, above, pp. 78–79.

126. Legends of John's advanced age are a function of Jesus's words about him to Peter at the close of the Gospel of John: "If it is my will that he remain until I come, what is that to you?" (Jn 21:22).

127. As in Bede's recounting of the herdsman Cædmon's premonitions of death, foreknowledge of one's own death is a sure sign of sanctity. See Bede, *History of the English Church*, Book 4, chapter 24.

128. The story of the manna given to the Israelites in the wilderness is recounted in Exodus 16:1–36.

Ælfric: St. Dionysius

129. The story of St. Paul's mission in Athens, including the conversion of Dionysius, is recounted in Acts 17. The events here are extra-biblical, showing the typical medieval conflation of Dionysius the Areopagite, the theologian known today as Pseudo-Dionysius, and St. Denis, the evangelist of France. The ultimate source is Hilduin's ninth-century *Life of Denis*. Hilduin found the details about the evangelization of France in Gregory of Tours. Dionysius's feast day is October 9.

130. For the natural signs accompanying Christ's death, see Matthew 27:45, 51–52.

131. See Acts 17:23.

132. Notice that this is not the euhemeristic interpretation of the gods (i.e., that they were sinful humans from the remote past) recounted by both Ælfric and Wulfstan in their sermons *On the False Gods*. See Introduction, note 114, above.

133. St. Paul's actions in healing the blind man loosely follow those of Jesus in John 9:1–39, who there heals a man born blind.

134. These books are the treatises written by an anonymous early sixth-century Syrian monk, who wrote falsely under the name of Dionysius. The treatises of Pseudo-Dionysius are *The Divine Names*, *The Mystical Theology*, *The Ecclesiastical Hierarchy*, and *The Celestial Hierarchy*, the last being the one that explains the nine orders of angels Ælfric mentions here. Pseudo-Dionysius also claims to have written a non-extant treatise called *Theological Representations*. There exists a number of *Letters* as well. Titus and Polycarp and John are recipients of three of the *Letters*, while the extant treatises are addressed to Timothy. For the standard English translation of the Dionysian corpus, see Colm Luibheid, trans., with Paul Rorem, *Pseudo-Dionysius: The Complete Works* (New York: Paulist Press, 1987).

135. The apostles martyred in Rome were Peter and Paul.

136. The Northmen, of course, did not inhabit the lands northeast of Paris until the early tenth century.

137. These helpers of Dionysius are traceable back beyond Hilduin to Gregory of Tours.

138. For this apostolic mimesis, see St. Paul's words in 1 Corinthians 11:1: "Be imitators of me, as I am of Christ."

139. Lawrence, deacon and martyr, was killed in Rome in 258, during the persecution of Valerian, by being roasted on a gridiron, or so the legend has it. Prudentius, Ambrose, and Augustine all mention his death.

140. Many of the early Roman martyrs were killed by wild beasts. The beasts here in their pacifism owe much to the lions who did not eat Daniel. See Daniel 6:10–24.

141. Again, this oven owes much to the one that did not roast Shadrach, Meshach, and Abednego. See Daniel 3:8–27.

142. Andrew's martyrdom, not recounted in either the Blickling Homily on St. Andrew or in the Old English poem *Andreas*, was crucifixion on an X-shaped cross.

Ælfric: St. Oswald

143. He arrived on the Isle of Thanet near Canterbury in 597. This is St. Augustine of Canterbury, not the more famous St. Augustine, bishop of Hippo, the theologian who wrote *The Confessions* and *The City of God* and so many other influential treatises.

144. King Oswald reigned from 633 to 641. Oswald's life, including most of the details related by Ælfric, is recounted by Bede in Book III, Chapters 1–13, of his *Ecclesiastical History*, the source for Ælfric's sermon. His saint's day is August 5.

145. The sojourn in Scotland was a political exile.

146. These are Eadwine's cousin Osric in Deira and his nephew Eanfrið in Bernicia. The two nations had been united as Northumbria but were again separated in response to Cadwallon's aggression. Oswald later reunited them when he defeated the British king in the Battle of Heavenfield, the story of which is recounted below.

147. This is perhaps a reference to Emperor Constantine's vision of the cross before the Battle of the Milvian Bridge in 310.

148. The resistance to bodily decay after death is one of the most frequent marks of sanctity found in the hagiographical writings of the Middle Ages.

149. This is a reference to Oswald's ascendancy to the role of over-king or "Bretwalda."

150. This is a reference to the origins of the famous York Minster, which, as it survives, lacks the original Anglo-Saxon work.

151. This was the famous "cross-vigil" posture recommended in the Irish and Anglo-Saxon penitentials as a posture of prayer for the penitent.

152. Penda was king of Mercia from 632 to 655.

153. Oswiu was king of Northumbria from 641 to 670. He defeated Penda at the Battle of Winwæd in 655.

Ælfric: On the Sacrifice of Easter

154. That is, Holy Saturday.

155. Ælfric's sources are the treatises both titled *De Corpore et Sanguine Christi* by Ratramnus and Radbert. Ratramnus, monk of Corbie, wrote a treatise calling for a symbolical interpretation of the eucharist, while his abbot, Radbert, called for an interpretation based on the real presence of Christ in the bread and wine. Ælfric evidently conflated the two sources either not realizing they were contradictory or attempting a synthesis.

156. See Exodus 12:1–8.

157. See Exodus 12:9–11.

158. See Exodus 12:29–36.

159. See Exodus 12:14–15.

160. See Exodus 14:1–31.

161. This is recounted in the latter chapters of Exodus and the book of Numbers. The incident of the water of Meribah is recounted in Exodus 17:1–7.

162. The important texts for this association of Christ with the sacrificial lamb are Isaiah 53:7, "He was oppressed, and he was afflicted, yet he opened not his mouth; like a lamb that is led to the slaughter, and like a sheep that before its shearers is dumb, so he opened not his mouth," and Revelation 5:6–10, "And between the throne and the four living creatures and among the elders, I saw a Lamb standing, as though it had been slain, with seven horns and with seven eyes, which are the seven spirits of God sent out into all the earth; and he went and took the scroll from the right hand of him who was seated on the throne. And when he had taken the scroll, the four living creatures and the twenty-four elders fell down before the Lamb, each holding a harp, and with golden bowls full of incense, which are the prayers of the saints; and they sang a new song, saying, 'Worthy art thou to take the scroll and to open its seals, for thou wast slain and by thy blood didst ransom men for God from every tribe and tongue

and people and nation, and hast made them a kingdom and priests to our God, and they shall reign on earth.'"

163. The Agnus Dei is part of the regular liturgy of the eucharist, immediately preceding the priest's consumption of the bread and wine.

164. Eating and drinking "spiritually" is Ratramnus's way of explaining the symbolic rather than real nature of the eucharist.

165. Compare John 6:22–40.

166. These are the words of institution in the mass. See Matthew 26:26–28: "Now as they were eating, Jesus took bread, and blessed, and broke it, and gave it to the disciples and said, 'Take, eat; this is my body.' And he took a cup, and when he had given thanks he gave it to them, saying, 'Drink of it, all of you; for this is my blood of the covenant, which is poured out for many for the forgiveness of sins.'"

167. Following Ratramnus, Ælfric makes here his strongest case for the symbolic presence of Christ in the eucharist. What follows immediately after this statement closely paraphrases Ratramnus.

168. The story that follows is taken secondhand from *The Lives of the Fathers*. Radbert, arguing against Ratramnus, used this anecdote that he found in *The Lives of the Fathers* as proof for the real presence. The anecdote became a medieval commonplace; readers of the Vulgate French *Quest of the Holy Grail* or Malory's version of the Grail-quest can recognize this story, for it becomes a vision Galahad sees on achieving the Grail.

169. See 1 Corinthians 10:1–6: "I want you to know, brethren, that our fathers were all under the cloud, and all passed through the sea, and all were baptized into Moses in the cloud and in the sea, and all ate the same supernatural food and all drank the same supernatural drink. For they drank from the supernatural Rock which followed them, and the Rock was Christ. Nevertheless with most of them God was not pleased; for they were overthrown in the wilderness. Now these things are warnings for us, not to desire evil as they did."

170. John 4:13–14: "Jesus said to her, 'Every one who drinks of this water will thirst again, but whoever drinks of the water that I shall give him will never thirst; the water that I shall give him will become in him a spring of water welling up to eternal life."

171. Cf. John 6:22–40.

172. See John 6:53–58: "So Jesus said to them, 'Truly, truly, I say to you, unless you eat the flesh of the Son of man and drink his blood, you have no life in you; he who eats my flesh and drinks my blood has eternal life, and I will raise him up at the last day. For my flesh is food indeed, and my blood is drink indeed. He who eats my flesh and drinks my blood

abides in me, and I in him. As the living Father sent me, and I live because of the Father, so he who eats me will live because of me. This is the bread which came down from heaven, not such as the fathers ate and died; he who eats this bread will live for ever.'"

173. See 1 Corinthians 6:15: "Do you not know that your bodies are members of Christ?"

174. See 1 Corinthians 10:17: "Because there is one bread, we who are many are one body, for we all partake of the one bread."

175. See 1 Corinthians 11:27: "Whoever, therefore, eats the bread or drinks the cup of the Lord in an unworthy manner will be guilty of profaning the body and blood of the Lord."

176. See 1 Corinthians 5:6–8: "Your boasting is not good. Do you not know that a little leaven leavens the whole lump? Cleanse out the old leaven that you may be a new lump, as you really are unleavened. For Christ, our paschal lamb, has been sacrificed. Let us, therefore, celebrate the festival, not with the old leaven, the leaven of malice and evil, but with the unleavened bread of sincerity and truth."

177. Compare 1 Corinthians 5:6–8. See note 176, above.

178. This is a reference to the tongues of fire that appeared over the apostles' heads at Pentecost. See Acts 2:1–4: "When the day of Pentecost had come, they were all together in one place. And suddenly a sound came from heaven like the rush of a mighty wind, and it filled all the house where they were sitting. And there appeared to them tongues as of fire, distributed and resting on each one of them. And they were all filled with the Holy Spirit and began to speak in other tongues, as the Spirit gave them utterance."

179. See John 19:31–34: "Since it was the day of Preparation, in order to prevent the bodies from remaining on the cross on the sabbath (for that sabbath was a high day), the Jews asked Pilate that their legs might be broken, and they might be taken away. So the soldiers came and broke the legs of the first, and of the other who had been crucified with him; but when they came to Jesus and saw that he was already dead, they did not break his legs."

Wulfstan: On the False Gods

180. The story of the Tower of Babel is recounted in Genesis 11:1–9. Genesis 10:8–10 mentions Nimrod's association with Babel: "Cush became the father of Nimrod; he was the first on earth to be a

mighty man. He was a mighty hunter before the LORD; therefore it is said, 'Like Nimrod a mighty hunter before the LORD.' The beginning of his kingdom was Babel, Erech, and Accad, all of them in the land of Shinar."

181. The giants actually preceded Noah's Flood. See Genesis 6:4.

182. The linkage of pagan gods and goddesses with humans who purportedly lived in the remote past is a theory known as *euhemerism*. See Introduction, note 114, above.

183. The equivalency of Graeco-Roman deities with those of the Germanic tribes was traditional. Tacitus, for instance, in his *Germania*, uses the Roman names in his descriptions of the Germanic deities.

Wulfstan: On the Sevenfold Gifts of the Spirit

184. See Isaiah 11:1–3: "There shall come forth a shoot from the stump of Jesse, and a branch shall grow out of his roots. And the Spirit of the Lord shall rest upon him, the spirit of wisdom and understanding, the spirit of counsel and might, the spirit of knowledge and the fear of the Lord. And his delight shall be in the fear of the Lord."

185. Compare St. Paul's list of spiritual gifts in 1 Corinthians 12:1, 4–11: "Now concerning spiritual gifts, brethren, I do not want you to be uninformed....Now there are varieties of gifts, but the same Spirit; and there are varieties of service, but the same Lord; and there are varieties of working, but it is the same God who inspires them all in every one. To each is given the manifestation of the Spirit for the common good. To one is given through the Spirit the utterance of wisdom, and to another the utterance of knowledge according to the same Spirit, to another faith by the same Spirit, to another gifts of healing by the one Spirit, to another the working of miracles, to another prophecy, to another the ability to distinguish between spirits, to another various kinds of tongues, to another the interpretation of tongues. All these are inspired by one and the same Spirit, who apportions to each one individually as he wills."

186. The *sevenfold* nature of these gifts not only pertains to the number of gifts listed in Isaiah 11:2–3 but also to the traditional mystical valence of the number seven, one that is used to good effect in the book of Revelation; see Revelation 5:6 (see note 162, above).

187. See Job 28:28: "Behold, the fear of the Lord, that is wisdom; and to depart from evil is understanding"; see also Psalm 111:10: "The fear of the LORD is the beginning of wisdom; a good understanding have all those who practice it."

188. The specific condemnation of hypocrisy here and the general condemnation of it throughout this sermon, owes much to Christ's recurring condemnation of hypocrites in the gospels. See, for instance, Matthew 6:2–16, Matthew 15:7, Mark 7:6, Matthew 16:3, Luke 12:56, Matthew 22:18, Matthew 23:13–15, and Matthew 24:51.

189. For Antichrist, see above, note 83.

Wulfstan: **Sermo Lupi ad Anglos**

190. *Lupus,* Latin for "Wolf," translates the first element in Wulfstan's name.

191. For the Antichrist, see above, note 83.

192. This is a reference to the nonpayment of tithes and other taxes that benefited the church.

193. God's servants are the clergy.

194. Wulfstan, as explained in the Introduction (see above, pp. 17, 50), was one of the chief law-writers of Anglo-Saxon England.

195. Wulfstan seems to mean here robbery of churches by the Anglo-Saxons themselves, though, of course, robbery of churches was one of the hallmarks of the Viking invasions.

196. Compare Matthew 10:21: "Brother will deliver up brother to death, and the father his child, and children will rise against parents and have them put to death."

197. Compare Philippians 3:18–19: "For many, of whom I have often told you and now tell you even with tears, live as enemies of the cross of Christ. Their end is destruction, their god is the belly, and they glory in their shame, with minds set on earthly things."

198. King Edward the Martyr was murdered in 978, three years after succeeding his father Edgar, by a thane of his half-brother Æþelræd, who then succeeded him. At the time of this sermon's composition Wulfstan was one of Æþelræd's counselors.

199. This is possibly a reference to the Viking custom of berserk fighting, when a martial trance made the berserker superhumanly strong.

200. This is a reference to the tribute money often exacted by the Vikings.

201. That is, the penitentials.

202. For Gildas and the influence of his jeremiad on Wulfstan's, see the Introduction, pp. 3–4, 37–38.

Bodley 343: The Temptation of Christ

203. The holy time of fasting is Lent.

204. See Matthew 4:1–2: "Then Jesus was led up by the Spirit into the wilderness to be tempted by the devil. And he fasted forty days and forty nights, and afterward he was hungry."

205. See Hebrews 4:15: "For we have not a high priest who is unable to sympathize with our weaknesses, but one who in every respect has been tempted as we are, yet without sin."

206. Matthew's account of the temptation is recounted in chapter 4:1–11, with parallel versions in Mark 1:12–13 and Luke 4:1–13.

207. Matthew 4:1.

208. Matthew 4:2.

209. Compare Exodus 24:12–18: "The LORD said to Moses, 'Come up to me on the mountain, and wait there; and I will give you the tables of stone, with the law and the commandment, which I have written for their instruction.' So Moses rose with his servant Joshua, and Moses went up into the mountain of God. And he said to the elders, 'Tarry here for us, until we come to you again; and, behold, Aaron and Hur are with you; whoever has a cause, let him go to them.' Then Moses went up on the mountain, and the cloud covered the mountain. The glory of the LORD settled on Mount Sinai, and the cloud covered it six days; and on the seventh day he called to Moses out of the midst of the cloud. Now the appearance of the glory of the LORD was like a devouring fire on the top of the mountain in the sight of the people of Israel. And Moses entered the cloud, and went up on the mountain. And Moses was on the mountain forty days and forty nights."

210. See 1 Kings 19:8: "And he [Elijah] arose, and ate and drank, and went in the strength of that food forty days and forty nights to Horeb the mount of God."

211. Matthew 4:3.

212. Genesis 1:3.

213. Matthew 4:4: "But he answered, 'It is written, "Man shall not live by bread alone, but by every word that proceeds from the mouth of God."'"

214. Matthew 4:5.

215. See 1 Corinthians 6:15. See note 173, above.

216. Matthew 4:6.

217. Compare Matthew 4:7: "Jesus said to him, 'Again it is written, "You shall not tempt the Lord your God."'"

218. See Matthew 4:8.

219. Matthew 4:9.

220. See Matthew 4:10: "Then Jesus said to him, 'Begone, Satan! For it is written, "You shall worship the Lord your God and him only shall you serve."'"

221. Matthew 4:11.

222. See Hebrews 1:14: "Are they [angels] not all ministering spirits sent forth to serve, for the sake of those who are to obtain salvation?" Compare note 33, above.

223. 2 Corinthians 6:2: "At the acceptable time I have listened to you, and helped you on the day of salvation." This in turn is a quotation of Isaiah 49:8.

224. For the tithe, see Leviticus 27:30–33: "All the tithe of the land, whether of the seed of the land or of the fruit of the trees, is the LORD's; it is holy to the LORD. If a man wishes to redeem any of his tithe, he shall add a fifth to it. And all the tithe of herds and flocks, every tenth animal of all that pass under the herdsman's staff, shall be holy to the LORD. A man shall not inquire whether it is good or bad, neither shall he exchange it; and if he exchanges it, then both it and that for which it is exchanged shall be holy; it shall not be redeemed." See also Genesis 28:22, where Jacob at Bethel says to God, "…of all that thou givest me I will give the tenth to thee."

Bodley 343: The Transfiguration of Christ

225. The fullest dominical discourse on this topic is the Olivet Discourse, found in Matthew 24—25; the homilist here, though, refers to Matthew 16:27: "For the Son of man is to come with his angels in the glory of his Father, and then he will repay every man for what he has done."

226. Matthew 16:28: "Truly, I say to you, there are some standing here who will not taste death before they see the Son of man coming in his kingdom." This seems to refer to the Judgment at the end of time, but it has been traditionally associated instead with the Transfiguration, the narrative of which immediately follows.

227. The story of the Transfiguration is related in Matthew 17:1–13; the homilist paraphrases it fairly accurately as he continues his homily.

228. Matthew 17:4.

229. Matthew 17:5.

230. Matthew 17:7.

231. See Matthew 7:13–14: "Enter by the narrow gate; for the gate is wide and the way is easy, that leads to destruction, and those who enter by it are many. For the gate is narrow and the way is hard, that leads to life, and those who find it are few."

232. The homilist's source at this point is Bede's *Homeliarum Evangelii Libri II*, which quotes Paul's letter to the Philippians 3:20, *"Nostra autem conuersatio in caelis est unde etiam Saluatorem expectamus Iesum Christum dominum nostrum,"* rendered in the RSV as, "But our commonwealth is in heaven, and from it we await a Savior, the Lord Jesus Christ." The homilist has mistranslated *conuersatio*, rendering it with three roughly equivalent words, *murhðe, wuldor,* and *blisse.*

233. Matthew 17:1.

234. In Matthew 16:28, he promised, "there are some standing here who will not taste death before they see the Son of man coming in his kingdom"; this verse is followed immediately with Matthew 17:1, "And after six days Jesus took with him Peter and James and John his brother, and led them up a high mountain apart."

235. Matthew 17:2.

236. 1 Corinthians 15:41–42: "There is one glory of the sun, and another glory of the moon, and another glory of the stars; for star differs from star in glory. So is it with the resurrection of the dead. What is sown is perishable, what is raised is imperishable."

237. See Matthew 25:31–46. See note 6, above.

238. Matthew 17:3.

239. Luke 9:30–31.

240. For Elijah's avoidance of earthly death, see 2 Kings 2:11–12: "And as they still went on and talked, behold, a chariot of fire and horses of fire separated the two of them. And Elijah went up by a whirlwind into heaven. And Elisha saw it and he cried, 'My father, my father! the chariots of Israel and its horsemen!' And he saw him no more."

241. Traditionally Elijah has been associated (along with Enoch) as one of the two witnesses mentioned in Revelation 11:3–13: "'And I will grant my two witnesses power to prophesy for one thousand two hundred and sixty days, clothed in sackcloth.' These are the two olive trees and the two lampstands which stand before the Lord of the earth. And if any one would harm them, fire pours from their mouth and consumes their foes; if any one would harm them, thus he is doomed to be killed. They have power to shut the sky, that no rain may fall during the days of their prophesying, and they have power over the waters to turn them into blood, and

to smite the earth with every plague, as often as they desire. And when they have finished their testimony, the beast that ascends from the bottomless pit will make war upon them and conquer them and kill them, and their dead bodies will lie in the street of the great city which is allegorically called Sodom and Egypt, where their Lord was crucified. For three days and a half men from the peoples and tribes and tongues and nations gaze at their dead bodies and refuse to let them be placed in a tomb, and those who dwell on the earth will rejoice over them and make merry and exchange presents, because these two prophets had been a torment to those who dwell on the earth. But after the three and a half days a breath of life from God entered them, and they stood up on their feet, and great fear fell on those who saw them. Then they heard a loud voice from heaven saying to them, 'Come up hither!' And in the sight of their foes they went up to heaven in a cloud. And at that hour there was a great earthquake, and a tenth of the city fell; seven thousand people were killed in the earthquake, and the rest were terrified and gave glory to the God of heaven."

242.   See 1 Corinthians 15:51–52: "Lo! I tell you a mystery. We shall not all sleep, but we shall all be changed, in a moment, in the twinkling of an eye, at the last trumpet. For the trumpet will sound, and the dead will be raised imperishable, and we shall be changed."

243.   Matthew 17:4.

244.   Revelation 21:22: "And I saw no temple in the city, for its temple is the Lord God the Almighty and the Lamb."

245.   Matthew 17:5.

246.   Matthew 17:6.

247.   Matthew 17:9.

Bodley 343: The Transience of Earthly Delights

248.   See note 10, above.

249.   See note 11, above.

250.   Compare Revelation 20:11–15: "Then I saw a great white throne and him who sat upon it; from his presence earth and sky fled away, and no place was found for them. And I saw the dead, great and small, standing before the throne, and books were opened. Also another book was opened, which is the book of life. And the dead were judged by what was written in the books, by what they had done. And the sea gave up the dead in it, Death and Hades gave up the dead in them, and all were judged by what they had done. Then Death and Hades were thrown into the lake

of fire. This is the second death, the lake of fire; and if any one's name was not found written in the book of life, he was thrown into the lake of fire."

251. See Matthew 24:29–31. See note 80, above.

252. For the following passage, see Matthew 25:31–46. See note 6, above.

253. The main source for this doctrine that the damned see the blessed in heaven is the parable of Dives and Lazarus. See Luke 16:19–28: "There was a rich man, who was clothed in purple and fine linen and who feasted sumptuously every day. And at his gate lay a poor man named Lazarus, full of sores, who desired to be fed with what fell from the rich man's table; moreover the dogs came and licked his sores. The poor man died and was carried by the angels to Abraham's bosom. The rich man also died and was buried; and in Hades, being in torment, he lifted up his eyes, and saw Abraham far off and Lazarus in his bosom. And he called out, 'Father Abraham, have mercy upon me, and send Lazarus to dip the end of his finger in water and cool my tongue; for I am in anguish in this flame.' But Abraham said, 'Son, remember that you in your lifetime received your good things, and Lazarus in like manner evil things; but now he is comforted here, and you are in anguish. And besides all this, between us and you a great chasm has been fixed, in order that those who would pass from here to you may not be able, and none may cross from there to us.' And he said, 'Then I beg you, father, to send him to my father's house, for I have five brothers, so that he may warn them, lest they also come into this place of torment.'"

254. See Job 1:21. See note 122, above.

255. Compare Revelation 22:3–5: "There shall no more be anything accursed, but the throne of God and of the Lamb shall be in it, and his servants shall worship him; they shall see his face, and his name shall be on their foreheads. And night shall be no more; they need no light of lamp or sun, for the Lord God will be their light, and they shall reign for ever and ever."

256. This passage is conventional in that it elaborates the famous *ubi sunt* motif, the elegiac lament for the glories that have passed. Compare the famous *ubi sunt* passage in the Old English poem *The Wanderer*, lines 92–96.

257. Compare Matthew 7:7–11: "Ask, and it will be given you; seek, and you will find; knock, and it will be opened to you. For every one who asks receives, and he who seeks finds, and to him who knocks it will be opened. Or what man of you, if his son asks him for bread, will give him a stone? Or if he asks for a fish, will give him a serpent? If you then, who are

evil, know how to give good gifts to your children, how much more will your Father who is in heaven give good things to those who ask him!"

258. Perhaps this is a reference to Luke 7:37–38, 47–48: "And behold, a woman of the city, who was a sinner, when she learned that he was sitting at a table in the Pharisee's house, brought an alabaster flask of ointment, and standing behind him at his feet, weeping, she began to wet his feet with her tears, and wiped them with the hair of her head, and kissed his feet, and anointed them with the ointment.... 'Therefore I tell you, her sins, which are many, are forgiven, for she loved much; but he who is forgiven little, loves little.' And he said to her, 'Your sins are forgiven.'"

259. See Matthew 6:19–21. See note 10, above.

Cædmon's Hymn

260. For the story of Cædmon's composition of this hymn, see the Introduction to this volume, pp. 46–48.

261. The poem from this point paraphrases Genesis 1:1: "In the beginning God created the heavens and the earth."

Genesis A (Selection): "Abraham and Isaac"

262. That is, Abraham, who, perhaps to the surprise of modern readers, has been depicted in the preceding lines of *Genesis A* as a Germanic warlord. The story of Abraham's near sacrifice of Isaac is found in Genesis 22.

263. Compare Genesis 22:2: "Take your son, your only son Isaac, whom you love, and go to the land of Moriah, and offer him there as a burnt offering upon one of the mountains of which I shall tell you."

264. In Old English secular poetry the lord is usually depicted as one who gives rich gifts to his retainers, his band of thanes. "Ring-giver" is the common formula describing him.

265. Genesis gives no approximate age for Isaac at the time of his near sacrifice. When medieval commentators supply one, it ranges from infant up to young adult. Surprisingly the age thirty-three is frequently encountered—because of its allegorical connections with Christ's age of thirty-three years at his crucifixion.

266. See Genesis 22:4: "On the third day Abraham lifted up his eyes and saw the place afar off." The detail of the third day was, of course, traditionally associated with Christ's resurrection on the third day.

267. Compare Genesis 22:5: "Then Abraham said to his young men, 'Stay here with the ass; I and the lad will go yonder and worship, and come again to you.'"

268. See Genesis 22:7: "And Isaac said to his father Abraham, 'My father!' And he said, 'Here am I, my son.' He said, 'Behold, the fire and the wood; but where is the lamb for a burnt offering?'"

269. See Genesis 22:8: "Abraham said, 'God will provide himself the lamb for a burnt offering, my son.'"

270. See Genesis 22:12: "He said, 'Do not lay your hand on the lad or do anything to him; for now I know that you fear God, seeing you have not withheld your son, your only son, from me.'"

Genesis B (First Fragment): "Satan in Hell"

271. Pseudo-Dionysius, in *The Celestial Hierarchy*, posits the traditional nine orders of angels; he is likely drawing on the ancient tradition of ten orders created by God, one of which fell, with humankind eventually replacing the fallen order and restoring the perfect number.

272. The account in Genesis attributes the subsequent temptation of Adam and Eve to "the serpent" (Gn 3:1). For the association of Satan with this story, see Elaine Pagels, *The Origin of Satan* (New York: Random House, 1995), pp. 35–62.

273. Compare Isaiah 14:12–15: "How you are fallen from heaven, O Day Star, son of Dawn! How you are cut down to the ground, you who laid the nations low! You said in your heart, 'I will ascend to heaven; above the stars of God I will set my throne on high; I will sit on the mount of assembly in the far north; I will ascend above the heights of the clouds, I will make myself like the Most High.' But you are brought down to Sheol, to the depths of the Pit." The Vulgate gives "Lucifer" for "Day Star."

274. West and north are traditionally the directions of death and evil, respectively. The passage from Isaiah 14 quoted in note 273 immediately above specifies only the north.

275. East traditionally is the direction of resurrection.

276. "Satan" makes his first appearance in the Bible in the book of Job, where, attending God's court, he offers to tempt faithful Job. *Satan* in Hebrew means "adversary." See Job 1:6–12.

277. The failure of Satan's syntax here is perhaps mimetic of his broken state of mind.

278. Compare 1 John 1:5–6: "This is the message we have heard from him and proclaim to you, that God is light and in him is no darkness at all. If we say we have fellowship with him while we walk in darkness, we lie and do not live according to the truth...."

279. See Genesis 1:26: "Then God said, 'Let us make man in our image, after our likeness; and let them have dominion over the fish of the sea, and over the birds of the air, and over the cattle, and over all the earth, and over every creeping thing that creeps upon the earth.'"

280. The text breaks off here, for two leaves of the manuscript are missing at this point.

Judith

281. The poem as it stands in the manuscript starts in the middle of a sentence. The extent of what is missing has been debated. The poem recounts the concluding events of the book of Judith, narrating approximately the last five chapters of that sixteen-chapter book. The first eleven chapters together with the first seven verses of the twelfth recount the situation of which the events of the poem form a climax. The Assyrians under King Nebuchadnessar, facing battle against the Medes under King Arphaxad, send to their client-states, including Judea, for troops to help. When they refuse this help, Nebuchadnessar crushes the Medes without it and vows revenge on his client-states. He sends his army under the general Holofernes to exterminate the recalcitrant nations. Camped below the mountainous Judean city of Bethulia, he cuts off its water supply, causing the inhabitants much suffering. The elders consider capitulating, but Judith, a pious widow, reprimands them and then tells them to let her out through the city's gate with her handmaid, for she will subdue the invincible enemy. She makes her way to the Assyrian camp, where she pretends to be a traitor who will help them conquer the city. After a few days, Holofernes, smitten by her beauty—which is emphasized in the biblical text—plans a banquet so he can seduce her. The extant Old English poem begins here.

282. That is, her beauty.

283. Compare Judith 12:20: "Holofernes was so enchanted with her that he drank far more wine than he had drunk on any other day of his life" (Jerusalem Bible).

284. The following gleeful description of Holofernes's drunkenness is entirely the Old English poet's.

285. The biblical author makes a point of Judith regaling herself, not as in the poem, Holofernes providing her with gifts of rings and such so she may appear beautiful. See Judith 12:15: "At this she rose and put on her dress and all her feminine adornments" (Jerusalem Bible).

286. This curtain with one-way vision is an invention of the Old English poet.

287. This line lacks its b-verse.

288. Compare Judith 13:4–8: "By now everyone had left Holofernes and no one, either important or unimportant, was left in the bedroom. Standing beside the bed, Judith murmured to herself: 'Lord God, to whom all strength belongs, prosper what my hands are now to do for the greater glory of Jerusalem, now is the time to recover your heritage and further my designs to crush the enemies arrayed against us.' With that she went up to the bedpost by Holofernes' head and took down his scimitar; coming closer to the bed she caught him by the hair and said, 'Make me strong today, Lord God of Israel!'" (Jerusalem Bible).

289. Compare Judith 13:8. "Twice she struck at the nape of his neck with all her strength and cut off his head" (Jerusalem Bible).

290. Judith is able to escape so easily because for the previous three days Holofernes, trusting her as a traitor to the Israelites, has allowed her freedom of movement in and out of the Assyrians' camp.

291. Compare Judith 14:1–5: "Judith said, 'Listen to me, brother. Take this head and hang it on your battlements. When morning comes and the sun is up, let every man take his arms and every able-bodied man leave the town. Appoint a leader for these, as if you meant to march down to the plain against the Assyrian advance post. But you must not do this. The Assyrians will gather up their equipment, make for their camp and wake up their commanders; they in turn will rush to the tent of Holofernes and not be able to find him. They will then be seized with panic and flee at your advance. All you and the others who live in the territory of Israel will have to do is to give chase and slaughter them as they retreat.'"

292. The three carrion beasts of battle—wolf, raven, and eagle—are a frequent detail in Old English battle poems.

293. In the gospels gnashing of teeth is associated with damnation. See, for instance, Matthew 8:11–12: "I tell you, many will come from east and west and sit at table with Abraham, Isaac, and Jacob in the kingdom of heaven, while the sons of the kingdom will be thrown into the outer darkness; there men will weep and gnash their teeth."

294. As mentioned in texts from Tacitus's *Germania* through the Old English poem *The Battle of Maldon* (991), the retainers' duty was to die with their lord in battle. See the Introduction, pp. 40–41.

295. The book of Judith goes on to recount briefly the pertinent details of the rest of Judith's life. She lives in wealth and security, refusing all suitors, until she frees her handmaid from servitude and dies, honored by all, at age 105. See Judith 16:21–30.

Cynewulf: The Fates of the Apostles

296. "Listen," is the translation of the Old English *Hwæt*, the traditional opening of Old English poems (see, for instance, the opening of *Beowulf* and the opening of *Andreas*).

297. The language, of course, casts the apostles into the role of Germanic heroes.

298. In Acts 1, the casting of lots is used to choose Mathias, the apostle who replaced Judas.

299. Cynewulf here is responding to Christ's call for universal evangelism. See Matthew 28:16–20: "Now the eleven disciples went to Galilee, to the mountain to which Jesus had directed them. And when they saw him they worshiped him; but some doubted. And Jesus came and said to them, 'All authority in heaven and on earth has been given to me. Go therefore and make disciples of all nations, baptizing them in the name of the Father and of the Son and of the Holy Spirit, teaching them to observe all that I have commanded you; and lo, I am with you always, to the close of the age.'"

300. Traditionally, Peter and Paul were martyred in Rome under Nero's persecution. Compare John 21:18–19, in which Jesus seemingly predicts the manner of Peter's death (traditionally by upside-down crucifixion): "'Truly, truly, I say to you, when you were young, you girded yourself and walked where you would; but when you are old, you will stretch out your hands, and another will gird you and carry you where you do not wish to go.' (This he said to show by what death he was to glorify God.) And after this he said to him, 'Follow me.'" For Paul's imprisonment among the Romans, see Acts 27—28.

301. Traditionally, Andrew dies in Achaia by being crucified on an X-shaped cross. The Blickling Homily on St. Andrew and the Old English poem *Andreas* depict him being interrupted in his ministry in Achaia to rescue St. Matthew from the country of the cannibals.

302. For John's career, see Ælfric's sermon on him translated in this volume above, pp. 100–8.

303. This James is James the Great, son of Zebedee and brother of John. He was the first apostle to be martyred, having been slain by order of King Herod Agrippa; see Acts 12:1–2: "About that time Herod the king laid violent hands upon some who belonged to the church. He killed James the brother of John with the sword...." Traditionally, James's body was transported to Compostela in northern Spain, where a great center of pilgrimage arose in the high and later Middle Ages.

304. Traditionally, Philip the Apostle (sometimes confused with Philip the Deacon, mentioned in Acts 8; 21:8) preached the gospel in Phrygia and died at Hierapolis.

305. Traditionally Bartholomew (who is named Nathanael in the Gospel of John) made his way to India and Armenia, where he was martyred by flaying alive and beheading.

306. Thomas, the Doubter (see John 20:24–29), known also as Didymus (= "twin"), is said to have evangelized either Parthia or India, where he was martyred by being run through with a spear.

307. A mistake in orthography caused the Anglo-Saxons to think Matthew spent part of his evangelistic career in Mermedonia, the country of the cannibals, for in the original legend (the Greek *Praxeis Andreou*), it is Mathias. Traditionally Matthew (called Levi in the gospels of Mark and Luke) was associated not only as here with Ethiopia but also Persia and the Persian Gulf region.

308. This is James the Less, son of Alphaeus, the supposed author of the Epistle of James, traditionally martyred by being beaten to death with a fuller's club under the order of the Sanhedrin in A.D. 62.

309. Simon the Zealot is associated in some traditions with Edessa, in others Egypt, before joining Jude for the trip to Persia. With Jude he is said to have been martyred there in the city of Sufium by being hewn to death by pagan priests.

310. Jude, author of the Epistle of Jude, traditionally was martyred with Simon the Zealot in Persia.

311. Notice how Cynewulf includes St. Paul in the list of the Twelve. Judas, originally one of the Twelve, was of course excluded because of his betrayal of Jesus. In Acts 1, Mathias is chosen by lot to succeed him. Cynewulf ignores Mathias entirely. Traditionally, Mathias evangelized Cappadocia (some traditions link him to Ethiopia).

312. What follows are the names for the runes that anagrammatically spell out Cynewulf's name: Wealth (F), Joy (W), Ours (U), Water (L), Torch (C), Horn (Y), and Need (N).

Guthlac A

313. The unity of *Guthlac A* is in debate, with some suggesting that the first twenty-nine lines of the poem really belong to the previous poem in the Exeter Book, *Christ III*. See Alexandra Hennessey Olsen, *Guthlac of Croyland: A Study of Heroic Hagiography* (Washington, D.C.: University Press of America, 1981), pp. 21–22.

314. That is, the pious lay status, the monastic life, the life of the secular priests, and the life of the hermits. The poet is not referring to the various and sometimes competing monastic orders.

315. Compare Matthew 24:6–8: "And you will hear of wars and rumors of wars; see that you are not alarmed; for this must take place, but the end is not yet. For nation will rise against nation, and kingdom against kingdom, and there will be famines and earthquakes in various places: all this is but the beginnings of the birth-pangs."

316. See Genesis 1:3–31 for the six days of creation.

317. Matthew 22:14: "For many are called, but few are chosen."

318. Much of the impetus for both the monastic and eremitical movements came from the monks and solitaries in the Egyptian desert in the third and fourth centuries, most prominent among them being St. Antony. Athanasius's *Life of Antony* became the paradigm for many saints' lives, and *Guthlac A* is ultimately indebted to it. See Athanasius's *Life of Antony*.

319. Compare Ephesians 6:11–17: "Put on the whole armor of God, that you may be able to stand against the wiles of the devil. For we are not contending against flesh and blood, but against the principalities, against the powers, against the world rulers of this present darkness, against the spiritual hosts of wickedness in the heavenly places. Therefore take the whole armor of God, that you may be able to withstand in the evil day, and having done all, to stand. Stand therefore, having girded your loins with truth, and having put on the breastplate of righteousness, and having shod your feet with the equipment of the gospel of peace; besides all these, taking the shield of faith, with which you can quench all the flaming darts of the evil one. And take the helmet of salvation, and the sword of the Spirit, which is the word of God."

320.   Guthlac (672–714) was a nobleman of royal blood from Mercia. He was a thane and warrior in his teens and early twenties before fleeing the world to become first a monk at Repton and later (701) a hermit at Crowland (sometimes referred to as Croyland). There he inhabited a hermitage only accessible by boat.

321.   It was actually a fenland home. The poet is inexact in his topographical references.

322.   That is, the military life of a soldier.

323.   Guthlac's temptation to join a band of outlaws is important for subsequent events in this poem, for the demons who tempt him take on the vocabulary and aspects of earthly bandits.

324.   The term *march* or *marchland* refers to a border in dispute between hostile nations or groups of people. This border, however, through the poet's appropriation of political and military language, is a spiritual one.

325.   See note 319, above.

326.   The constant theme in the lives of hermit saints is the attack of demons to harass them (sometimes with physical violence) and tempt them. Athanasius's *Life of Antony* sets the pattern for the later lives, including Felix's Latin *Life of Guthlac* and this poem.

327.   For this possessiveness of the demons over their territory now claimed by Guthlac, compare Athanasius's *Life of Antony*: "Since he [Antony] did not allow them [his friends] to enter [his hermitage], those of his acquaintance who came to him often spent days and nights outside. They heard what sounded like clamoring mobs inside making noises, emitting pitiful sounds and crying out, 'Get away from what is ours! What do you have to do with the desert? You cannot endure our treachery!'" (p. 41).

328.   Compare Athanasius's *Life of Antony*: "When he discovered beyond the river a deserted fortress, empty so long that reptiles filled it, he went there, and took up residence in it. Then at once the creeping things departed, as if someone were in pursuit, and barricading the entrance once more, and putting aside enough loaves for six months (for the Thebans do this, and frequently they remain unspoiled for a whole year), and having water inside, he was hidden within as in a shrine. He remained alone in the place, neither going out himself nor seeing any of those who visited. For a long time he continued this life of discipline, receiving the loaves twice yearly from the housetop above" (pp. 40–41).

329.   Compare Psalm 23:4: "Even though I walk through the valley of the shadow of death, I fear no evil; for thou art with me; thy rod and thy staff, they comfort me."

330. Compare Athanasius's *Life of Antony*: "Six months had not passed since the death of his parents when, going to the Lord's house as usual and gathering his thoughts, he considered while he walked how the apostles, forsaking everything, followed the Savior, and how in Acts some sold what they possessed and took the proceeds and placed them at the feet of the apostles for distribution among those in need, and what great hope is stored up for such people in heaven....Immediately Antony went out from the Lord's house and gave to the townspeople the possessions he had from his forebears...." (p. 31).

331. There is a gap here in the text as it stands in the Exeter Book.

332. Compare Philippians 1:21: "For me to live is Christ, and to die is gain."

333. Compare the hideous noise demons make when they attack Antony in Athanasius's *Life of Antony*. See above, note 327.

334. In Athanasius's *Life of Antony* the demons also attack the saint, at one point leaving him unconscious so that he is presumed dead (see pp. 37–38).

335. This temporary giving over into the power of demons is reminiscent of God's allowing Satan to tempt Job. See Job 1:12.

336. There is a gap here in the text.

337. This is an ironic reference to the demons, who of course do not serve Guthlac.

338. This is the apostle Bartholomew, whom Guthlac has chosen for his patron. See above, note 305.

339. Guthlac died in 714.

340. Compare Revelation 22:3–4. See note 255, above.

Advent Lyrics

341. The text here is fragmentary, beginning in the middle of a sentence. This portion is based on the Great Antiphon for December 22, *O Rex gentium*: "*O Rex gentium, et desideratus earum, lapisque angularis, qui facis utraque unum: veni et salva hominem, quem de limo formasti*" (Benedictines of Solesmes, eds., *The Liber Usualis with Introduction and Rubrics in English* [Boston: McLaughlin and Reilly, 1950], p. 342). ("O King of the nations and their desire, stone of the corner who make both one, come and save man whom you made out of clay.")

342. See Ephesians 2:19–22: "So then you are no longer strangers and sojourners, but you are fellow citizens with the saints and members of

the household of God, built upon the foundation of the apostles and prophets, Christ Jesus himself being the cornerstone, in whom the whole structure is joined together and grows into a holy temple in the Lord; in whom you also are built into it for a dwelling place of God in the Spirit."

343. The following section is based on the Great Antiphon for December 20, *O Clavis David*: "*O Clavis David, et sceptrum domus Israel: qui aperis, et nemo claudit, claudis, et nemo aperit: veni, et educ vinctum de domo carceris, sedentem in tenebris et umbra mortis*" (*Liber Usualis*, p. 341). ("O Key of David and scepter of the House of Israel, who opens and no one closes, you close and no one opens: come and lead the prisoners out of the house of prison who sit in darkness and the shadow of death.")

344. This attention to the Virgin, characteristic of the *Advent Lyrics* as a whole, is lacking in the original antiphon.

345. This section is based on one of the so-called "added" O-antiphon. These antiphons were composed in imitation of the Great Antiphons for Advent and are often included in antiphonaries along with them. See Robert B. Burlin, *The Old English Advent: A Typological Commentary* (New Haven, Conn.: Yale University Press, 1968), pp. 42–43. The source for this section reads, "*O Hierusalem, civitas Dei summi: leva in circuitu oculos tuos, et vide Dominum tuum, quia jam veniet solvere te a vinculis.*" ("O Jerusalem, city of the great God: lift up your eyes round about and see your Lord, for soon he will come to release you from your chains.") See also the antiphon for the vespers for the third Sunday in Advent: "*Jerusalem gaude gaudio magno, quia veniet tibi Salvator, alleluia*" (*Liber Usualis*, p. 133). ("Jerusalem, rejoice with great joy because a Savior will come to you, alleluia.")

346. The source for this is another of the added antiphons: "*O Virgo virginum, quomode fiet istud, quia nec primam similem visa es nec habere sequentem? Filiae Hierusalem, quid me admiramini? Divinum est mysterium hoc quod cernitis.*" ("O Virgin of virgins, how shall this be? For never was there one like you, nor will there ever be. Daughters of Jerusalem, why do you look wondering at me? What you behold is a divine mystery.") See also the antiphon for the Magnificat of vespers for the third Sunday in Advent: "*Beata es Maria, quae credidisti: perficientur in te quae dicta sunt tibi a Domino, alleluia.*" (You are blessed, Mary, because you believed. What was said to you by the Lord is perfected in you. Alleluia.")

347. One of Mary's traditional epithets was *maris stella*, "Star of the sea."

348. The source for the following section is the Great Antiphon for December 21: "*O oriens, splendor lucis aeternae, et sol justitiae: veni, et illu-*

mina sedentes in tenebris et umbra mortis" (Liber Usualis, p. 342). ("O East, splendor of eternal light, and sun of justice, come and illumine those who sit in darkness and the shadow of death.")

349. The source for the following section is the Great Antiphon for December 23, *"O Emmanuel, Rex et legifer noster, expectatio gentium et Salvator earum: veni ad salvandum nos, Domine Deus noster" (Liber Usualis*, p. 342). ("O Emmanuel, King and Lawgiver, expectation of nations and their Savior: come for our salvation, our Lord God.")

350. Compare Isaiah 7:14: "Therefore the Lord himself will give you a sign. Behold, a young woman shall conceive and bear a son, and shall call his name Immanuel." (Immanuel, i.e., "God with us").

351. The story of Melchizedek's blessing of Abraham is found in Genesis 14:17–20: "After his [Abraham's] return from the defeat of Chedorlaomer and the kings who were with him, the king of Sodom went out to meet him at the Valley of Shaveh (that is, the King's Valley). And Melchizedek king of Salem brought out bread and wine; he was priest of God Most High. And he blessed him and said, 'Blessed be Abram by God Most High, maker of heaven and earth; and blessed be God Most High, who has delivered your enemies into your hand!' And Abram gave him a tenth of everything." The author of the Epistle to the Hebrews (thought in the Middle Ages to be St. Paul) made much of Melchizedek; see Hebrews 6:19—7:10, 7:15–17: "We have this as a sure and steadfast anchor of the soul, a hope that enters into the inner shrine behind the curtain, where Jesus has gone as a forerunner on our behalf, having become a high priest for ever after the order of Melchizedek. For this Melchizedek, king of Salem, priest of the Most High God, met Abraham returning from the slaughter of the kings and blessed him; and to him Abraham apportioned a tenth part of everything. He is first, by translation of his name, king of righteousness, and then he is also king of Salem, that is, king of peace. He is without father or mother or genealogy, and has neither beginning of days nor end of life, but resembling the Son of God he continues a priest for ever. See how great he is! Abraham the patriarch gave him a tithe of the spoils. And those descendants of Levi who receive the priestly office have a commandment in the law to take tithes from the people, that is, from their brethren, though these also are descended from Abraham. But this man who has not their genealogy received tithes from Abraham and blessed him who had the promises. It is beyond dispute that the inferior is blessed by the superior. Here tithes are received by mortal men; there, by one of whom it is testified that he lives. One might even say that Levi himself,

who receives tithes, paid tithes through Abraham, for he was still in the loins of his ancestor when Melchizedek met him....This becomes even more evident when another priest arises in the likeness of Melchizedek, who has become a priest, not according to a legal requirement concerning bodily descent but by the power of an indestructible life. For it is witnessed of him, 'Thou art a priest for ever, after the order of Melchizedek.'" The last sentence of this passage is a reference to Psalm 110:4.

352. The following section, famous for its proto-dramatic rendering of the tension between Joseph and Mary at the discovery of her pregnancy, does not have an immediate source in the antiphons. *Eala*, the Old English word translated "O," had the secondary meaning, "Alas," as it should be construed here. The ultimate source, though, is Matthew 1:18–19: "Now the birth of Jesus Christ took place in this way. When his mother Mary had been betrothed to Joseph, before they came together she was found to be with child of the Holy Spirit; and her husband Joseph, being a just man and unwilling to put her to shame, resolved to divorce her quietly."

353. The source for the following section is an antiphon that may have been part of the liturgy for the Vigil of Christmas (see Burlin, *Advent*, p. 132): "*O Rex pacifice, Tu ante saecula nate: per auream egrede portam, redemptos tuos visita, et eos illuc revoca unde ruerunt per culpam.*" ("O King of peace, you who were born before all ages: come out by the golden gate, visit them you have redeemed, and lead them back to that place from which they fell by sin.") Compare the antiphon for first vespers on Christmas Day: "*Rex pacificus magnificatus est, cujus vultum desiderat universa terra*" (*Liber Usualis*, p. 364). ("The King of peace is magnified whose face all the world has desired.")

354. This is an expansion of Genesis 1:3: "And God said, 'Let there be light'; and there was light."

355. The reference here is to the psalm often associated with Advent, Psalm 24:7–10: "Lift up your heads, O gates! and be lifted up, O ancient doors! that the King of glory may come in. Who is the King of glory? The LORD, strong and mighty, the LORD, mighty in battle! Lift up your heads, O gates! and be lifted up, O ancient doors! that the King of glory may come in. Who is this King of glory? The LORD of hosts, he is the King of glory!"

356. The source for this section is one of the additional antiphons: "*O mundi Domina, regio ex semine orta, ex tuo jam Christus processit alvo, tanquam sponsus de thalamo; hic jacet in presepio qui et sidera regit.*" ("O Lady of

the world, sprung of royal seed: from your womb Christ came forth, as a bridegroom from his chamber; he lies in a manger who also rules the stars.")

357. For the angel Gabriel's annunciation, see Luke 1:26–38: "In the sixth month the angel Gabriel was sent from God to a city of Galilee named Nazareth, to a virgin betrothed to a man whose name was Joseph, of the house of David; and the virgin's name was Mary. And he came to her and said, 'Hail, O favored one, the Lord is with you!' But she was greatly troubled at the saying, and considered in her mind what sort of greeting this might be. And the angel said to her, 'Do not be afraid, Mary, for you have found favor with God. And behold, you will conceive in your womb and bear a son, and you shall call his name Jesus. He will be great, and will be called the Son of the Most High; and the Lord God will give to him the throne of his father David, and he will reign over the house of Jacob for ever; and of his kingdom there will be no end.' And Mary said to the angel, 'How can this be, since I have no husband?' And the angel said to her, 'The Holy Spirit will come upon you, and the power of the Most High will overshadow you; therefore the child to be born will be called holy, the Son of God. And behold, your kinswoman Elizabeth in her old age has also conceived a son; and this is the sixth month with her who was called barren. For with God nothing will be impossible.' And Mary said, 'Behold, I am the handmaid of the Lord; let it be to me according to your word.' And the angel departed from her."

358. See note 350, above.

359. No antiphonal source has been found for the following section.

360. Two trinitarian antiphons comprise the source for the following section: *"Te jure laudant, te adorant, te glorifcant omnes creaturae tuae, O beata Trinitas"* (see Burlin, *Advent*, p. 163). ("All your creatures justly praise you, worship you, glorify you, O blessed Trinity.") And *"O beata et benedicta et gloriosa Trinitas, Pater et Filius et Spiritus sanctus"* (see Burlin, *Advent*, p. 163). ("O hallowed and blessed and glorious Trinity, Father and Son and Holy Spirit.")

361. The source for the following section is an antiphon from the Octave of Christmas, *"O admirabile commercium, Creator generis humani animatum corpus sumens, de Virgine nasci dignatus est: et procedens homo sine semine, largitus est nobis suam deitatem"* (see Burlin, *Advent*, p. 170). ("O admirable exchange: the Creator of humankind, assuming a human body, deigned to be born of a Virgin, and becoming man without man's seed, bestowed on us his divinity.")

The Lord's Prayer I

362. There are two versions of the Lord's Prayer in the Bible: "Our Father who art in heaven, Hallowed be thy name. Thy kingdom come. Thy will be done, On earth as it is in heaven. Give us this day our daily bread, and forgive us our debts, as we also have forgiven our debtors. And lead us not into temptation, but deliver us from evil" (Mt 6:9–13); and "Father, hallowed be thy name. Thy kingdom come. Give us each day our daily bread; and forgive us our sins, for we ourselves forgive every one who is indebted to us; and lead us not into temptation" (Lk 11:2–4). The Old English poet, like almost everyone, prefers the version found in the Gospel of Matthew.

Psalm 121

363. The text of Psalm 121 is as follows: "I lift up my eyes to the hills. From whence does my help come? My help comes from the LORD, who made heaven and earth. He will not let your foot be moved, he who keeps you will not slumber. Behold, he who keeps Israel will neither slumber nor sleep. The LORD is your keeper; the LORD is your shade on your right hand. The sun shall not smite you by day, nor the moon by night. The LORD will keep you from all evil; he will keep your life. The LORD will keep your going out and your coming in from this time forth and for evermore."

Soul and Body II

364. The reference here is the doctrine that the soul must be separated from the body from the moment of death until the general resurrection at the end of time that immediately precedes the Last Judgment.

365. The b-verse is missing here.

366. Compare Genesis 3:19: "In the sweat of your face you shall eat bread till you return to the ground, for out of it you were taken; you are dust, and to dust you shall return."

367. For the Last Judgment, see Matthew 25:31–46 and Revelation 20:11–15. See notes 6 and 80, above.

Judgment Day I

368. The reference is to the destruction of the earth attending Noah's Flood. See Genesis 6:9—8:22.

369. That is, the devils.

370. Compare the conditions in the New Jerusalem in Revelation 21:22–27.

371. For the Judgment Day, see Matthew 25:31–46 and Revelation 20:11–15. See notes 6 and 80, above.

372. The poet depicts the cross as a ship's mast.

373. See Matthew 25:32–33: "Before him will be gathered all the nations, and he will separate them one from another as a shepherd separates the sheep from the goats, and he will place the sheep at his right hand, but the goats at the left." The left (Latin, *sinister*) is the locus of the damned.

374. The reference is to the New Jerusalem. See Revelation 21:10–14.

375. See Ezekiel 37:5–6: "Thus says the Lord GOD to these bones: Behold, I will cause breath to enter you, and you shall live. And I will lay sinews upon you, and will cause flesh to come upon you, and cover you with skin, and put breath in you, and you shall live; and you shall know that I am the LORD."

376. For the apocalyptic trumpets, see Revelation 8:6—9:20; 11:15–19.

The Phoenix

377. Compare the description of the New Jerusalem in Revelation 21:22—22:5: "And I saw no temple in the city, for its temple is the Lord God the Almighty and the Lamb. And the city has no need of sun or moon to shine upon it, for the glory of God is its light, and its lamp is the Lamb. By its light shall the nations walk; and the kings of the earth shall bring their glory into it, and its gates shall never be shut by day—and there shall be no night there; they shall bring into it the glory and the honor of the nations. But nothing unclean shall enter it, nor any one who practices abomination or falsehood, but only those who are written in the Lamb's book of life. Then he showed me the river of the water of life, bright as crystal, flowing from the throne of God and of the Lamb through the middle of the street of the city; also, on either side of the river, the tree of life with its twelve kinds of fruit, yielding its fruit each month; and the leaves

of the tree were for the healing of the nations. There shall no more be anything accursed, but the throne of God and of the Lamb shall be in it, and his servants shall worship him; they shall see his face, and his name shall be on their foreheads. And night shall be no more; they need no light of lamp or sun, for the Lord God will be their light, and they shall reign for ever and ever."

378.   Compare Isaiah 40:4–5: "Every valley shall be lifted up, and every mountain and hill be made low; the uneven ground shall become level, and the rough places a plain. And the glory of the LORD shall be revealed, and all flesh shall see it together, for the mouth of the LORD has spoken."

379.   The reference is to Noah's Flood. See Genesis 7:6–24.

380.   Compare Genesis 2:8–9: "And the LORD God planted a garden in Eden, in the east; and there he put the man whom he had formed. And out of the ground the LORD God made to grow every tree that is pleasant to the sight and good for food, the tree of life also in the midst of the garden, and the tree of the knowledge of good and evil."

381.   The east, traditionally, is the direction of resurrection. Typically, medieval churches were constructed with their altars toward the east—a possible response to 1 John 1:5. See note 278, above.

382.   This is a possible allegorical parallel to Revelation 20:5–7, 9b: "The rest of the dead did not come to life until the thousand years were ended. This is the first resurrection. Blessed and holy is he who shares in the first resurrection! Over such the second death has no power, but they shall be priests of God and of Christ, and they shall reign with him a thousand years. And when the thousand years are ended, Satan will be loosed from his prison....but fire came down from heaven and consumed them...."

383.   These lines are an allegorical reference to the relationship of Father and Son within the Trinity.

384.   See Genesis 1:27: "So God created man in his own image, in the image of God he created him; male and female he created them."

385.   See Genesis 3:1: "Now the serpent was more subtle than any other wild creature that the LORD God had made."

386.   See Genesis 3:23–24: "...therefore the LORD God sent him forth from the garden of Eden, to till the ground from which he was taken. He drove out the man; and at the east of the garden of Eden he placed the cherubim, and a flaming sword which turned every way, to guard the way to the tree of life."

387. For Judgment day, see Matthew 25:31–46 and Revelation 20:11–15. See notes 6 and 80, above.

388. See Ezekiel 31:5–8: "So it towered high above all the trees of the forest; its boughs grew large and its branches long, from abundant water in its shoots. All the birds of the air made their nests in its boughs; under its branches all the beasts of the field brought forth their young; and under its shadow dwelt all great nations. It was beautiful in its greatness, in the length of its branches; for its roots went down to abundant waters. The cedars in the garden of God could not rival it, nor the fir trees equal its boughs; the plane trees were as nothing compared with its branches; no tree in the garden of God was like it in beauty."

389. See Job 19:25–26: "For I know that my Redeemer lives, and at last he will stand upon the earth; and after my skin has been thus destroyed, then from my flesh I shall see God."

390. See Revelation 21:23. See note 90, above.

391. See Revelation 14:1–5: "Then I looked, and lo, on Mount Zion stood the Lamb, and with him a hundred and forty-four thousand who had his name and his Father's name written on their foreheads. And I heard a voice from heaven like the sound of many waters and like the sound of loud thunder; the voice I heard was like the sound of harpers playing on their harps, and they sing a new song before the throne and before the four living creatures and before the elders. No one could learn that song except the hundred and forty-four thousand who had been redeemed from the earth. It is these who have not defiled themselves with women, for they are chaste; it is these who follow the Lamb wherever he goes; these have been redeemed from mankind as first fruits for God and the Lamb, and in their mouth no lie was found, for they are spotless."

392. These concluding ten lines of the poem are macaronic, alternating Old English and Latin phrases.

The Dream of the Rood

393. "Listen" translates the Old English word *Hwæt*, the traditional opening of Old English poems like *Beowulf* and *Andreas*.

394. This translation preserves the manuscript reading, but many editors emend it to "All the angels of the Lord beheld it there." See the Introduction above, pp. 42–43.

395. The hill, of course, is Golgatha or Calvary. See Matthew 27:33 and parallels.

396. See Matthew 27:51: "And behold, the curtain of the temple was torn in two, from top to bottom; and the earth shook, and the rocks were split."

397. According to the theory of Gustav Aulen in his *Christus Victor*, the earlier Middle Ages held less to a sacrificial image of Christ's atonement, in which he was the passive victim sacrificed to God for humanity's sins, but instead to a martial metaphor, in which he does battle with (or in some instances tricks) the Devil and thus releases humanity from the Devil's possession. See Gustav Aulen, *Christus Victor* (New York: Macmillan, 1951), p. 59. Compare Gordon D. Kaufman, *Systematic Theology: A Historicist Perspective* (New York: Scribners, 1968), p. 394.

398. Note the rood's association of his own wounds with Christ's.

399. See Matthew 27:45: "Now from the sixth hour there was darkness over all the land until the ninth hour."

400. That is, the hands of Nicodemus and Joseph of Aramathea, who have come to bury Jesus. See Matthew 27:57–60 and John 19:38–42.

401. Traditionally, the true cross was found in 327 by St. Helena, Emperor Constantine's mother. Cynewulf relates the story in his Old English poem *Elene*.

402. Compare Luke 1:42: "Blessed are you among women."

403. For Judgment Day, see Matthew 25:31–46 and Revelation 20:11–15. See notes 6 and 80, above.

Maxims II

404. The Anglo-Saxons sometimes referred to the ruins left among them by the Romans as the work of giants.

405. The reference is to the ancient sport of falconry.

406. See Genesis 1:20–22: "And God said, 'Let the waters bring forth swarms of living creatures, and let birds fly above the earth across the firmament of the heavens.' So God created the great sea monsters and every living creature that moves, with which the waters swarm, according to their kinds, and every winged bird according to its kind. And God saw that it was good. And God blessed them, saying, 'Be fruitful and multiply and fill the waters in the seas, and let birds multiply on the earth.'"

407. See Genesis 1:14–15: "And God said, 'Let there be lights in the firmament of the heavens to separate the day from the night; and let them be for signs and for seasons and for days and years, and let them be lights in the firmament of the heavens to give light upon the earth.'"

Bibliography

Primary Texts Used for the Translations in the Volume:

Bethurum, Dorothy, ed. *The Homilies of Wulfstan*. Oxford: Clarendon Press, 1957. (*On the False Gods, On the Sevenfold Gifts of the Spirit, Sermo Lupi ad Anglos*)

Dobbie, Elliott Van Kirk, ed. *The Anglo-Saxon Minor Poems*. Anglo-Saxon Poetic Records 6. New York: Columbia University Press, 1942. (*Maxims II, Cædmon's Hymn*)

————. *Beowulf and Judith*. Anglo-Saxon Poetic Records 4. New York: Columbia University Press, 1953. (*Judith*)

Godden, Malcolm, ed. *Ælfric's Catholic Homilies: The Second Series*. Early English Text Society, Supplementary Series 5. London: Oxford University Press, 1979. (*On the Sacrifice of Easter*)

Irvine, Susan, ed. *Old English Homilies from MS Bodley 343*. Early English Text Society 302. Oxford: Oxford University Press, 1993. (*The Temptation of Christ, The Transfiguration of Christ, The Transience of Earthly Delights*)

Krapp, George Philip, ed. *The Junius Manuscript*. Anglo-Saxon Poetic Records 1. New York: Columbia University Press, 1931. (Selections from *Genesis A* and *Genesis B*)

————. *The Paris Psalter and The Meters of Boethius*. Anglo-Saxon Poetic Records 5. New York: Columbia University Press, 1932. (*Psalm 121*)

————. *The Vercelli Book*. Anglo-Saxon Poetic Records 2. New York: Columbia University Press, 1932. (*The Fates of the Apostles, The Dream of the Rood*)

317

Krapp, George Philip, and Elliott Van Kirk Dobbie, eds. *The Exeter Book.* Anglo-Saxon Poetic Records 3. New York: Columbia University Press, 1936. (*Advent Lyrics, Guthlac A, The Phoenix, Soul and Body II, Judgment Day I, The Lord's Prayer I*)

Morris, R., ed. *The Blickling Homilies.* Early English Text Society 58, 63, 73. London: Oxford University Press, 1874–80, reprinted 1967. (*The End of the World, The Birth of John the Baptist, The Dedication of St. Michael's Church, St. Andrew*)

Scragg, D. G., ed. *The Vercelli Homilies and Related Texts.* Early English Text Society 300. Oxford: Oxford University Press, 1992. (*The Day of Judgment, Christmas Day, Rogation Day*)

Skeat, Walter W., ed. *Ælfric's Lives of Saints.* 2 vols. Early English Text Society 76, 82, 94, 114. London: Oxford University Press, 1881–1900, reprinted 1966. (*St. John the Apostle, St. Dionysius, St. Oswald*)

Secondary Sources:

Albertson, Clinton, S.J. *Anglo-Saxon Saints and Heroes.* New York: Fordham University Press, 1967.

Allen, Michael J. B., and Daniel G. Calder, trans. *Sources and Analogues of Old English Poetry: The Major Latin Texts in Translation.* Cambridge: D. S. Brewer, 1976.

Amos, Ashley Crandell. *Linguistic Means of Determining the Date of Old English Literary Texts.* Cambridge, Mass.: Medieval Academy of America, 1980.

Apel, Willi. *Gregorian Chant.* Bloomington, Ind.: Indiana University Press, 1958, 1990.

Aulen, Gustav. *Christus Victor.* New York: Macmillan, 1951.

Barlow, Frank. *Edward the Confessor.* Berkeley and Los Angeles: University of California Press, 1970.

Benario, Herbert W., trans. *Tacitus: Agricola, Germany, Dialogue on Orators.* New York: Bobbs-Merrill, 1967.

Benedictines of Solesmes, The, eds. *The Liber Usualis with Introduction and Rubrics in English.* Boston: McLaughlin and Reilly, 1950.

Bieler, Ludwig. "The Irish Penitentials: Their Religious and Social Background," *Studia Patristica* 8 (1966): 329–39.

Biller, Peter, and A. J. Minnis, eds. *Handling Sin: Confession in the Middle Ages.* Rochester, N.Y.: York Medieval Press, 1998.

BIBLIOGRAPHY

Blair, Peter Hunter. *An Introduction to Anglo-Saxon England*. Cambridge: Cambridge University Press, 1959, 1977.

———. *The World of Bede*. Cambridge: Cambridge University Press, 1970, 1990.

Blake, N. F. "The Form of *The Phoenix*." Pages 268–78 in Martin Stevens and Jerome Mandel, eds. *Old English Literature: Twenty-two Analytical Essays*. Lincoln, Neb.: University of Nebraska Press, 1968.

Bodden, Mary Catherine. "The Preservation and Transmission of Greek in Early England." Pages 53–63 in Paul E. Szarmach, ed. *Sources in Anglo-Saxon Culture*. Kalamazoo, Mich.: Medieval Institute Publications, 1986.

Boenig, Robert. *The Acts of Andrew in the Country of the Cannibals: Translations from the Greek, Latin, and Old English*. New York: Garland, 1991.

———. "The Anglo-Saxon Harp." *Speculum* 71 (1996): 290–320.

———. *Saint and Hero: Andreas and Medieval Doctrine*. Lewisburg, Pa.: Bucknell University Press, 1991.

———. "Very Sharp/Unsharp, Unpeace/Firm Peace: Morphemic Ambiguity in *Beowulf*." *Neophilologus* 76 (1992): 275–82.

Bolton, W. F. *Anglo-Latin Literature*. Princeton, N.J.: Princeton University Press, 1967.

———. *Alcuin and Beowulf*. New Brunswick, N.J.: Rutgers University Press, 1978.

Brechter, Dom Suso. *Die Quellen zur Angel-sachsenmission Gregors des Grossen*. Munster, Westphalia: Aschendorff, 1941.

Bruce-Mitford, Rupert. *The Sutton Hoo Ship Burial*. 3 vols. London: British Museum, 1975–83.

Burlin, Robert B. *The Old English Advent*. New Haven, Conn.: Yale University Press, 1968.

Bynum, Caroline Walker. *The Resurrection of the Body in Western Christianity, 200–1336*. New York: Columbia University Press, 1995.

Camille, Michael. *The Gothic Idol: Ideology and Image-Making in Medieval Art*. Cambridge: Cambridge University Press, 1989.

Cassidy, Frederic G., and Richard Ringler, eds. *Bright's Old English Grammar and Reader*. 3d. ed. New York: Holt, Rinehart, and Winston, 1971.

Chase, Colin. ed. *Two Alcuin Letter-Books*. Toronto: University of Toronto Press, 1975.

———. *The Dating of Beowulf*. Toronto: University of Toronto Press, 1981.

Clader, Nigel. *The Comet Is Coming*. New York: Viking Press, 1980.

Colgrave, Bertram, and R. A. B. Mynors, eds. and trans. *Bede's Ecclesiastical History of the English People*. Oxford: Clarendon Press, 1969.

Creed, Robert P. "A New Approach to the Rhythm of *Beowulf.*" *Publications of the Modern Language Association* 81 (1966): 22–33.

Davidson, Clifford, and Thomas H. Seiler, eds. *The Iconography of Hell*. Kalamazoo, Mich.: Medieval Institute Publications, 1992.

Davies, John. *A History of Wales*. London: Penguin, 1993.

Deansley, Margaret. "The Capitular Text of the *Responsiones* of Pope Gregory I to St. Augustine." *Journal of Ecclesiastical History* 11 (1961): 231–34.

Deansley, Margaret, and Paul Grosjean, S.J. "The Canterbury *Editio* of the Answers of Pope Gregory I to St. Augustine," *Journal of Ecclesiastical History* 10 (1959): 1–49.

Donaldson, E. Talbot, trans. *Beowulf: A New Prose Translation*. New York: Norton, 1966.

Emmerson, Richard K. *Antichrist in the Middle Ages*. Seattle: University of Washington Press, 1981.

———. "From Epistola to Sermo: The Old English Version of Adso's Libellus de Antichristo." *Journal of English and Germanic Philology* 82 (1983): 1–10.

Emmerson, Richard K., and Bernard McGinn, eds. *The Apocalypse in the Middle Ages*. Ithaca, N.Y.: Cornell University Press, 1992.

Farmer, David Hugh. *Oxford Dictionary of Saints*. Oxford: Oxford University Press, 1992.

Foley, John Miles. "Literary Art and Oral Tradition in Old English and Serbian Poetry." *Anglo-Saxon England* 12 (1983): 183–214.

Foley, Trent. *Images of Sanctity in Eddius Stephanus' Life of Bishop Wilfred, an Early English Saint's Life*. Lewiston, N.Y.: Edwin Mellen, 1992.

Frantzen, Allen J. *The Literature of Penance in Anglo-Saxon England*. New Brunswick, N.J.: Rutgers University Press, 1983.

Frantzen, Allen, and John D. Niles, eds. *Anglo-Saxonism and the Construction of Social Identity*. Gainesville, Fla.: University Press of Florida, 1997.

Fulk, R. D. *A History of Old English Meter*. Philadelphia: University of Pennsylvania Press, 1992.

Gatch, Milton McCormick. "Eschatology in the Anonymous Old English Homilies." *Traditio* 21 (1965): 117–65.

Gordon, R. K., trans. *Anglo-Saxon Poetry*. London: Dent, 1926.

Greenfield, Stanley B. *A Critical History of Old English Literature*. New York: New York University Press, 1965.

Gregg, Robert C., trans. *Athanasius: The Life of Antony and The Letter to Marcellinus*. New York: Paulist Press, 1980.

Healey, Antonette diPaolo. *The Old English Vision of St. Paul*. Cambridge, Mass.: Medieval Academy of America, 1978.

Herm, Gerhard. *The Celts*. New York: St. Martin's Press, 1976.

Hilgarth, J. N., ed. *Christianity and Paganism, 350–750*. Philadelphia: University of Pennsylvania Press, 1969.

Hill, David. *An Atlas of Anglo-Saxon England*. Toronto: University of Toronto Press, 1981.

Hoppin, Richard. *Medieval Music*. New York: Norton, 1978.

Howe, Nicholas. *Migration and Mythology in Anglo-Saxon England*. New Haven, Conn.: Yale University Press, 1989.

Jolly, Karen Louise. *Popular Religion in Late Saxon England*. Chapel Hill, N.C.: University of North Carolina Press, 1996.

Kaufman, Gordon D. *Systematic Theology: A Historicist Perspective*. New York: Scribners, 1968.

Kiernan, Kevin S. *Beowulf and the Beowulf Manuscript*. New Brunswick, N.J.: Rutgers University Press, 1984.

Kinard, J. P. *A Study of Wulfstan's Homilies*. Baltimore: John Murphy, 1897.

Kirby, D. P., ed. *Saint Wilfred at Hexham*. Newcastle upon Tyne: Oriel Press, 1974.

Kirk, G. S. *The Songs of Homer*. Cambridge: Cambridge University Press, 1962.

Knowles, Dom David. *The Monastic Order in England: A History of Its Development from the Times of St. Dunstan to the Fourth Lateran Council, 940–1216*. 2d ed. Cambridge: Cambridge University Press, 1963.

Lapidge, Michael. "The School of Theodore and Hadrian." *Anglo-Saxon England* 15 (1986): 45–72.

———. "The Study of Greek at the School of Canterbury in the Seventh Century." Pages 169–94 in Michael W. Herren, ed. *The Sacred Nectar of the Greeks: The Study of Greek in the West in the Early Middle Ages*. London: King's College, University of London, 1988.

Lapidge, Michael, ed. *Archbishop Theodore: Commemorative Studies on His Life and Influence*. Cambridge: Cambridge University Press, 1995.

Lapidge, Michael, and Helmut Gneuss, eds. *Learning and Literature in Anglo-Saxon England: Studies Presented to Peter Clemoes on the Occasion of His Sixty-Fifth Birthday*. Cambridge: Cambridge University Press, 1985.

Lapidge, Michael, and Michael Herren, trans. *Aldhelm: The Prose Works*. Ipswich: D. S. Brewer, 1979.

Lee, Alvin A. *The Guest-Hall of Eden: Four Essays on the Design of Old English Poetry.* New Haven, Conn.: Yale University Press, 1972.

Lerer, Seth. *Literacy and Power in Anglo-Saxon Literature.* Lincoln, Neb.: University of Nebraska Press, 1991.

Leyerle, John. "The Interlace Structure of *Beowulf.*" *University of Toronto Quarterly* 37 (1967): 1–17.

Lord, Albert B. *The Singer of Tales.* Cambridge, Mass.: Harvard University Press, 1960.

Luibheid, Colm, trans., with Paul Rorem. *Pseudo-Dionysius: The Complete Works.* New York: Paulist Press, 1987.

Lutz, Cora E. *Schoolmasters of the Tenth Century.* Hamden, Conn.: Archon Books, 1977.

MacCana, Proinsias. *Celtic Mythology.* London: Hamelyn, 1970.

Macy, Gary. *The Theologies of the Eucharist in the Early Scholastic Period.* Oxford: Clarendon Press, 1984.

Magoun, Francis P., Jr. "The Oral-Formulaic Character of Anglo-Saxon Narrative Poetry." *Speculum* 28 (1953): 446–67.

Marsden, John. *The Fury of the Norsemen.* New York: St. Martin's Press, 1993.

Mayr-Harting, Henry. *The Coming of Christianity to Anglo-Saxon England.* 3d ed. University Park, Pa.: Pennsylvania State University Press, 1991.

McGinn, Bernard. *Antichrist: Two Thousand Years of the Human Fascination with Evil.* San Francisco: HarperSanFrancisco, 1994.

McGinn, Bernard. "The End of the World and the Beginning of Christendom." Pages 58–89 in Malcolm Bull, ed. *Apocalypse Theory and the Ends of the World.* Oxford: Blackwell, 1995.

McGinn, Bernard, ed. *Apocalyptic Spirituality: Treatises and Letters of Lactantius, Adso of Montier-en-Der, Joachim of Fiore, The Spiritual Franciscans, Savonarola.* New York: Paulist Press, 1979.

———. *Visions of the End: Apocalyptic Traditions in the Middle Ages.* New York: Columbia University Press, 1979.

McIntosh, Angus. "Wulfstan's Prose." *Proceedings of the British Academy* 35 (1949): 117–18.

McNeill, John T. *A History of the Cure of Souls.* New York: Harper & Row, 1951.

McNeill, John T., and Helen M. Gamer. *Medieval Handbooks of Penance.* New York: Columbia University Press, 1938.

Meyvaert, Paul. "Les Responsiones de S. Grégoire le Grand à S. Augustin de Cantorbéry." *Revue d'Histoire Ecclesiastique* 54 (1959): 879–94.

BIBLIOGRAPHY

Meyvaert, Paul. "Diversity Within Unity, a Gregorian Theme," *Heythorp Journal* 4 (1963): 141–62.

———. "Bede's Text of the *Libellus Responsionum* of Gregory the Great to Augustine of Canterbury." Pages 15–33 in Peter Clemoes and Kathleen Hughes, eds. *England Before the Conquest: Studies in Primary Sources Presented to Dorothy Whitelock*. Cambridge: Cambridge University Press, 1971.

Miller, Thomas, ed. *The Old English Version of Bede's Ecclesiastical History of the English People*. Early English Text Society 95, 96, 110, 111. London: Oxford University Press, 1890–98, reprinted 1959, 1963.

Mortimer, Robert Cecil. *The Origins of Private Penance in the Western Church*. Oxford: Clarendon Press, 1939.

Murphy, G. Ronald, S.J. *The Saxon Savior: The Germanic Transformation of the Gospel in the Ninth-Century Heliand*. New York: Oxford University Press, 1989.

Murray, Hilda M. R., ed. *Erthe upon Erthe, Printed from Twenty-four Manuscripts*. Early English Text Society 141. London: Oxford University Press, 1911.

Nordenfalk, Carl. *Celtic and Anglo-Saxon Painting*. New York: George Braziller, 1977.

North, John. *The Norton History of Astronomy and Cosmology*. New York: Norton, 1995.

O'Keeffe, Katherine O'Brien. *Visible Song: Transitional Literacy in Old English Verse*. Cambridge: Cambridge University Press, 1990.

Oakley, Thomas P. "Celtic Penance: Its Sources, Affiliation, and Influence." *Irish Ecclesiastical Review* 52 (1938): 198–264.

Oakley, Thomas P. "The Origins of Irish Penitential Discipline." *Catholic Historical Review* 19 (1933–34): 320–32.

Olsen, Alexandra Hennessey. *Guthlac of Croyland: A Study of Heroic Hagiography*. Washington, D.C.: University Press of America, 1981.

Page, R. I. *Runes*. Berkeley and Los Angeles: University of California Press, 1987.

Pagels, Elaine. *The Origin of Satan*. New York: Random House, 1995.

Petersen, Rodney L. *Preaching in the Last Days: The Theme of "Two Witnesses" in the Sixteenth and Seventeenth Centuries*. New York: Oxford University Press, 1993.

Pierce, Rosamund. "The 'Frankis' Penitentials." *Studies in Church History* 2 (1975): 31–39.

Pope, John C. *The Rhythm of Beowulf*. 2d ed. New Haven, Conn.: Yale University Press, 1966.

Pope, John E. *The Homilies of Ælfric: A Supplementary Collection*. 2 vols. Early English Text Society 259, 260. London: Oxford University Press, 1967, 1968.

Pyles, Thomas, and John Algeo. *The Origin and Development of the English Language*. 3d ed. New York: Harcourt, Brace, Jovonovich, 1982.

Rice, Robert C. "The Penitential Motif in Cynewulf's *Fates of the Apostles* and in His Epilogues," *Anglo-Saxon England* 6 (1977): 105–19.

Robinson, Fred C. *Beowulf and the Appositional Style*. Knoxville, Tenn.: University of Tennessee Press, 1987.

Rosenwein, Barbara H. *Rhinoceros Bound: Cluny in the Tenth Century*. Philadelphia: University of Pennsylvania Press, 1982.

Ross, Anne. *Pagan Celtic Britain: Studies in Iconographical Tradition*. Chicago: Academy Chicago Publishers, 1967, 1996.

Schlauch, Margaret. "The 'Dream of the Rood' as Prosopopoeia." Pages 23–34 in *Essays and Studies in Honor of Carelton Brown*. New York: New York University Press, 1940.

Scragg, D. G., ed. *The Battle of Maldon*. Manchester: Manchester University Press, 1981.

Sheedy, Charles E., C.S.C. *The Eucharistic Controversy of the Eleventh Century Against the Background of Pre-Scholastic Theology*. Washington, D.C.: Catholic University of America Press, 1947.

Sherley-Price, Leo, and R. E. Latham, trans. *Bede: A History of the English Church and People*. Harmondsworth: Penguin, 1955, 1968.

Sisam, Kenneth. *Studies in the History of Old English Literature*. Oxford: Clarendon Press, 1962.

Smith, A. H. *The Parker Chronicle, 832–900*. London: Methuen, 1935.

Smyth, Alfred P. *King Alfred the Great*. Oxford: Oxford University Press, 1995.

Swanton, Michael. *Anglo-Saxon Prose*. London: Dent, 1975.

Sweet, Henry, ed. *King Alfred's Orosius*. Early English Text Society 78. London: Oxford University Press, 1883, reprinted 1959.

———. *King Alfred's West Saxon Version of Gregory's Pastoral Care*. Early English Text Society 45, 50. London: Oxford University Press, 1871–72, reprinted 1958.

Vauchez, André. *The Spirituality of the Medieval West from the Eighth to the Twelfth Century*. Trans. Colette Friedlander. Kalamazoo, Mich.: Cistercian Publications, 1993.

Watkins, Oscar D. *A History of Penance*. 1920. Reprinted New York: Burt Franklin, 1961.

BIBLIOGRAPHY

Whitelock, Dorothy. "Archbishop Wulfstan, Homilist and Statesman." *Transactions of the Royal Historical Society*, 4th Series 24 (1942): 25–45.

Wilson, David Fenwick. *Music of the Middle Ages: Style and Structure*. New York: Macmillan, 1990.

Wilson, David M. *The Bayeaux Tapestry: The Complete Tapestry in Color with an Introduction, Description, and Commentary*. New York: Alfred A. Knopf, 1985.

Winterbottom, Michael, trans. *Gildas: The Ruin of Britain and Other Works*. Totowa, N.J.: Roman and Littlefield, 1978.

Woolf, Rosemary. "The Ideal of Men Dying with Their Lord in the *Germania* and in *The Battle of Maldon*." *Anglo-Saxon England* 5 (1976): 63–81.

Wrenn, C. L. *A Study of Old English Literature*. New York: Norton, 1967.

Index

References in **boldface** are to material in Introduction.

INDEX

Other Volumes in This Series

Other Volumes in This Series

Other Volumes in This Series